Moderate Liberalism and the Scottish Enlightenment

To the memory of my father, Christos Vassiliou

Moderate Liberalism and the Scottish Enlightenment

Montesquieu, Hume, Smith and Ferguson

CONSTANTINE CHRISTOS VASSILIOU

EDINBURGH
University Press

Edinburgh University Press is one of the leading university presses in the UK. We publish academic books and journals in our selected subject areas across the humanities and social sciences, combining cutting-edge scholarship with high editorial and production values to produce academic works of lasting importance. For more information visit our website: edinburghuniversitypress.com

Edinburgh University Press Ltd
13 Infirmary Street
Edinburgh EH1 1LT

First published in hardback by Edinburgh University Press 2023

Typeset in 11/13 Adobe Sabon by
IDSUK (DataConnection) Ltd

A CIP record for this book is available from the British Library

ISBN 978-1-3995-2119-2 (hardback)
ISBN 978-1-3995-2120-8 (paperback)
ISBN 978-1-3995-2121-5 (webready PDF)
ISBN 978-1-3995-2122-2 (epub)

The right of Constantine Vassiliou to be identified as the author of this work has been asserted in accordance with the Copyright, Designs and Patents Act 1988, and the Copyright and Related Rights Regulations 2003 (SI No. 2498).

Contents

Preface: A Liberal Framework for Inspiring Magnanimity in the Modern Commercial World

I wish to begin with a brief biographical note to provide a more human introduction to a scholarly project which developed out of an abiding preoccupation with the promise and betrayal of elites in the modern commercial world. Having been raised in a middle-class suburb of Montreal, Quebec, I had the good fortune to attend an elite prep school throughout my childhood. I was afforded this privilege by dint of coming of age before a prolonged period of quantitative easing, when the personal sacrifices of my first-generation Canadian, restaurant-owning parents were still sufficient for giving their children access to an education typically reserved for the Brahmin classes of Montreal's anglophone community. My family's fortunes took a turn for the worse after a disgruntled restaurant competitor[1] with connections to an underworld – which keeps itself tethered to industries that operate with large cash flows – made a nearly successful attempt on my, my father's and my brother's life. The incident generated spectacular news headlines,[2] causing unwarranted reputational damage to my family and an extended period of severe financial hardship, marked with bankruptcies and painful home foreclosures initiated by predatory lenders. Despite these challenges, I continued attending the same prep school thanks to a series of ostensibly imprudent financial decisions, justified by an assured expectation that the social capital I was accruing would yield long-term bountiful returns.

The sudden change of material circumstances had me reconciling a culture that is sometimes rough around the edges with one whose 'commercial' manners I came to appreciate, recognising how they could help lubricate the personal frictions I constantly encountered with the chaotic situations that followed my family's misfortune. What I had come to value most was not the economic ladder that my privilege gave me access to, but a moral orientation – to be kind, not to bully, to stand out of respect when a superior entered the room, to say grace before meals, to respect the rules of fair play in competitive sports, and to maintain a healthy contempt for money – the last of which I naively internalised having not yet absorbed Adam Smith's warning about emulating the nobility without acquiring the virtues requisite for achieving nobility.[3] What first seemed as affectations that the upwardly mobile needed to imbibe became a trove of resources for navigating a world that suddenly did not make sense to a traumatised child. I felt gifted having acquired an understanding of 'aristocratic' manners, honour codes and norms, convinced that they should be distributed more widely, since being elite did not necessarily mean being rich, but being 'noble'.

I eventually became sensitised to the class difference between me and my former peers whom I resented for spending their summers in Paris writing in journals during our college years, while I remained tethered to a struggling family restaurant business. This new contention tempered my contempt for money, feeding into my decision to pursue what became a brief career in banking, the final years of which entailed a trading position and a decent vantage point for observing the unfolding financial crises of those years. It was then that I realised that the commercial elite culture I had embraced was as shallow as the skin-deep manners I had come to fetishise. I witnessed the practical consequences of a banking culture on Wall Street that incentivised economic actors to not be responsible in their day-to-day commercial activities. The ignoble activities that precipitated the Great Recession were as vicious and ruthless as the scheming villains I encountered when ensconced in Montreal's restaurant ecosystem, although performed in nicer attire than the latter's gawdy narco-fashion, which, in hindsight, was a more authentic representation of honour achieved without virtue.

In retrospect, it is unsurprising that when I began my doctorate in political science at the University of Toronto my intimations led me to a thinker who came from the lower ranks of France's nobility: Charles-Louis de Secondat, baron de La Brède et de Montesquieu. The Bordeaux aristocrat was under no illusions about the pathological problems that stunted France's ancien régime, which became amplified with the rapid pace of commercial innovation in the early eighteenth century. As I immersed myself in Enlightenment political thought, I became convinced that contentious discussions triggered by the Great Recession – concerning the culture of Wall Street and the proper scope of government oversight – might be soberly illuminated by the work of this great thinker who confronted in his own time the hazards of financial speculation. Montesquieu was a seminal figure who astutely observed France's transition from an orderly but stultifying feudal order to a technologically progressive but often unstable commercial society. While he appreciated some of the social mores and manners seen among France's nobility, he nonetheless valued the increasing quality of life delivered by modern commerce. In examining this tension that runs the gamut of Montesquieu's writings, I unearthed a wider, underexplored strand of foundational eighteenth-century liberal thought, which includes key thinkers of the Scottish Enlightenment who recognised that a free and equal society is not a self-correcting wind-up toy, that its stability depended on maintaining a deep sense for the public good among its citizens. Their preoccupation with the role of the nobility in commercial society reflects a shared concern about the new sources of despotism in eighteenth-century Europe, of which they theoretically respond to by scaffolding a sphere of public honour which hovers above the marketplace.

Montesquieu, David Hume, Adam Smith and Adam Ferguson, the principal thinkers I cover throughout the book, represent an axis point in the history of political thought, being among the earliest thinkers to predict the eventuality of market society. They presciently observed that, if we look at the direction of human activity outside the commercial sphere, everyone will end up living commercial lives one way or the other. Despite their optimism about the modern commercial world, they were preoccupied with how commercial mores will come to dominate our psychological dispositions. Today we will find a cottage industry of political theorists and public intellectuals who respond to similar concerns about the moral possibilities of market society.[4] They raise questions about how market rationality has permeated nearly all spheres of human activity. In the academy some have sounded the alarm over a pernicious spirit of careerism underwriting our research and pedagogy.[5] Our dating world increasingly resembles an awkward online auction that atrophies our capacity to connect,[6] yielding pathological behaviours typically detailed in a Michel Houellebecq novel. The recreational sports we play are more likely directed by algorithms than a coach's old-fashioned instincts. It is no coincidence that *Moneyball* (2011), an adapted screenplay[7] about the important role Wall Street–derived statisticians played in building a winning team, is the best-known baseball movie of the last twenty years – a far cry from *Field of Dreams*!

In their own time, Montesquieu and his Scottish counterparts were attuned to the pathological features of commerce, and liberal modernity more generally, but they understood that commerce was power in the eighteenth century, that nations cannot turn the clock back. Instead, they found vestigial sources of virtue within Europe's most advanced nations, which were indispensable for keeping everything on an even keel and locking in the gains of modern commerce. They warned against letting commercial mores go unleashed but doubted the practicality of resuscitating an organic sense of the public sphere, as experienced in the ancient Roman republic or the Greek polis. Rather, they provided readers with competing theories of honour that aim towards a more balanced conception of commerce and virtue, avoiding the clash between a liberalism of self-interest and a republicanism of selfless civic virtue.

In unearthing hinge-points that link Montesquieu with his Scottish counterparts on questions concerning the nature of honour and its function in commercial and political life, I develop two narrative arcs throughout *Moderate Liberalism and the Scottish Enlightenment*, which reach a nexus with the following paradoxical claim: as societies become increasingly liberal and open, they will be unable to survive without an aristocratic ethos that provides a sense of honour among citizens. Our sustained attention to this paradox will yield important questions concerning our own politically and economically fragile times.

First, in comparing the sentimental bases of Montesquieu's, Hume's, Smith's and Ferguson's respective theories, *Moderate Liberalism and the Scottish Enlightenment* offers an important contribution to contemporary theory that is preoccupied with how varied forms of populism have shaken our liberal democratic foundations. A moral ecology of liberal theory today has origins in neo-Kantian political thought, which might sometimes be insensitive to the role of sentiments in human relationships that Montesquieu and his Scottish counterparts carefully considered in their theorising. Despite their enthusiasm for commerce, they shared the view that engaging with one another in a rational technocratic fashion would inevitably lead to despotism. Rather, they presupposed that people are most functional in political life through empathy and sought ways to prevent commerce from stifling human beings' sociable impulses. I present Montesquieu and his Scottish counterparts as proto-liberal thinkers who channel and moderate existing institutions to enliven the just sentiments while containing the pernicious ones. In considering how their theories responded to the hazards of eighteenth-century finance, this book captures the sense of chaotic change that disrupts the sentiments they had deemed necessary for securing the modern commercial world's emergent liberal practices. It will demonstrate how their moderate liberalism is not wholly derivative of intellectual or instrumental virtue but is, rather, grounded in social contingency. In examining their respective visions of free, moderate government, we will see how their theories distinctly preserve a civic space, meant to nourish citizens' sense of interpersonal magnanimity and to temper their inward-looking passions.

Second, by comparing Montesquieu, Hume and Smith's theoretical responses to the hazards of eighteenth-century high finance, readers will discover a shared affinity for France's and Britain's delicate distinctions of rank. Montesquieu's penchant for the titled nobility suggests a continual need to preserve non-commercial sources of virtue in the modern world. Conversely, Hume and Smith held that a well-ordered commercial meritocracy would sufficiently foster social responsibility among Britain's elites. In pressing these two perspectives against one another, this book provokes readers to critically reflect upon current-day features of capitalism which have crystalised over the past three centuries. Hume's and Smith's optimism that commercial society *itself* could provide us with our moral bearings will raise questions about how the accelerated growth of automation, shadow derivatives markets, and cryptocurrencies, for example, are reconfiguring our commercial interactions. Alternatively, Montesquieu's persistent warnings that untethered commercial meritocracy fosters a toxic winner-take-all mentality constitute a compelling case for needing to counteract commercial ambition with non-commercial distinction. In writing during Europe's transition from a feudal order towards a more liberal commercial world, Montesquieu and his Scottish counterparts were attuned to their nations' new 'aristocracies' and sought ways to cultivate a deep sense for the public good in them. Considering the transition our current liberal order is undergoing, their political projects offer useful frameworks for engaging with our own emerging 'elites', whose innovative projects risk producing sources of despotism inconceivable prior to the twenty-first century.

Given the logarithmic rise of populism since the Great Recession, evidenced by a routinisation of demagogic dog-whistle rhetoric that recalls the darkest crisis points of the twentieth century, it is understandable how one would look askance towards scholarly attempts at theorising such an amorphous term – elite – to frame our civic challenges. Yet, this theme occupied a critical dimension of Montesquieu and his Scottish counterparts' liberal thought. They recognised that, to maintain their viability, large liberal societies needed an axiology of value that transcends the plurality of inescapable unequal relationships contained within.

In a recent article which examines the failures of America's 'new aristocracy', Patrick Deneen claims that, in an increasingly secular and progressive age of liberal capitalism, modern elites are unaware of their privileged status because they lack the *noblesse oblige* and Protestant impulses that animated their socially responsible forerunners in the early twentieth century.[8] The argument follows that the logical progression of liberalism led to the abandonment of *noblesse oblige*, providing a final death blow to chivalry in the modern age. Deneen provides a compelling analysis of class inequality but hyperbolises the distinction between the two groups of 'elites' that he details. Despite past examples of philanthropy, the historiography of this period is in violent agreement about the trail of debt and poverty post–Gilded Age elites left behind, which Franklin D. Roosevelt had to remedy by expanding the welfare state. Nonetheless, Deneen's critique of contemporary liberalism compels us to reflect on what it means to be a knight in the twenty-first century.

Francis Fukuyama's classic commentary offers a friendlier critique of liberalism. Yet, his 'End of History' thesis is much maligned today precisely because it presciently recognised how the material comforts liberalism yields will insufficiently satisfy human beings.[9] He takes it for granted that honour is an assertion of our freedom and that liberal democracies need to channel human beings' natural desire for recognition to maintain their viability. We want to be seen, and he perceives the state to be our principal outlet for recognition. Fukuyama provides a favourable view of Enlightenment political thought, identifying sources of civic redemption within liberalism itself. He admires the United States' Founding Fathers for realising that, however biologically encoded it may be in our natures, *thùmos* simply cannot be eradicated.[10] Our political culture today empirically confirms this claim, that *megalothùmia* cannot be overcome.[11] However, Fukuyama's preoccupation with the genealogy of American liberalism eclipses the wide panorama of foundational liberal thinkers who distinctly theorised honour. Their projects evoked alternative sources to classical Rome and

Christianity for inspiring a civic-minded, moderate disposition among citizens in commercial Europe.

In examining how Montesquieu and his Scottish counterparts adapted their liberal theories to the financialisation of European governments, *Moderate Liberalism and the Scottish Enlightenment* demonstrates how eighteenth-century honour is not a pre-modern chivalric anachronism, but a conceptual lens for identifying an emotional quality that is necessary for twenty-first-century citizenship. It will provide readers with a heuristic for identifying when commercial innovation poses a threat to our liberal foundations, and a framework for balancing commercial ends with the public good *under conditions of liberal democracy*. In an age of polarised extremes, we have already seen how restive democracies have flirted with populist, illiberal responses to our elites' recent indiscretions. Montesquieu's, Hume's, Smith's and Ferguson's foundational theories offer us more viable, middle-ground prescriptions that are sensitive to the emotional constitution of a liberal society. This underappreciated facet of their political thought is undoubtedly germane today as external and internal critics of liberalism question the viability of our hyper-individualistic liberal democratic culture.

Notes

1. Geoff Baker, 'Man fears 2nd attempt on life after pipe bomb failed', *The Gazette* [Montreal], 16 Apr. 1994, https://advance-lexis-com. ezproxy.lib.uh.edu/api/document?collection=news&id=urn:contentI tem:3SR8-X150-002G-H3W9-00000-00&context=1516831
2. Aaron Derfel, Ann Carroll and Eddie Collister, 'Police disarm car bomb that caused traffic chaos', *The Gazette* [Montreal], 12 Nov. 1993, https://advance-lexis-com.ezproxy.lib.uh.edu/api/document?co llection=news&id=urn:contentItem:3SR8-XFB0-002G-H2JG-00000- 00&context=1516831
3. Adam Smith, *Theory of Moral Sentiments* (London: Henry G. Bohn, 1853), Part I, Sec. 3, Chap. 3, 88.
4. Cf. Wendy Brown, *Undoing the Demos: Neoliberalism's Stealth Revolution* (Princeton: Princeton University Press, 2015); Patrick J. Deneen, *Why Liberalism Failed* (New Haven: Yale University Press, 2018); Michael Sandel, *The Tyranny of Merit: What's Become of the Common Good* (New York: Farrar, Straus and Giroux, 2020).
5. George Thomas, 'Liberal Education and American Democracy', *The American Interest*, 24 Aug. 2015, https://www.the-american-interest. com/2015/08/24/liberal-education-and-american-democracy/

6. Ashley Fetters, 'The Five Years That Changed Dating', *The Atlantic*, 21 Dec. 2018.

7. Michael Lewis, *Moneyball: The Art of Winning an Unfair Game* (New York: W. W. Norton & Co. 2004).

8. Patrick J. Deneen, 'The Ignoble Lie: How the New Aristocracy Masks its Privilege', *First Things*, Apr. 2018, https://www.firstthings.com/article/2018/04/the-ignoble-lie.

9. Francis Fukuyama, *The End of History and the Last Man* (New York: Free Press, 1992).

10. Ibid., 187.

11. Ibid., 19.

Acknowledgements

This book could not have been written without a community of scholars, friends and institutions.

I am grateful to Edinburgh University Press's Board of Directors for their commitment to this project and to my anonymous readers for their generous feedback. To an early-career scholar, the tempestuous world of academic publishing is daunting, but I was able to navigate it thanks to Ersev Ersoy, Vasileios Syros and Beatriz Lopez's continual encouragement and advice. I am also deeply grateful to my research assistant, Jonah McCoy, and copyeditor, Robert Tuesley Anderson, for their fastidious work during the critical late stages of the project.

Many institutions hosted important discussions that shaped earlier iterations of this book: UCL/QMUL's London Summer School in Intellectual History; Eighteenth-Century Scottish Studies Society; Kinder Institute on Constitutional Democracy; International Society for Eighteenth-Century Studies; Southern Political Science Association; University of Toronto Political Theory Research Workshop; *Starting Points Journal*; *Lumen*; *Eighteenth-Century Scotland*.

I am grateful to the research librarians and staff who generously (and patiently!) assisted me during my time at Bibliothèque de l'Arsenal; Bibliothèque national de France; Folger Shakespeare Library; William Andrews Clark Library; National Library of Scotland; British Library; Thomas Fisher Library; Robarts Library.

I am grateful to the exceptional scholars who critiqued earlier versions of the manuscript: Alexander Broadie, Paul Carrese, David Carrithers, Henry C. Clark, Carli Conklin, Alin Fumurescu,

Alan Gibson, Khalil Habib, Avi Lifschitz, Andrea Radasanu, Helena Rosenblatt, Andrew Sabl, Jay Sexton, Rick Sher, Vickie Sullivan, Aaron Zubia.

The University of Toronto, a long-standing model for studies in the history of political thought, was an ideal hub for discussing the themes in this book. I am especially thankful to Ryan Balot, Joseph Carens, Simone Chambers, Andrew Gross, Ryan Hurl, Mark Lippincott, Nicholas Marler, Clifford Orwin, Jose Parra, Lincoln and Lindsay Mahon-Rathnam, Sarah Rich-Zendel, Faisal Saadatmand and Igor Shoikhedbrod, for our rich and refreshing conversations.

'Tell me and I forget, teach me and I may remember, involve me and I learn,' said Benjamin Franklin. I have been blessed to discover so many generous mentors and guides whose ecumenical collegiality was indispensable throughout this project: Edward Andrew, Ronald Beiner, Jeffrey Church, Aurelian Craiutu, Donald Drakeman, Justin Dyer, Dustin Gish, Michael Mosher, Emily Nacol, Robert Sparling, Lee Ward, and Stuart Warner. I am especially indebted to my dear friends, Professors Rebecca Kingston and James Moore. Rebecca's scholarship and supervision now serve as my model when advising researchers. James is a stalwart scholar who introduced me to the exciting ideas of the Scottish Enlightenment; I cannot think of a better way to honour his mentorship than placing my manuscript with Edinburgh University Press.

'No man is a failure who has friends,' writes Clarence in *It's a Wonderful Life*. I am grateful to wonderful friends whose diversity of perspectives have helped me communicate my research to engaged citizens beyond the academy: Sara Druggett, Phillip Karpowicz, Sandra Kassis, Eric Lothman, Peter Lund, Dylan Rajguru, Eric Rosset, Niharika Thanki, Tri Vinh Van and Robert Wheaton.

'Now abideth faith, hope, and love, and of these the greatest is love' (I Corinthians 13:13). This book owes its deepest intellectual debt to the following people. I am grateful to my late grandmother and matriarch, Eleni Vassiliou, for infusing my family with a profound spirit of *agapé*. Christopher James Aranda's magnanimity, sense of duty, and fertile mind echoes throughout this entire book. I am grateful to my brother and most loyal supporter, Anthony Vassiliou. His empathy and conviviality preserve my faith in the everyday kindness of a healthy liberal society. I will be forever grateful to my late father, Christos Vassiliou, whose larger-than-life sacrifices have given me a fighting shot at a privileged academic life. Memories of his stoicism furnished the energy needed to finish this book. Finally, I am most grateful to my mother, Connie Rapatsoulea Vassiliou. Due to the prejudices of her time, only her friends and family could benefit from the warmth of her wisdom, but ever since I left my career in finance to write this book, her support has been unwavering, despite the prejudices of my time.

Introduction: Montesquieu's Moderate Liberalism and the Scottish Enlightenment

This book points to a perennial problem in liberal modernity: how to balance commercial considerations with the public interest. We do not need to look further back than the subprime crisis and the subsequent Great Recession to see the practical results of an ethos that assumes an unproblematic reconciliation of these ends. An illustrative example is the establishment of Fannie Mae and Freddie Mac, US government–sponsored corporations created by the Roosevelt administration in response to the United States' banking crisis during the 1930s. Such initiatives show how moral hazard may become a concern under any regulatory system. Despite their benevolent origins and effectiveness in stabilising banks during the Great Depression, these institutions provided private financiers and bankers with a disincentive to judiciously consider risk in their day-to-day lending practices.[1] They inadvertently encouraged financiers to provide loans for the purposes of reselling them to larger institutions that securitised them and assumed the entire risk. The resulting economic fallout eroded citizens' trust in public institutions. What is more, the subsequent piecemeal erosion of the Dodd–Frank regulatory regime in the United States – established in 2010 to rein in the excesses of Wall Street – has fed into a culture of populism, reflected by the hostility of underprivileged classes towards public and private elites whose indiscretions became an acknowledged cause for their overarching financial distress. *Moderate Liberalism and the Scottish Enlightenment* considers this dilemma through the lenses of Enlightenment-era political philosophers who met similar challenges during capitalism's nascent stages. Their works contain elegant theories of moderate government, germane to our own thinking about political morality in liberal modernity.

Montesquieu is well known as a paragon of the 'Moderate Enlightenment' – a theorist of constitutional balance. However, underexplored affinities between him and key figures in the Scottish Enlightenment can enlarge our understanding of their moderation. They highlight that it is not a merely legalistic notion but a deeper vision of how commercial ends and public spiritedness may be harmonised. In recounting how Montesquieu and his Scottish contemporaries responded to the civic challenges associated with Europe's gradual financialisation, I recapture a conceptual space in the famous eighteenth-century commerce and virtue debates. I present Montesquieu as a pivotal figure in these debates.[2] His theoretical assessment of commercial society made him a powerful interlocutor with his Scottish contemporaries. He had a deliberately ambivalent position throughout his writings, being a promoter of commerce who nonetheless warned how it could become a handmaid of despotism if left untamed. With his Mandevillean enthusiasm for commerce on the one hand, and his nostalgia for the classical politics of the ancients on the other, Montesquieu rejected the dichotomy that politics must either be wholly grounded in genuine morality or commercial self-interest. This book will provide a comparative analysis of Montesquieu, David Hume, Adam Smith and Adam Ferguson's political thought, to highlight an important facet of their moderate liberalism: a shared propensity for social distinctions, which aimed to accommodate virtue in a society preoccupied with self-interested commerce.

This book challenges those who associate Montesquieu's well-known admiration for commercial England with a radically liberal political philosophy that seeks to accelerate the dismantling of Europe's pre-modern structures of social and political management. Scholars have notably emphasised the following passage in Book 3.3 of *The Spirit of the Laws*, which on its face reads as a neutral instantiation of the eighteenth-century commerce and virtue debates, to support their claim: 'The political men of Greece who lived under popular government recognized no other force to sustain it than virtue. Those of today speak to us only of manufacturing, commerce, finance, wealth, and even luxury.'[3] According to Thomas Pangle, Montesquieu's stark opposition between the virtue of the ancients and the inward-looking commercial ethos of the moderns provides the groundwork for a liberal philosophy that precludes the possibility of classical virtue in the modern commercial world. Andrew Bibby accepts Pangle's premise but focuses a good part of his analysis on Book 23 of *The Spirit of the Laws*.[4] There

Montesquieu exhibits his expertise in banking and paper money, proving that he fully aligns himself with the political men of today.

Catherine Larrère convincingly rejects such 'monist' accounts of Montesquieu's constitutionalism, noting how they betray a primary feature of his liberal political philosophy, namely, a 'pluralist vision of the political good'.[5] She argues that Montesquieu's deliberately neutral distinction between economies of commerce (England) and economies of luxury (France) corresponds with his 'external' (constitutional) pluralism. He attunes readers to the 'several paths commerce can take in modern times'.[6] It follows, then, that Montesquieu deliberately blurs the distinction between the ancients and moderns in 3.3, to highlight the multiple intermediate possibilities for approximating virtue in the modern commercial world, with some nations better equipped to accommodate certain modes of high finance than others.

This book stakes a distinct claim about the Bordeaux aristocrat's proto-liberalism. Montesquieu is a distant admirer of commercial England who rejects the island nation as a wholesale political model for France. I present him as a thinker who recognised how institutions and existing social affectations that prima facie seem non-liberal may help sustain eighteenth-century Europe's emergent liberal practices: religious toleration, a right to private property, and institutional checks and balances that guarantee the impartial administration of law and justice. I situate him alongside the civic republican tradition, with Hume, Smith and Ferguson, recapturing a moderate perspective in foundational liberal thought that accepts commerce as the organising principle of the modern world but nonetheless recognises how certain pre-modern institutions and practices need to be channelled and moderated to counterpoise its most vicious features which threaten to reverse the gains of liberal modernity. A further investigation into how they uniquely reconcile private commercial gain with the public good will reveal less strict conceptions of liberalism and republicanism, illustrating the possibility that one may accept the general principles of modernity while maintaining a healthy scepticism towards commerce.

Eighteenth-century Commerce

In the eighteenth century the term 'commerce' had a much broader meaning than it does today. It meant a communication among different peoples, rather than simple material exchange, although it also referred to agriculture, manufacturing, arts, fishing, finance and navigation.[7] While Montesquieu uses the term broadly (communication) and narrowly, he rarely treats the different usages of 'commerce' in isolation from one another. Progress in the arts and manufacturing enhances communication among peoples, and communication among peoples fuels progress in the arts. Moreover, Montesquieu rarely considered the challenges of modern commerce *sui generis* vis-à-vis broader political challenges that preoccupied him. As we shall see, considerations over the various modes of interrelated eighteenth-century commercial activities – state and individual finance, traffic of goods, and the cosmopolitan exchange of knowledge and norms – informed his theory of free, moderate government.

A comparative study of how Montesquieu and his Scottish counterparts theoretically responded to the exigencies of modern commerce during capitalism's nascent stages will give readers a unique vantage point, wherefrom commerce was not seen as merely an economic phenomenon, but a cultural phenomenon as well. Albert Hirschman's classic commentary showcases how our sustained attention to the intellectual history of this period may illuminate promising features of capitalism that have been eclipsed by the historical circumstances of the last three centuries.[8] To current-day readers, capitalism might understandably seem like an agent of unpredictability and instrumentalisation as episodic economic crises have yielded an abiding sense of precarity among citizens, mirroring a constant disruption to the liberal commercial world's existing norms, mores and modes of communication. However, the rise of capitalism had more of a glacial quality to it, emerging 'out of the old to a greater extent than has generally been appreciated'.[9] The political philosophy of the seventeenth and eighteenth centuries responded enthusiastically to the burgeoning commercial world. Thinkers from this period witnessed a greater degree of predictability in human affairs that they associated with a growing desire for commercial gain across the population.[10] Montesquieu is the principal hero of Hirschman's story. He observed that commerce cured Europe from the 'ills of Machiavellianism', a testament to how the calculated pursuit of self-interest opposes the unruly passions that underpinned political management in previous ages. Hirschman states, Montesquieu 'saw nothing but douceur'[11] in human beings' desire for gain, evidenced by its alchemising effects on the prince's will to dominate.

Indeed, Montesquieu recognised the overall benefits of modern commerce. However, France's economic challenges in the wake of the War of the Spanish Succession (1701–14) made him attuned to its inherent dangers, namely, its potential impact on the civic personality. First, he warned that, although commerce forged new social bonds, it concomitantly produced an ethos that privileges self-interested ends over considerations for the common good. Second, he cautioned readers that modern commerce may produce a spirit of apathy among citizens in the face of despotic activity and injustice. Third, he observed that commercial innovation, specifically in the arts of high finance, opened new avenues for corruption among political and economic elites that inched free, moderate nations towards despotism. Montesquieu observed these dangers unfolding at varying degrees among European nations. However, in his immediate context, France, he was mostly preoccupied with how unchecked high finance may exploit and amplify the other dangers associated with modern commerce, and generate the conditions for unstable, despotic government.

France's debt crisis following the War of the Spanish Succession made government actors more amenable to 'financial engineering' schemes, which opened new avenues for corruption in commercial and political life. In an infamous episode known as 'Le système' (The System), John Law (1671–1729), a Scottish financier who served as Controller General of French Finances (1716–21), persuaded the French regent, Philippe II, duc d'Orléans, to sign off on a series of disastrous fiscal and monetary decisions, culminating in the infamous collapse of the 'Mississippi Bubble'. The System's collapse led to financial loss and social instability. Similar episodes took place across Europe at that time, compelling thinkers to reconceptualize the tension between commercial self-interest and civic virtue. In *Revolutionary Commerce*, Paul Cheney convincingly states that Montesquieu's response to Law's System reflects his broader goal to curtail the forces of 'primitive globalization' by nestling commercial life 'within the political and social hierarchies inherited from Europe's feudal monarchies'.[12] The Law debacle injected instability and unpredictability into human affairs,[13] amplifying the pathological features of modern commerce. The events surrounding the System's collapse reinforced Montesquieu's concern with maintaining a balance between the contribution of the 'monied class' to public life and the continuing role for aristocratic government.

Central Argument

In considering the institutional and intellectual context of Law's System in France, the first chapters of this book will cast light on why Law features as Montesquieu's avatar for despotism throughout his political writings. I explain that Law threatened to produce a despotism of the most pernicious sort. Unlike traditional threats to free, moderate government, which stemmed from absolute princely rule or clerical power, the form of despotism that concerned Montesquieu *most* came from a fusion of financial and political power. Law's System threatened existing intermediary institutional bodies, which were instrumental for checking centralised power,[14] and for inspiring a deep sense of the common good among the wider citizen body. More specifically, the Bordeaux aristocrat feared that Law's financial system fed into an emerging commercial culture of the time, which perceived money and personal wealth, rather than public spiritedness, as the greatest arbiter of social standing and recognition. In response to this perceived cultural pathology, Montesquieu reinvigorates France's vestigial institutions of honour to foster a hierarchy of value in the public mind that privileges civic engagement over wealth and commercial success. I then consider how David Hume and Adam Smith's theoretical responses to the financial crises of 1720 – both of which mirror Montesquieu's preoccupation with social distinctions – uniquely integrate within their broader visions of politics.

Later chapters consider how Montesquieu, Hume, Smith and Ferguson's political economy concerns shaped their understandings of liberty and modern honour. Montesquieu and Hume chiefly preoccupied themselves with the civic challenges posed by innovations in high finance, whereas Smith and Ferguson had to contend with the added concern over how *commercial specialisation* stifled the civic personality and threatened European liberty. In examining their responses to these challenges, *Moderate Liberalism and the Scottish Enlightenment* maps out the trajectories of two distinct conceptions of free, moderate government, identifiable in the political thought of Montesquieu and Hume. I will then trace the ongoing unfolding of these ideas as the object of commercial considerations shifted a generation later. My analysis illuminates a strand of foundational liberal thought, paradoxically concerned with how pre-modern institutions may be harnessed to preserve liberty and political order in the modern commercial world. It builds on the scholarship that recognises how Montesquieu's *Spirit of the Laws* shifted the discourse in Scotland from a politics informed by jurisprudence and theoretical conjecture to a politics grounded in historicity by emphasising his shared sensitivity with Hume, Smith and Ferguson to the fragility of liberty and the destabilising features of modern commerce.[15] They shared the view that the liberal commercial world could not sustain itself if we remove honour from the public sphere. Their liberal theories point to an idea of justice that cannot be encapsulated by abstract principles a priori but by the hierarchy of relationships that exist within pluralistic liberal nations; with the mere existence of certain hierarchical honours, moral behaviour comes as an emergent property. I argue that their preoccupation with European honour is emblematic of a politics of 'fellow feeling' and 'empathy', which formed the basis of a healthy liberal society.

Montesquieu and the Moderate Enlightenment

The term 'moderation' is often employed as a pejorative descriptor in contemporary political discourse, mirroring some of the historiography in eighteenth-century political thought. It is therefore important to differentiate Montesquieu and his contemporaries' usage of the term 'moderation' from its more familiar usage that implies a reactionary preference for order over justice. The latter might bring to mind Martin Luther King Jr's 'Letter from a Birmingham Jail', which famously excoriates the 'white moderate' who is sympathetic but unwilling to disturb the political order in the face of absolute injustice.[16] King privileges an 'extremism of love' and 'extremism of justice' over a moderate propensity for order that he associates with the 'white moderate'.[17] Montesquieu's 'moderate' approximates the principles of King's paragon citizen, with his warning to readers not to conflate his usage of the term with that of the French moralists[18] which connotes 'faintheartedness and . . . laziness of soul'.[19] Montesquieu's moderation aims to enable courage – a spirit of resistance among citizens in the face of injustice – in the modern commercial world.

Some situate Montesquieu among a group of Enlightenment thinkers who had a reactionary impulse facing the tearing down of Europe's existing pre-modern institutions. For instance, in distinguishing between the radical and moderate Enlightenments, of which Montesquieu purportedly falls in the latter category, Jonathan Israel explains, 'It was a battle between . . . progress that drives toward equality and democracy and seeks to enlighten everyone, and marginal reform of the existing order of monarchy and privilege.'[20] Israel's account erringly treats a thinker's commitment to formal democratic equality as a litmus test for determining whether Montesquieu merits a place on the 'right side' of Enlightenment history. While Montesquieu's vision of politics accepts a circumscribed role for the illiberal clergy in the administration of the state, and it moreover extolls 'inegalitarian' institutions of honour, his political moderation cannot simply be equated to a reactionary embrace of tradition.[21] Montesquieu tolerates and adapts pre-modern institutions to preserve the gains of modern commerce, and to save the modern order from itself. Israel's heuristic obfuscates Montesquieu's moderate liberalism – an outlook that fully embraces our Enlightenment ideals and practices.

Dennis Rasmussen's recent commentary provides a more judicious account of Enlightenment moderation, situating Montesquieu within a tradition of pragmatists who commonly grounded their visions of politics in experience and empiricism.[22] However, he and other interpreters dubiously claim that commerce unqualifiedly constituted Montesquieu's moderate vision of politics, ignoring abiding anxieties about how a commercial culture may produce the conditions for despotic rule.[23] Commerce supported the principles of free, moderate government. At the same time, it was a source of immoderation and despotism if left unchecked. An important feature of Montesquieu's moderation is that *commerce itself* needs to be moderated.

Aurelian Craiutu's account captures the multifaceted nature of Montesquieu's moderation,[24] urging scholars to remap what he eloquently describes as 'the lost archipelago' of modern political thought. If we lose the moderate perspective of these thinkers, it is a loss that does not simply have ramifications for eighteenth-century intellectual history, but also for the currency of ideas available to support our liberal foundations. *Moderate Liberalism and the Scottish Enlightenment* charts a new passageway towards an island of eighteenth-century moderation, which is particularly sensitive to the role of sentiments in our moral and political reasoning.[25]

Montesquieu's Moderation

Montesquieu's slippery usage of the term 'moderation' throughout *The Spirit of the Laws* has yielded divergent interpretations among scholars examining this theme.[26] He first invokes the term to distinguish good regimes from despotic regimes. In Part I, he details three typologies of free, moderate government, emphasising the central importance of their animating *principles*, or 'the human passions that set [government] in motion.'[27] He later explains that 'the corruption of each government almost always begins with that of its principles,'[28] implying that laws and institutions alone are insufficient for maintaining liberty and guaranteeing the impartial administration of justice. Free, moderate government demands the population's emotional investment into their country's laws and institutions. In the absence of a spirited citizenry, government will inevitably collapse into its default form: despotism. Republican, aristocratic, and monarchical governments – Montesquieu's three archetypal moderate regimes in *The Spirit of the Laws* – become despotic when the spirit of virtue or honour no longer animates their populations respectively.

Scholars will sometimes conclude that Montesquieu's tripartite regime classification points towards an ideal typology extolled throughout his works. Their disagreement over his actual preferred regime testifies to the Bordeaux aristocrat's pluralism concerning this question. In reality, Montesquieu invokes moderation as a theory of institutional balance which umbrellas over multiple, imperfect constitutional possibilities. He writes:

> In order to form a moderate government, one must combine powers, regulate them, temper them, make them act; one must give one power a ballast, so to speak, to put it in a position to resist another; this is a masterpiece of legislation that chance rarely produces and prudence is rarely allowed to produce. By contrast, a despotic government leaps to view, so to speak; it is uniform throughout; as only passions are needed to establish it, everyone is good enough for that.[29]

There are two key propositions contained in this touchstone definition of moderation that will be unpacked throughout this book.

1. *A nation's institutional sources of moderation may become despotic if left unchecked.* Montesquieu's prescription that each source of political power should 'resist another' will frustrate our efforts to classify any one institution of moderation as an unalloyed good. Multiple spheres of human activity derived from institutional, commercial and political life needed to be counteracted to prevent despotism. Montesquieu does not make an exception for the institutions most closely correlated with honour and virtue. This may seem contradictory considering how these 'principles' distinctly provide the fulcrum for maintaining free, moderate government. However, 28.41, which examines political moderation

at the level of individual psychology, helps us make sense of this ambiguity. He writes:

> By a misfortune attached to the human condition, great men who are moderate are rare; and, as it is always easier to follow one's strength than to check it, perhaps, in the class of superior people, it is easier to find extremely virtuous people than extremely wise men.
>
> The soul takes such delight in dominating other souls; even those who love the good love themselves so much that no one is so unfortunate as to distrust his good intentions; and, in truth, our actions depend on so many things that it is a thousand times easier to do good than to do it well.[30]

Indeed, virtue and honour spring free, moderate government into motion, but principled ambition may lead to despotism since genuinely virtuous people '[take] such delight in dominating other souls'. As such, it is not only our innate desire to increase power which needs to be tamed to maintain this 'masterpiece of legislation', but also the passions that enable human beings' highest moral possibilities.

2. *Various modes of government may be free and moderate.* At most, the commercialisation of Europe has afforded nations new opportunities to draw lessons from each other's best practices; but their unique circumstances preclude the possibility of finding an alternative, superlative regime beyond their frontiers. Montesquieu's aphoristic style undercuts attempts at identifying an ideal regime that anchors his vision of politics. *The Spirit of the Laws* is a dialectical, not a propositional, work. It induces readers to establish their political horizons by examining their *own* institutional sources of liberty and moderate government.[31] As Montesquieu candidly states in his prefatory remarks, he would be the happiest of mortals if his reader finds 'new reasons for loving his duties, his prince and his laws and that . . . each could better feel his happiness in his own country, government, and position . . .'[32] His tripartite regime classification more judiciously serves as a rubric for assessing the emotional health of one's nation, and identifying its particular sources of free, moderate government. However, Montesquieu's nostalgic tenor in his account of the classical politics of Greece and Rome throughout Part I of *The Spirit of the Laws*, his two superlative republican models, reflects his overall doubt that selfless civic virtue could reliably animate citizens in a commercial world of diminished souls. His lamentations intimate

that honour, or human beings' primordial desire for preferences and distinctions, is a more fungible currency in an emerging liberal world characterised by 'political men who speak to us only of manufacturing, commerce, finance, wealth, and even luxury'.[33] This book's examination of Montesquieu's idea of honour will extend beyond the scope of Montesquieu's archetypal monarchy as detailed in *The Spirit of the Laws*, unearthing a facet of his thought, which escapes the unhelpful dichotomy that free societies can be maintained strictly through virtue in the classical sense, or by legal restraints alone.

The 'Tale of the Troglodytes': Commerce and Virtue in the Modern Commercial World

Recent scholars challenge the historiography of eighteenth-century political economy that assumes commerce and virtue were held in opposition to each other, demonstrating how the most renowned boosters of modern commerce filtered ancient philosophical ideas into their political arguments.[34] For instance, in Melissa Lane's recent analysis of David Hume's and Adam Smith's thought, she explains how both held that scientific literacy was sacrosanct for meaningful civic engagement, yet she convincingly shows how they equally shared their ancient Greek counterparts' anxieties about the civic challenges their nations would face if a spirit of *pleonexia*, or 'an immoderate, overreaching desire for more than one's share',[35] took firm hold over the population. As we shall see, Montesquieu's earliest writings warn readers that free, commercial nations were not immune to the dangers of *pleonexia*.[36] In his immediate context, he bemoaned France's transition into a society that increasingly considered wealth as the only barometer of value and social distinction. It is a concern that looms large in his 'Tale of the Troglodytes' – an allegory from *Persian Letters* that warns about the despotic dangers inherent to a political community anchored by self-interested commerce alone. Next, I examine Montesquieu's famous allegory to illuminate a central challenge he presents to his readers: how to satisfy commercial ends while preserving civic virtue in an eighteenth-century context? It is a challenge that occupied a critical dimension of Hume, Smith and Ferguson's thought, and one that Montesquieu himself grapples with throughout his political writings.[37]

Montesquieu introduces the allegory in Letter 10 of the *Persian Letters*, when Mirza presses his friend and mentor, Usbek, to elaborate on an earlier assertion he made, that men 'were born in order to be virtuous, and that justice is a quality that is as much a part of them as their own existence'.[38] Usbek responds that certain truths need to be felt,[39] implying a relationship between justice and the populace's emotional constitution. He then recounts a stadial history of the Troglodytes to support his claim.

The mythical tale encompasses two familiar modes of political organisation that mirror the eighteenth-century commerce and virtue debates. The first took shape in the wake of a successful coup that the Troglodytes orchestrated, overthrowing a tyrannical king of foreign origin. The king's brutality will become seared into the Troglodytes' historical memory in successive generations. Having associated their obedience with the king's illegitimate rule, the newly liberated Troglodytes resolved that 'all individuals . . . would no longer obey anyone; that each would look solely to his own interests, without consulting those of others'.[40] Their constitution was infused with a spirit of avaricious greed, which eventually spiralled out of control. Usbek's description of the early Troglodytes approximates a Hobbesian state of nature marked by famine, vast material inequality and commercial dishonesty, to which the Troglodytes were desensitised having always been 'strangers to the principles of justice and equity'. The situation proved ungovernable. The Troglodytes' founding maxims – 1) 'to submit to no one' and 2) 'that each should follow his own interest, without any attention to others' – stunted their capacity to identify their individual interests with the public interest, and fostered an aversion to rule, even among the most highly esteemed Troglodytes who refused to busy themselves with the public 'affairs to the neglect of [their] own'.[41] But it was the Troglodytes' dishonesty in daily commerce that led to their ultimate demise. Usbek recounts to Mirza that the Troglodytes faced a deadly disease outbreak and turned to a renowned doctor for his assistance. However, the doctor refused them, recalling how they had swindled him the last time he helped them manage an outbreak. The doctor then excoriated the Troglodytes, diagnosing them with a more virulent, incurable disease. '[Y]ou have a poison in your soul more mortal than the one for which you want to be cured; you do not deserve to occupy a place on earth, because you have no humanity, and the rules of equity are to you unknown.'[42] Nearly all the Troglodytes died as a result, an ignominious decline that casts doubt over a nation's viability once the population becomes infused with a spirit of avaricious greed.

Only two extraordinary men survived the plague. 'They were humane; they knew justice; they loved virtue.'[43] The men formed and sustained a new union – a republic that recalls to the reader the virtue of classical Athens and Rome – maintained by 'the uprightness of their hearts, as by the corruption of those of others ...' for whom they 'felt nothing but pity'.[44] This stage of Troglodyte history ushered in their halcyon days, affording a life according to justice, morality, and benevolence. Citizens committed themselves to the commonweal and exhibited a sense of propriety and honesty in their commercial interactions. Even though their wealth attracted envy and aggression from their neighbours, external threats were easily quenched since their overall prosperity was anchored by a martial spirit that made the self-ruling Troglodytes ferocious towards anyone who menaced their fellow citizens. In addition, the Troglodytes' new-found happiness and prosperity yielded a spirit of religiosity and reverence for the gods 'that improved their morals'. However, this more humane and equitable stage of Troglodyte history was short-lived. As commerce expanded, a growing desire for private gain overwhelmed the altruistic part of the soul most satiated by justice and virtue.[45] Civic virtue became too burdensome. The Troglodytes eventually appointed a king who was renowned for his magnanimity, thus relieving themselves of any burdens associated with affairs of state. The tale ends with the newly appointed king delivering a speech which recalls the Troglodytes' miserable ancestors, lamenting how they willingly made themselves subjects 'to satisfy ambition, amass riches, a life of ease and self-indulgent pleasure; and that, as long as [they] avoid serious crime'.[46] Such institutional arrangements were intolerable during simpler ages, whereas now the Troglodytes unwittingly submitted to the absolute care of his magistracy, giving up their true happiness in exchange for peace, security and material wealth.

The allegory's conclusion is rather ambiguous, mirroring Montesquieu's ambivalent stance in the eighteenth-century commerce and virtue debates. Usbek illustrates the possibility that commerce and virtue are reconcilable. Yet, we learn that as commercial progress disrupts the equilibrium, citizens will grow soft and incapable of fulfilling their civic responsibilities. Scholars have noted how Montesquieu developed a theoretical response to this dilemma in his later writings, arriving at different conclusions over which regime – a moderate monarchy or a commercial republic – provides the best conditions for reconciling commercial gain with the public interest.[47] Their divergent claims are a testament to Montesquieu's view that commercial modernity may sling in different directions. Montesquieu already begins to develop a sophisticated theoretical response to this dilemma in *Persian Letters*, with Usbek's response to Mirza after the latter pressed his mentor to weigh in on a philosophical debate he was having with Rica, on 'whether men are happy due to the pleasures and satisfaction of the senses or to the practice of virtue'.[48] One will recall that Usbek demurs from giving a rational defence of his position, stating 'there are certain truths for which it is not enough to be persuaded, but which one must also be made to feel'.[49] These prefatory remarks to the Troglodyte allegory cast light upon the dramatic tale's dual purpose: to educate Mirza on how to 'feel' the correctness of his claims concerning justice and happiness,[50] and to demonstrate that justice does not merely depend on a nation's juridical structures but on the quality of its citizens' emotional constitution.

Commerce tends towards producing a feeling for exact justice, as Montesquieu will later state in an often-cited passage from *The Spirit of Laws*, atrophying 'those moral virtues that make it so that one does not always discuss one's own interests alone and that one can neglect them for those of others'.[51] What may be interpreted as an acceptable compromise in *The Spirit of the Laws* is in fact a political problem that preoccupied Montesquieu throughout his writings. In his *Treatise on Duties*, written four years after *Persian Letters*, he distinguishes between exact justice, or a strict adherence to laws, and justice of a more general kind, echoing the Troglodyte king's ominous warning in Letter 14 of *Persian Letters*. A general feeling of justice 'detach(es) man from himself to attach him to his neighbour . . . without that everything is common, and there remains nothing but a base self-interest, which is properly nothing more than the animal instinct of all men'.[52] When a state simply functions as a vehicle for Hobbesian material comforts, the character of its citizens will approximate the wickedness and brutishness of the miserable Troglodytes in Letter 11 of *Persian Letters*. His unpublished essay thus clarifies the Troglodyte dilemma: commercial prosperity confers happiness; it concomitantly blunts a general feeling of justice that once 'made citizens attentive, helpful, tender, affectionate, and sensitive'.[53] How, then, does the modern legislator balance commerce and virtue in a post-classical republican world, while preserving a general feeling of justice that makes free, moderate government viable?

It is unclear whether Montesquieu is nostalgically calling for a return to Europe's republican past or settling for its current monarchical paradigm so long as the magistrate guarantees its subjects' personal liberty – a question that has been a subject of debate among his interpreters. The following passage from Montesquieu's addendum to the 'Tale of the Troglodytes', published in his *Pensées*, merits full quotation because it provides scholars with meaningful clues for understanding his own response to this challenge. When the king asks his Troglodyte subjects whether they prefer riches or virtue, one of them replies:

> [W]e are happy; we are working on an excellent foundation. Dare I say it? It is you alone who will decide whether riches are pernicious to our people or not. If they see that you prefer wealth to virtue, they will soon accustom themselves to doing likewise, and in that, your taste will govern theirs. If you raise a man to office or bring him into your confidence solely because he is rich, be assured that you will be striking a mortal blow to his virtue, and that you will be imperceptibly creating as many dishonest people as there are men who will have noticed that cruel distinction. You know, my Lord, the basis on which your people's virtue is founded: it is education. Change that education, and whoever was not bold enough to be criminal will soon blush at being virtuous.[54]

To this the king responds:

> Troglodytes . . . wealth is going to enter your midst. But I declare that if you are not virtuous, you will be one of the unhappiest peoples in the world. In the state you are in, I need only to be more just than you; this is the mark of my royal authority, and I can find none more august. If you seek to distinguish yourselves solely by wealth, *which is nothing in itself*, I will certainly have to distinguish myself by the same means, and not remain in a state of poverty that you disdain . . . O Troglodytes! We can be united by a beautiful bond: if you are virtuous, I will be; if I am virtuous, you will be.[55]

What readers learn from Montesquieu's unpublished letter is that the softer virtues are not wholly endogenous to commercial society, contrary to what some scholars have suggested.[56] Unchecked commerce atrophies citizens' moral sensibilities.[57] As individuals 'distinguish themselves by wealth', they yield a government whose officeholders increasingly reflect their diminished selves. As commerce expands, people no longer know what to value, and are too ashamed to display their virtue when the only recognition of true worth stems from material wealth. Commerce is not the original sin. Rather, the Troglodytes reflect a society that loses its moral hierarchy when commerce reaches *ubiquity*. The allures of fashion and ornamentation penetrate the civic mind, and citizens judge words and deeds by the barometer of wealth and nothing else. They conflate the public and private sphere since no other barometer for judgement exists under conditions where wealth becomes so ubiquitous that people 'blush at being virtuous'. Montesquieu warns that unchecked commerce leaves citizens with no criteria to evaluate character. They give more consideration to the strengths and virtues of commerce than the higher virtues that will today 'astonish our small souls!'[58] When higher offices are filled wholly on the basis of individual wealth, spectators remain silent.

Notwithstanding Montesquieu's concerns about the pathological features of modern commerce, he was nonetheless a booster of commerce. He observed how the spirit of commerce made civilisations more open, benevolent and humane,[59] shedding new avenues for moral and political progress, unavailable to the great republican regimes of previous ages. This greater flexibility permitted legislators to return citizens to 'their duties by their political and civil laws',[60] while respecting the general spirit of the nation they find themselves in. It is clear that, for Montesquieu, these gains would have been impossible under the conditions of 'equilibrium' one finds among the self-governing Troglodytes in Letter 13 of *Persian Letters*. Notwithstanding his sanguinity, the looming possibility of a society that does not know how to value anything else except for money deeply troubled Montesquieu throughout his writings, recognising how an unmitigated desire for gain may accommodate a desire for power.

The implicit question that Montesquieu poses with his provocative tale is how do modern commercial nations foster a sociable, other-regarding spirit among an increasingly inward-looking citizenry that is readily willing to exchange its liberty for personal ease and comfort? Hume, Smith and Ferguson will uniquely respond to the allegory's theoretical challenge, each arriving at a unique framework for approximating virtue in their respective theories.[61] They share Montesquieu's premise that the means by which to balance the pursuit of wealth and the public good is a rare nexus between the desire for honour through wealth and public acclaim. Yet, like Montesquieu, they reject the *agon* that characterised pre-modern honour-loving cultures. *Moderate Liberalism and the Scottish Enlightenment* will detail how they each pacify honour by channelling it within the commercial world.

Chapter Overview

The first chapter emphasises the impact of the events surrounding John Law's System on Montesquieu's intellectual formation. It explains how France's series of bankruptcies and experimental paper money schemes following the War of the Spanish Succession permitted Law to introduce his innovative schemes to France. Historical and institutional considerations will provide the backdrop for understanding how questions concerning eighteenth-century political economy were at the forefront of Montesquieu's mind as he developed his theory of free, moderate government. The chapter then examines competing accounts of 'political moderation' in the works and notes of Jean-François Mélon and John Law himself, to distinguish Montesquieu's own account, which emphasises the importance of maintaining a civically minded nobility to counteract centralised power.

I then examine how Montesquieu's concerns about Law's despotism loomed large in his earlier writings with a distinct focus on *Persian Letters*, to gain an entry point into his theoretical response to the wealth and virtue problem that he presents in his 'Tale of the Troglodytes'. As we shall see, Paris was not free from the inescapable pathologies of commercial modernity which Law himself embodied and amplified by instituting his System. However, Montesquieu held that these corrupting forces may be confined by France's longstanding honour-yielding institutions, namely the *parlements*.

Chapter 2 establishes the tangible roots of Montesquieu, Hume and Smith's respective ideas of honour, demonstrating how concerns over finance informed their respective liberal theories. First, it considers Montesquieu's response to the fiscal and monetary crises that plagued France between the time of Louis XIVs death in September 1715 and the collapse of John Law's System in November 1720. It then examines David Hume's preoccupation with eighteenth-century high finance. Mirroring Montesquieu, Hume feared that the paper money economy would disturb European nations' social distinctions, whose maintenance he deemed necessary for preserving free, moderate government in the modern commercial world. Finally, I compare Trenchard and Gordon ('Cato') and Montesquieu's responses to the collapse of the South Sea Bubble in England, examining how they informed Adam Smith's theoretical response to the financial bubbles of 1720. In pressing their distinct responses to the hazards of high finance against one another, this chapter illuminates a moderate perspective in the eighteenth-century commerce and virtue debates, which embraces commerce but harnesses existing honour-yielding institutions to produce a civic republican counterpoise to its excesses.

Chapter 3 considers Montesquieu's response to James Harrington's republican project. It interrogates his two unflattering references to Harrington in *The Spirit of the Laws*, to highlight Montesquieu's emphasis on the ineluctable role of raw emotion in the moral and political reasoning of political *and* philosophical 'legislators'. I explain that Montesquieu sympathised with Harrington's republican sensibilities, but, observing how innovation in high finance forged new dysfunctional features into European economies, he concluded that Harrington's civic republican theory was obsolete in the modern commercial world. Law's System symbolised challenges of which Harrington did not have the wherewithal to consider prior to Europe's financial revolutions. In Montesquieu's view, the emergence of paper money, public debt and financial speculation demanded an alternative foundation for free, moderate government.

Chapter 4 interrogates Montesquieu's and Hume's comparative analyses of Britain and France, to illuminate the conditions that enable liberty in their respective visions of politics. In the first part, I explain how both thinkers ground their theories of free, moderate government on the social passions they deemed necessary for providing vigour and stability to their nations' laws. Hume observed how eighteenth-century French salons created a tactile sociability mechanism that permitted various classes of society to congregate and engage in delightful, polite conversations about philosophy, history, politics and the various issues of the day. The pleasure derived from the commercial transmission of ideas and values that took place in the salons tempered the political factionalism, which, in Hume's view, posed the greatest threat to European nations. Montesquieu appreciated France's culture of commercial sociability as well. Yet, he would not have shared Hume's optimism that commerce alone can produce self-sufficient mores. Building off this point of contrast, I explain how Montesquieu's analysis of England led him towards a more robust conception of free, moderate government, which emphasises the importance of preserving non-commercial sources of public sentiment.

Building on the previous chapter's themes, Chapter 5 considers the historical and intellectual context that informed Hume's and Montesquieu's understandings of modern liberty. I examine the continuities and disjunctures between Montesquieu's and Hume's conceptions of modern honour vis-à-vis Bernard Mandeville's. I then interrogate Montesquieu and Hume's disagreement over questions concerning the relationship between liberty and honour, and the role of the nobility in commercial society. I begin by comparing their respective genealogies of modern liberty. Montesquieu traces its origins in France to Saint Louis's judicial reforms, whereas Hume follows James Harrington, tracing its origins in Britain to Henry VII's property reforms. My analysis shows how they each accepted commerce as the organising principle of the modern world and a progenitor of moral activity in eighteenth-century Europe, although at different degrees. Commerce was co-equal with liberty for Hume. By contrast, Montesquieu feared that the salutary distinctions associated with commerce could potentially collapse into wealth distinction alone, stifling other important barometers of value in a political community. In contrast to Hume, who categorically privileged commercial honour over ancient and feudal modes, Montesquieu had deeper reservations concerning a political culture whose animating 'principles' were borne via commerce alone.

Chapter 6 reconstructs a pluralistic theory of honour that runs the gamut of Montesquieu's political writings. It is grounded in the idea that existing political and institutional configurations need to reflect human beings' divided wills. His theory suggests the possibility that honour-loving may be harnessed to enliven human beings' social affections. It is why Montesquieu held that the liberal commercial world could not sustain itself if honour were removed from the public sphere. As such, he provides readers with a lens to recognise when commercial honour has gone awry, and a framework for achieving public honour that is not sacrificial. Finally, I demonstrate how Montesquieu's pluralistic conception of honour *necessarily* includes quotidian and loftier forms. To support my analysis, I return to the legacy of Saint Louis, explaining how the Capetian monarch's important judicial reforms provided Montesquieu with the institutional groundwork for a theory of free, moderate government which aims to enlarge citizens' sense of interpersonal magnanimity.

Chapter 7 examines how Adam Smith and Adam Ferguson adapted Montesquieu's moderation to their respective theories of politics. It explains that Montesquieu and his Scottish counterparts accept the possibility of multiple intermediate positions between fully embracing a classical republican or a commercially grounded vision of politics. They show readers that one does not need to jump directly from Rome or Sparta to the Mandevillean beehive; however, the means through which they approximate political virtue differ. Echoing Hume, Smith presupposes that modern commerce itself may produce the social and political virtues that satisfy the modern world's political exigencies, whereas Montesquieu and Ferguson emphasised the need to harness pre-modern institutions and manners to counterbalance commercial mores.

Moderate Liberalism and the Scottish Enlightenment will help illuminate post–Cold War attempts at dealing with the explosion of liberal capitalism as the de facto global standard. Francis Fukuyama, who famously proclaimed that there is no viable alternative to this dominant ideology, examined its deep roots to discover sources for taking advantage of it while counteracting its pathologies. The subsequent third-way politics of the 1990s and centrist attempts to counteract the recent wave of populism in the West each aim to protect the existing liberal economic order from more debased forms. Their attempts at moderating the excesses of liberal capitalism mirror the moderate compromises that Montesquieu and his Scottish counterparts deemed necessary for guaranteeing a free and stable order under conditions of modern commerce. This book will carefully reconstruct their respective visions of free, moderate government so that the limits and potential of this analogy can be fully understood.

Notes

1. 'Wonderful While it Lasted', *The Economist*, 30 Nov. 2013, https://www.economist.com/finance-and-economics/2013/11/30/wonderful-while-it-lasted
2. Mark Hulliung, *Montesquieu and the Old Regime* (Los Angeles: University of California Press, 1976); Céline Spector, *Montesquieu: pouvoirs, richesses et sociétés* (Paris: Presses universitaires de France, 2004); Thomas Pangle, *The Theological Basis of Liberal Modernity in Montesquieu's Spirit of the Laws* (Chicago: Chicago University Press, 2010); Iain McDaniel, *Adam Ferguson in the Scottish Enlightenment* (Cambridge, MA: Harvard University Press, 2013); Dennis Rasmussen, *The Pragmatic Enlightenment: Recovering the Liberalism of Hume, Smith, Montesquieu, and Voltaire* (Cambridge: Cambridge University Press, 2014).
3. Montesquieu, *The Spirit of the Laws*, ed. and trans. Anne M. Cohler, Basia C. Miller and Harold S. Stone (Cambridge: Cambridge University Press, 1989), 3.3, 22. Emphasis added.
4. Andrew Bibby, *Montesquieu's Political Economy* (New York: Palgrave Macmillan, 2016), ch. 5.

5. Catherine Larrère, 'Montesquieu and Liberalism: The Question of Pluralism', in *Montesquieu and His Legacy*, ed. Rebecca Kingston (Albany: SUNY, 2009), 283.

6. Ibid., 282.

7. Francois-Veron de Forbonnais, 'Commerce', in *Encyclopédie, ou Dictionnaire raisonné des sciences, des arts et des métiers, etc*, ed. Denis Diderot and Jean le Rond d'Alembert, University of Chicago: ARTFL Encyclopédie Project (Spring 2021 Edition), ed. Robert Morrissey and Glenn Roe, http://encyclopedie.uchicago.edu/, 691.

8. Albert Hirschman, *The Passions and the Interests: Political Arguments for Capitalism before Its Triumph* (Princeton: Princeton University Press First Printing Classics Edition, 2013), 132.

9. Ibid., 4.

10. Ibid., 48.

11. Ibid., 78.

12. Paul Cheney, *Revolutionary Commerce: Globalization and the French Monarchy* (Cambridge, MA: Harvard University Press), 54.

13. Anoush Terjanian, *Commerce and its Discontents in Eighteenth-century Political Thought* (Cambridge: Cambridge University Press, 2013), 27.

14. Scholars have already noted Montesquieu's significant concerns over how new modes of government finance disrupted revenue flows to France's nobility, weakening its political power. She correctly cites Montesquieu's affinity for France's *parlements*, whose titled office-holders performed an indispensable judiciary role in counteracting the Bourbon Crown's imperial ambitions. Judith Shklar, *Montesquieu* (Oxford: Oxford University Press, 1987), 80, 115. Law's System renewed Louis XIV's previous efforts to merge 'reason of state' and commerce – a mercantilist trend in French political economy that may only be arrested by the moderating power of the nobility. Istvan Hont, *Jealousies of Trade* (Cambridge, MA: Harvard University Press, 2005), 105.

15. James Moore, 'Montesquieu and the Scottish Enlightenment', in *Montesquieu and His Legacy*, ed. Rebecca Kingston (Albany: SUNY Press, 2008), 180; Mark Hulliung, *Enlightenment in Scotland and France: Studies in Political Thought*, Routledge Research in Early Modern History (London and New York: Routledge, 2019); Alexander Broadie, *Agreeable Connexions: Scottish Enlightenment Links with France* (Edinburgh: Birlinn, 2012).

16. I am thankful to Ronald Beiner, who in reading an earlier version of the manuscript, directed me to Martin Luther King Jr's famous letter, which questions the normative value of political moderation under circumstances of absolute injustice. Ronald Beiner, 'Commentary on "Montesquieu's Moderation"', University of Toronto, 19 August 2019.

17. 'Was not Jesus an extremist for love: "Love your enemies, bless them that curse you, do good to them that hate you, and pray for them which despitefully use you, and persecute you." Was not Amos an extremist for justice: "Let justice roll down like waters and righteousness like an ever flowing stream." Was not Paul an extremist for the Christian gospel: "I bear in my body the marks of the Lord Jesus." Was not Martin Luther an extremist: "Here I stand; I cannot do otherwise, so help me God."' Martin Luther King Jr, 'Letter from a Birmingham Jail', African Studies Center–University of Pennsylvania, https://www.africa.upenn.edu/Articles_Gen/Letter_Birmingham.html.

18. Georges Benrekassa, 'Moderation', in *A Montesquieu Dictionary*, ed. Catherine Volpilhac-Auger. Lyon: ENS Lyon, September 2013. http://dictionnaire-montesquieu.ens-lyon.fr/en/article/1376477506/en/

19. Montesquieu, *The Spirit of the Laws*, 3.4, 25.

20. Jonathan Israel, *A Revolution of the Mind: Radical Enlightenment and the Intellectual Origins of Modern Democracy* (Princeton: Princeton University Press, 2009), 33.

21. Ibid., 19.

22. He correctly identifies commerce as a principal source of moderation in eighteenth-century Europe, arguing that commercial exchange relations helped forge social bonds on a more benign foundation that reflected the emerging liberal order. Rasmussen, *Pragmatic Enlightenment*, 268.

23. Such accounts, which present Montesquieu as an unqualified booster of modern commerce, have yielded conflicting monist accounts of his *summum bonum*. Cf. Paul Rahe, *Montesquieu and the Logic of Liberty* (New Haven: Yale University Press, 2010); Pangle, *The Theological Basis of Liberal Modernity*; Spector, *Montesquieu*.

24. Aurelian Craiutu, *A Virtue for Courageous Minds: Moderation in French Political Thought, 1748–1830* (Princeton: Princeton University Press, 2012), 36.

25. Moore, 'Montesquieu and the Scottish Enlightenment', 180.

26. Cf. Paul O. Carrese, *Democracy in Moderation: Montesquieu, Tocqueville, and Sustainable Liberalism* (Cambridge: Cambridge University Press, 2016); Rasmussen, *Pragmatic Enlightenment*; Duncan Kelly, *The Propriety of Liberty: Persons, Passions and Judgment in Modern Political Thought* (Princeton: Princeton University Press, 2011); Donald Desserud, 'Commerce and Political Participation in Montesquieu's Letter to Domville', *History of European Ideas* 25.3 (1999): 135–51.

27. Montesquieu, *The Spirit of the Laws*, 3.1, 21.

28. Ibid., 8.1, 112.

29. Ibid., 5.14.

30. Ibid., 28.41, 595.

31. 'I should like to seek out in all the moderate governments we know the distribution of the three powers and calculate thereupon the degrees of liberty each one of them can enjoy. But one must not always so exhaust a subject that one leaves nothing for the reader to do. It is not a question of making him read but of making him think.' Montesquieu, *The Spirit of the Laws*, 11.20, 186.
32. Ibid., 'Preface', xliv.
33. Ibid., 2.3, 23.
34. Helena Rosenblatt, *The Lost History of Liberalism: From Ancient Rome to the Twenty-first Century* (Princeton: Princeton University Press, 2018); Melissa Lane, *Eco-Republic: What the Ancients Can Teach Us about Ethics, Virtue, and Sustainable Living* (Princeton: Princeton University Press, 2012).
35. Lane, *Eco-Republic*, 32.
36. Cf. Chapter 1. Interestingly, Montesquieu employs mythical Greek allegory to recount the Law debacle in his earlier writings, shining a spotlight on how free, dynamic commercial nations are not immune to the dangers of *pleonexia*.
37. Cf. Michael Sonenscher, who observes traces the maturation of a theory of honour that bypassed the warning about wealth and power that Montesquieu had issued at the end of the unpublished sequel of the Troglodyte history. Sonenscher, *Before the Deluge*, 100–3.
38. Montesquieu, *Persian Letters*, trans. and ed. Stéphane Douard and Stuart Warner (South Bend: St. Augustine's Press, 2017), 18.
39. Ibid., 19.
40. Ibid.
41. Ibid., 20.
42. Ibid., 21.
43. Ibid., 22.
44. Ibid.
45. Ibid.
46. Ibid.
47. Cecil Courtney, cited in Andrew Scott Bibby, *Montesquieu's Political Economy* (New York: Palgrave MacMillan), 27; Donald Desserud, 'Virtue, Commerce and Moderation in "The Tale of the Troglodytes": Montesquieu's *Persian Letters*', *History of Political Thought* 12.4 (1991), 624; Michael Sonenscher, *Before the Deluge: Public Debt, Inequality, and the Intellectual Origins of the French Revolution* (Princeton: Princeton University Press, 2007), 100–3.
48. Montesquieu, *Persian Letters*, Letter 10, 18.
49. Ibid., Letter 11, 19.
50. For an excellent discussion, see Ryan Hanley's 'Distance Learning: Political Education in the *Persian Letters*', *Review of Politics* 83.4 (2021): 533–54.
51. Montesquieu, *The Spirit of the Laws*, 20.2, 339.

52. Montesquieu, *Treatise on Duties*, in *Montesquieu: Discourses, Dissertations, and Dialogues on Politics, Science, and Religion* (Cambridge: Cambridge University Press, 2020), 113.

53. Ibid., 127. Fred Dallmayr's recent analysis demonstrates how high the stakes were for free, commercial nations, presenting the Troglodyte allegory as a warning 'that people should not abandon the practice of ethical life in favor of formal legal structures and procedures behind whose screen they might sink into lethargy or selfish greed'. 'Montesquieu's *Persian Letters*: A Timely Classic', *Montesquieu and His Legacy*, ed. Rebecca Kingston (Albany: University of New York Press, 2009), 246.

54. Montesquieu, *My Thoughts*, trans. and ed. Henry C. Clark (Indianapolis: Liberty Fund, 2012), 464.

55. Ibid.

56. According to Donald Desserud, the unpublished Troglodyte letter corroborates the view of scholars who identify England as Montesquieu's most preferred regime in *The Spirit of the Laws*, since it is the only constitution that permits commerce to flourish alongside political virtue. Desserud suggests that commercial engagement itself is the principal source of civic learning for Montesquieu. As readers observe in 19.27, commercial England 'produces citizens who consider and deliberate, but over matters they have a passionate concern'. Desserud, 'Virtue, Commerce and Moderation', 624.

57. In Nelson's view, the allegory reveals Montesquieu's preference for the Greek republican model because it most accords with human nature. Nelson identifies the happiest citizens in the 'Athenian republic', since this regime satisfies both the higher and lower individual needs, thus most conforming to reason and nature. Accordingly, a more robust normative and prescriptive strain exists in the political thought of Montesquieu than one would initially suppose. Eric Nelson, *The Greek Tradition in Republican Thought* (Cambridge: Cambridge University Press, 2004), 193. However, a number of passages from Book 19 of *The Spirit of the Laws* belie the criteria for happiness that Nelson teases out from the Troglodyte allegory, as we shall see in Chapter 4 of this book.

58. Montesquieu, *The Spirit of the Laws*, 4.4, 35.

59. Ibid., 20.1, 338.

60. Ibid., 1.1, 5.

61. Richard Sher, 'From Troglodytes to Americans: Montesquieu and the Scottish Enlightenment on Liberty, Virtue, and Commerce', in *Republicanism, Liberty, and Commercial Society, 1649–1776*, ed. David Wootton (Stanford: Stanford University Press, 1994), 369.

Chapter 1

From High Society to High Finance: John Law's System and the Spectre of Modern Despotism

The designing knave of the present day is not more scrupulous, nor the visionary fool less sanguine, than the knave and the fool of the last century.[1]

London Gazette, 1825

During the early eighteenth century Europe was rattled by a series of financial shocks, stemming from the impropriety of government and economic actors who grew increasingly interdependent as governments relied on private lenders for imperial expansion. New institutional arrangements redefined the relationship between class and power and led to original notions of political justice, inconceivable in the pre-modern economic era. Political thinkers increasingly placed emphasis on how existing notions of freedom could be squared with bringing unwieldy and chaotic economic situations under political control. Some concerned themselves with how commerce stifled the civic character, while others held a more optimistic view, suggesting commerce was a source of political stability that engendered certain forms of virtue commensurate with eighteenth-century political exigencies. Montesquieu sought to reconcile these two positions throughout his political works.

This chapter builds on the existing literature which considers how the failure of John Law's System and its reverberations shaped Montesquieu's political thought.[2] Its primary aim is to trace the tangible roots of Montesquieu's ambiguity over the relationship between commerce and liberty – a principal theme in this book's subsequent chapters.

The first part reconstructs the context of John Law's System. Here, I explain how the confluence of France's existing monetary and fiscal regime and its experimentation with new modes of high finance during the War of the Spanish Succession, ripened the conditions for Law to introduce his System to the Regency following Louis XIV's death in 1715. The second part examines Montesquieu's and Law's competing conceptions of political moderation, highlighting the former's abiding preoccupation with France's titled nobility. Here, readers will discover why Law had become such a worrisome figure. The Scottish financier's System undermined France's remnant honour-yielding institutions, which, in Montesquieu's view, were indispensable for counteracting the Bourbon Crown's despotic tendencies.

John Law's System: Its Antecedents and Subsequent Collapse

The War of the Spanish Succession (1701–14) had devastating consequences on France's economic, social and political order. It was left insolvent with unsustainable debt, leading to a series of currency devaluations as it struggled to meet its ballooning war costs. France's public credit suffered as a result, spurring a vicious economic cycle of high rates of interest for public and private borrowing, followed by an increase in taxes on French citizens to support interest payments on its national debt.[3] Moreover, the Treaty of Utrecht – which formally ended the war in 1713 – included several commercial guarantees for England and Holland, giving France's neighbours a comparative advantage in global trade.[4]

France's weakened position in global commerce only deepened its existing fiscal and monetary crises. Its high tax burdens had put additional downward pressure on the country's manufacturing and international trade, which led to high unemployment and poverty across its urban centres. Meanwhile, England, which equally confronted a high debt burden following the War of the Spanish Succession, had secured good public credit and emerged economically more stable than France, despite the latter's relatively abundant population and wealth of natural resources. England demonstrated greater capacity for prudent fiscal and monetary management than France whose territorial 'victories' during the wars led to a series of economic crises that culminated in John Law's scheme following the death of Louis XIV.

England had two structural advantages over France that enabled it to secure public confidence in its credit: its existing central bank, established shortly following the Glorious Revolution (1688–9), and its efficient, highly centralised taxation system.[5] With respect to its monetary regime, the Bank of England forged a mutually beneficial, interdependent relationship with a new, growing class of private economic actors known as 'the monied interest', whose wealth largely depended on very liquid, mobile capital commonly referred to as paper money. On the one hand the increased liquidity enabled the Bank of England to borrow easily accessible funds from financial speculators against reliable future revenues to support ongoing war costs.[6] On the other hand private financiers had greater incentive to finance commercial enterprises against their own future revenues. Paper money accessible at the bank provided merchants and manufacturers greater liquidity and access to loans guaranteed by short-term future revenues.[7]

Although France accelerated its modernisation reforms throughout the seventeenth century by professionalising its army, centralising its bureaucracy and confining important decision-making processes to the Court, it continued to lag behind England's highly efficient and centralised tax regime.[8] Indeed, France may have proliferated its commerce throughout the seventeenth and eighteenth centuries with relatively equal, if not greater, vigour as compared with England.[9] However, it never succeeded in building an efficient fiscal-military state analogous to its cross-Channel rival's, since its taxation system remained inefficient, decentralised and largely feudal.[10] Unlike England, France continued to rely on its corrupt, predatory and deeply unpopular feudal tax-farming regime for raising a significant portion of its public revenues, which dangerously blurred the line between their fiscal and monetary activities. The country's high debt accumulated during the latter years of Louis XIV's reign only increased popular resentment towards the financier class and the ancillary classes that supported tax farming in French society. These classes disproportionally, if not exclusively, profited from the fiscal and monetary regime in place, while they stifled growth and productivity in all other sectors of the French economy. What is more, France's tax collection system lacked transparency,[11] which led to a greater degree of suspicion among French subjects, accompanied with wild and fantastical stories about greater corruption and conspiracies than were actually taking place.[12] In England taxation authority came from the people's representatives, which provided greater legitimacy and less resistance to higher imposts. By contrast, in France the people were taxed disproportionately vis-à-vis the nobility.[13] Yet interestingly, Britain's taxation was more regressive since the majority of its revenues relied on sales taxes as opposed to the land taxes which supplied the French Crown, notwithstanding existing exemptions for the Church and nobility.[14] Despite the economic inequalities that Britain's taxation model reproduced, its predictable revenues, which translated into greater creditworthiness, enabled the Bank of England to carry larger debt ratios than France, at relatively low interest rates.[15]

Moreover, Louis XIV's encroachment on the *parlements*' political power compounded France's fiscal and monetary problems. He filled the courts with officers loyal to the Crown, and increasingly curtailed their right of remonstrance. These measures impeded their ability to customarily check the Crown's sovereignty. Subsequently, the *parlements*' relative lack of authority permitted the Crown to strengthen its alliance with France's leading private financiers, upon whom it increasingly relied on for facilitating public revenues as Louis XIV entangled France in a series of wars, exhausting its tax base.[16] By contrast, their English parliamentary counterparts had greater institutional capacity to 'restrain malfeasance and secure public accountability'[17] among government and economic actors, while working in harmony with the Crown and Lords towards common ends. The English Parliament had the political power to circumscribe the sinister activities of private financiers and government actors who jointly participated in public finance.

Two principal factors contributed to France's economic failure:[18] the limitless profiteering of private financiers who exploited new opportunities created by Louis XIV's wars,[19] and fiscal and monetary mismanagement on the part of the Crown's ministers,[20] whose reforms triggered a series of bankruptcies, raising the cost of short-term credit. France's decentralised collection of revenues (tax farming) coupled with its increasingly centralised decision-making apparatus tightened an already unhealthy partnership between the Crown and a class of private financiers who then profited over a series of paper money schemes that France's ministers desperately approved after the tax base reached its limits.

France's tenuous financial situation made its senior ministers amenable to various experiments with paper money, which had a lasting effect on its political economy. First, it permitted the Crown to further consolidate its power. Indeed, France already had a systematically corrupt taxation system replete with inefficiencies, yet these inefficiencies naturally checked the Bourbon Crown's absolutism and territorial ambitions.[21] Conversely, the introduction of paper money created new avenues for raising public revenues, making the Crown less reliant on its tax collection system for short-term expenditures. Second, France's paper money experimentation prior to Louis XIV's death ripened the conditions for the Conseil de Finance – a network of private bankers, dealers and deputies from the provinces who advised the Crown on fiscal and monetary issues – to approve Law's System.[22]

John Law's System

John Law (1671–1729), a Scottish financier notorious for his gambling affliction,[23] introduced his System to France to modernise its economy and, more imminently, to resolve its monetary and fiscal crises. He wrote: 'The means for restoring order and public confidence is to establish commerce on true and necessarily new principles because France still has not had the fortune of enjoying good Credit.'[24] Law observed that both England and Holland sustained good public credit throughout the War of the Spanish Succession and that they attracted greater capital investment than France. He wanted France to model itself after England,[25] which had previously managed its own period of economic instability when it founded the Bank of England shortly following the Glorious Revolution. The country's newly established paper-based economy gave it greater monetary flexibility and left it in a better position overall to finance future war costs. Law successfully solicited his scheme to the French regent, Philippe II, duc d'Orléans (1674–1723) – after failing to persuade officials to approve a similar project in his native Scotland – and received authorisation to establish the Banque générale in 1716. The bank's mission was to gradually substitute paper money for the relatively illiquid gold standard that had persevered despite previous ministers' experimentations with various forms of currency. Law held that this would narrow the existing gap between depositors and debtors, and lead to a greater circulation of money and a fructuous rise in manufacturing and employment.[26] Moreover, Law planned to reduce the French kingdom's war debt burden by lowering interest rates on the *rentes*, which would in turn force debtholders to convert their holdings into public stock. Here, he faced stark opposition from France's *parlements*, whose representatives had most to gain from the relatively decentralised fiscal and monetary regime.

Louis XIV had weakened the French *parlements* when he under-mined their political right of remonstrance against Crown policy pronouncements in 1678.[27] The *parlements* nonetheless continued to perform indispensable state administrative functions that upheld the social order. Their noble members presided over trials, led the policing of the state and continued to register the Crown's policy pronouncements.[28] Meanwhile, the Bourbon king accelerated his sale of public offices to bourgeois aspirants,[29] whose kinship with merchants and traders[30] best qualified them for reconciling private commercial ends with the public interest. What is more, in being the most educated among the privileged classes, the newly minted officeholders' administrative competence made them indispensable for managing an increasingly complex modern state apparatus.

However, Louis XIV's death in 1715 left behind a political power vacuum that France's various intermediary bodies sought to fill.[31] Philippe II, duc d'Orléans, exploited these competing political ambitions by restoring the Parlement de Paris's right of remonstrance in exchange for their acquiescence in his claim on the Regency, which Louis XIV's surviving will had put into dispute.[32] However, the partnership forged by the duc d'Orléans and the Parlement de Paris reached an abrupt end shortly after, when the former authorised his close friend, John Law, to initiate his System.

On 2 May 1716 the Regency published consecutive *lettres patentes* that declared the establishment of the Banque générale. The Crown gave Law carte blanche over the institution's admin-istration for a minimum of twenty years.[33] It stated that the cen-tral bank would resolve each of France's pressing economic issues. Again, usury would decline, the transition to paper money would attract international trade, and the flow of money between Paris and the provinces would rise.[34] Law concurrently argued that lower rates of interest would increase employment and, in turn, lessen the individual tax burden among a majority of France's 18 million people whom the Crown relied on for its revenue.[35] Law held that noble families would generally benefit from his system, since low interest rates reduced the private debt that a majority of landowners held.[36]

In reality, Law's System was actually a scourge to France's inter-mediary political bodies, since it threatened to overturn the existing fiscal and monetary regime that guaranteed their economic wellbe-ing, but the System nonetheless provided the Parlement de Paris with an opportunity to demonstrate its newly restored political right of remonstrance.[37] During the System's early inception the Parlement protested against the issuance of paper money and targeted Law directly in its request to limit foreigners' powers in the administration of French finances.[38] The remonstrances, moreover, argue that a country's 'real' wealth had to be based on agriculture, manufacturing and population, rather than fictitious mobile capital.[39]

The regent perceived the Parlement de Paris's attempts to circumscribe Law's mandate as a threat to France's overall creditworthiness and a personal affront to his already tenuous political authority.[40] This suspicion prompted him to order the nation's first *lit de justice* in over a century; he issued a series of edicts that diluted the intermediary body's power of remonstrance against issues concerning finances and prohibited it from interfering with France's fiscal administration, which in turn gave the Crown unchecked authority to override *any* further remonstrances.[41]

The new measures permitted Law to advance his scheme with minimal opposition. He formed a public joint-stock company by merging the Mississippi Company – a state-owned conglomerate in the Americas – with what came to be called the Banque royale. The merger nudged bondholders to exchange their debt holdings for newly available and more lucrative public shares. The conversion scheme incrementally eliminated France's more than two billion livres' debt, enabling the Crown to afford its bloated administrative costs. In the short term Law's System helped improve France's economic situation. Lower interest rates assuaged private debt burdens, employment steadily increased, new colonies developed as commerce in Asia expanded, and domestic manufacturing grew steadily.[42]

Nicholas Dutot (1684–1741), a former employee and friend of Law's, credits Law's System for rendering the old method of doing commerce ineffective and for grounding France's economy in real wealth. He explains that monetary and fiscal easing eliminated usury and reduced foreign borrowing, while sums lent to manufacturers and traders at lower rates of interest augmented foreign trade.[43] Moreover, productivity grew in the countryside, which encouraged expatriates to return home after previously stagnant economic conditions had forced them to seek employment in neighbouring countries.[44]

Notwithstanding these achievements, the exuberance associated with the Mississippi Company's fortunes compelled the bank to continue issuing liquid paper stock at a rate that surpassed the real wealth of France's economy. In his post-mortem following the System's collapse, Dutot argued that France's economy was grounded in real wealth, since 'credit and confidence were established to benefit the state'.[45] Despite the System's success, paper money value needed to correspond with specie value and the real wealth of the economy. Dutot explains that Law's System had successfully achieved this balance when share value reached its zenith by March 1720, trading at fifty times its original worth.[46] Unlike his most ardent defenders who remained wedded to a two-currency regime, Law wanted to eliminate specie currency in its entirety. On 5 March 1720, the date Dutot marks as an inflection point in France's transformation from a real-wealth into an imaginary-wealth-based economy, the Regency issued an *arrêt* whose dictates accelerated the monetary conversion that Law initiated a couple of years earlier.[47] The *arrêt* argued that, as long as specie currency existed in the economy, individuals would hoard their money, and particular interests would continue to trump the public interest.[48] The *arrêt* produced greater speculative exuberance, inflating the Mississippi Company shares at an alarming rate. Realising that it was overheating the market, Law's ministry followed with an unpopular *arrêt* on 21 May 1720, which reduced the share value. The bad optics of this latest measure undermined France's creditworthiness, as Jean-François Melon (1675–1738) explained in his *Political Essay upon Commerce* (1734):

> This measure ignited the Public: the universal hurt the Regent, who then agreed to reverse the measure, but credit and confidence had been entirely lost at this point. It seemed that since that moment, every decision was made haphazard: what was initiated one day was destroyed the next, and the imbalance between banknotes and specie led to perpetual disorder, which would only come to an end. . .in November 1720.[49]

From an investor's perspective, the Regency tacitly acknowledged that the stock price was overvalued. The admission triggered an abrupt sell-off after two consecutive years of uninterrupted growth. Incensed, the public called for a reversal of the unpopular 21 May *arrêt*, and the Regency conceded. However, the Crown's capitulation only worsened the crisis as the sudden course reversal further shook public confidence in the state's creditworthiness. The price of the Mississippi stock collapsed and dragged the value of the new currency down with it. It reached its nadir by November 1720, when the stocks became worthless, leaving specie as the only remaining financial instrument of real value.[50]

Montesquieu's Response to Law's System: A New Mode of Despotism

According to Céline Spector, debates that emerged between Montesquieu and the *parlements* on the one side, and Law and his supporters on the other, reflected two competing visions of society.[51] Law and his followers promoted a system that centralised power and increased the rights of the sovereign, while forging conditions of equality among citizens. Montesquieu and the *parlements'* most vociferous critics of the System favoured social inequalities and hierarchical stratifications over an equal but enervated citizenry. They preferred that sovereign power remain diffuse and reliant on the mediating powers of the *parlements*.[52] Having said that, both Law and Montesquieu held that their prescriptions promoted a spirit of free, moderate government, although in very different ways.

In 2.4 of *The Spirit of the Laws*, Montesquieu writes:

> Mr Law, equally ignorant of the republican and of the monarchical constitutions, was one of the greatest promoters of despotism that had until then been seen in Europe. Besides the changes he made, which were so abrupt, so unusual, and so unheard of, he wanted to remove the intermediate ranks and abolish the political bodies; he was dissolving the monarchy by his chimerical payments and seemed to want to buy back the constitution itself.[53]

Law violated two guiding principles of moderate legislation that Montesquieu details throughout *The Spirit of the Laws*. First, the Scottish financier's 'abrupt . . . unusual, and so unheard of . . .' changes betrayed France's 'general spirit'. Second, his assault on France's intermediary bodies threatened to remove the principal source of restraint on monarchical power. Montesquieu provides little else in *The Spirit of the Laws* to explain what made Law so treacherous. Recent interpreters have downplayed Montesquieu's unflattering remarks about Law. Bibby suggests that the Scottish financier's imprudent disregard for France's existing institutions pales compared to the radically liberal agenda Montesquieu himself advances in *The Spirit of the Laws*. He correctly notes that Montesquieu's aversion to national banks and state enterprises distinctly pertained to Europe's existing continental monarchies,[54] not post–Financial Revolution England.[55] The argument follows that Montesquieu's admiration of England's political economy in 19.27, and his sophisticated analysis of monetary finance in Book 23, prove that he 'was well aware of the destructive capacity of commerce, and indeed, actively promoted it'.[56] Unless France jettisons its antiquated feudal institutions and practices, Law-type figures will continue to menace *European* monarchies.

Montesquieu's treatment of Law in his earlier writings suggests a different story. His commercial descriptor ('promoter') coheres with a more sustained critique of the Scottish financier that Montesquieu provides in *Persian Letters*. He describes Law's despotism with greater rhetorical flourish in Letter 142, where he recounts the myth of the 'Son of Aeolus'.[57] Trained by his father in the art of capturing wind, Aeolus's son (Law) headed for Betica (France) where 'gold glittered everywhere',[58] to persuade its citizens to exchange their gold and silver for his invisible commodity. He advises them to 'arise, and if you have creditors, go pay them with what you have imagined, and tell them to imagine in their turn'.[59] When the people hesitate and choose to hoard their gold instead, he says to them: 'I swear by my sacred goatskins, that if those people do not bring it to me, I shall punish them severely.'[60] In reality, state authorities prosecuted Law's dissenters and threatened shopkeepers who refused to keep pace with the higher rate of inflation that resulted from the forced conversion. Law deemed any citizen who subverted his currency conversion scheme as an enemy of the state, since 'anyone who prevents the gains that arrive from the circulation [of wealth] is a bad citizen; in such cases the sovereign can coerce citizens [into converting their currency] in order to serve the state's ends.'[61] He justified the state's despotic power, arguing that it suppressed particular interests that subverted the public interest.[62]

Law held that his system of Court capitalism produced a spirit of moderation in the prince that counterbalanced his despotic power. Conversely, in a decentralised system, where power is dispersed among the Crown, *parlements* and private bankers, particular interests pull the state in different directions. He explained that France's *parlements* were too weak to moderate 'la puissance suprême' of the prince, even with their fully restored right of remonstrance,[63] whereas, when politics and commerce are combined, the Crown's interests converge with the people's interests. He writes:

> When there is but one sole interest, one credit, and one supreme power in a fertile, well-situated, and well-populated extended kingdom, everything then operates by the same spring; the common interest becomes the interest of each particular individual; the head's interest is inseparable from those of the members, and neither can subsist without the other.[64]

In sum, Court capitalism unites all individual interests with the interests of the prince and produces a tempered, friendly despotism over the people.

Melon's *Political Essay upon Commerce* offers a qualified defence of John Law's System. Melon states that, although Law's System destroyed 'annuitant families'[65] and disturbed the social and political order, it nonetheless increased French commerce dramatically. Law's scheme re-established public credit and eliminated usury. Money circulated to the provinces that had suffered most during Louis XIV's reign, and French merchant ships sailing to the Americas doubled.[66] He writes: 'We may also see, that as a Bank under prudent Regulations and Management, is a great means of multiplying the common Measure of Commerce, it is of great Use to have one established in every trading Country.'[67] Melon held that in the first half of his mandate, Law managed the state finances with moderation and skill, in contrast to previous administrators whose immoderation and incompetence led France through a series of bankruptcies, destroying its public credit. According to Melon, the Crown turned despotic at the same time Law nationalised the Banque générale, changing its name to the Banque royale in 1718.

Melon holds that to maintain free, moderate government the legislator must accept some of the people's prejudices. He states: 'A proper Deference ought to be paid to the general Opinion and Clamours of Persons, who are best acquainted with the Grievances they complain of, or apprehend; for too great a Neglect in such a case, may introduce Panick, and Mischiefs which no Subsequent Care, may be able to remove, or remedy.'[68] While Montesquieu shares Melon's conviction that moderation is premised on the legislator's ability to distinguish between governing by law and by custom, he expresses reservations about whether this temper would prevail without proper institutional checks on such power. Montesquieu had the opportunity to meet Law in Venice seven years following the System's collapse. He observed, that despite Law's captious nature, the Scottish gambler loved his ideas more than money.[69] It was not Law's self-interested love of gain but his unchecked authority that tempted him to immoderately impose his vision on France, riding roughshod over its customary institutions and practices.

Indeed, Montesquieu observed how commercial self-interest could moderate the passions of the king and his powerful ministers, and acknowledged its potential for curing Europe from the ills of Machiavellianism.[70] He writes: 'And, happily, men are in a situation such that, though their passions inspire in them the thought of being wicked, they nevertheless have an interest in not being so.'[71] However, great enterprises '[are] not for monarchies, but for the government of the many'[72] where power is diffuse, and a vigilant representative parliamentary body checks the affairs of government and economic actors. He recognises the limits of the *parlements'* political powers in France, and for this reason argues that commercial and political interests should remain separate in monarchies.[73]

Montesquieu's lampooning of Law throughout his works should not be conflated with an otherwise tempered appreciation for Europe's burgeoning paper money economy, as others have noted. In Part IV of *The Spirit of the Laws*, he first establishes the relationship between mobile capital and liberty in his historical account of the ascent of paper money dating back to the late medieval period. At this time central authorities periodically targeted Jews and confiscated their land and goods at will.[74] Montesquieu recounts how many Jews were driven out of France and settled in Lombardy. Here, they invented financial instruments called 'letters of exchange' which allowed them to hide their wealth and engage in free commerce, undetected by central authorities.[75] Their innovation had a revolutionary effect on commerce since 'goods could be sent everywhere and [left] no trace anywhere'.[76] Paper money facilitated capital in a way that prevented the Crown from tracing its direction at any given time. It became increasingly difficult to enact policies that would regulate commerce. As Montesquieu writes, 'great acts of authority were so clumsy that experience itself has made known that only goodness of government brings prosperity.'[77] Certainly, letters of exchange, and mobile capital in general, cured Europe of Machiavellianism and had a moderating effect on princes, since their interest in the free flow of commerce counterbalanced their passions, which (previously) provoked various forms of wickedness.[78] Montesquieu's historical account of the free flow of paper money helps the reader further understand his anxieties concerning John Law's System, which brought mobile capital under the political control of the executive. Law's policies reversed the tide initiated in Lombardy during the late medieval period.

Although Montesquieu's qualified approval of paper money and public credit in *The Spirit of the Laws* suggests he evolved on issues concerning financial speculation, Michael Mosher explains that the Bordeaux aristocrat nonetheless maintained a republican aversion to Law's scheme throughout his writings.[79] Law symbolised France's accelerated transition towards an economy based on fictional wealth, characterised by dangerous risk-taking. His measures, according to Montesquieu, would inevitably produce a spirit of unchecked equality among citizens, a chief characteristic of despotic regimes.

Law's assault on the existing social and institutional order in place nudged France towards forms of equality that threatened its political liberty. In *The Spirit of the Laws*, he explains that even republics, animated by the principle of equality, needed hierarchical stratifications. It is why he praises both Solon and Tullius, whose reforms injected a spirit of aristocracy in Athens and Rome – the two paragon models of classical republican government. Montesquieu writes, 'In the popular state, the people are divided into certain classes. Great legislators have distinguished themselves by the way they have made this division, *and upon it the duration and prosperity of democracies have always depended*' (emphasis added).[80] Montesquieu is less concerned with socioeconomic equality than he is in avoiding an extreme spirit of political equality where citizens no longer accept being ruled and judged by their peers. He feared that, in the absence of intermediary bodies, a spirit of irreverence would grow among citizens, who would refuse to accept the rule of superiors holding public offices and would prefer to rule for themselves in all matters. Under such conditions, civic institutions lose their gravitas, and the people become corrupt once 'the restraint of commanding will be as tiresome as that of obeying had been'.[81] As people lose their appetite for self-rule and their liberty becomes too burdensome, '[a] single tyrant rises up' and restores order through his despotic rule.[82] Indeed, France was not a republic, but its perceived financial mismanagement and administrative incompetence produced a spirit of *extreme* equality among its subjects, further ripening the conditions for despotism.

Law's System equally threatened to produce a spirit of *base* equality among citizens, in so far as it fostered an unmitigated pursuit of luxury that rendered them equally apathetic in the face of injustices committed by the Crown. Montesquieu explains that a nation's liberty depended on greater passions than those that motivate distinction through luxury alone. Paris was not free from ambition, greed, vanity, dishonesty and false hope. Montesquieu accepted these inescapable features of modern commercial life. This is why some align him with Bernard Mandeville, whose *Fable of the Bees* famously collapses the distinction between private and public interest. Indeed, Mandeville echoes throughout *Persian Letters*, in so far as Montesquieu associates vanity with public wealth.[83] As

Usbek writes to Rhédi in Letter 106, '[Vanity] commands and is obeyed more promptly than our monarch would be, because interest is the greatest monarch on earth', without which 'this state would be one of the most miserable that has been in the world'.[84] At the same time, Montesquieu provides multiple vignettes that associate vanity with a spirit of malaise in French commercial life, inviting readers to contemplate its hazards.[85] Some have suggested that Montesquieu is deliberately ambiguous in his treatment of Parisian vanity, to highlight a core obstacle that is stunting France's capacity to adapt to the modern commercial world, namely, an abiding patrician's scorn towards self-interested commerce among France's bloated, non-commercial aristocratic classes.[86] Here, Bibby argues that Montesquieu responds to this challenge in *The Spirit of the Laws* with a theory of honour calibrated to the pursuit of wealth and commercial distinction.

Vanity is a principal animating force in commercial life that Montesquieu embraces throughout his writings. However, Usbek's analysis of France's honour culture in Letters 88–92 of *Persian Letters*, which culminates in a panegyric on the *parlements'* salutary role in French society, suggests a continual need for a non-commercial species of honour to exist *alongside* modes of recognition related to vanity and the pursuit of wealth.[87] What explains Montesquieu's propensity for France's social distinctions? To begin answering this question we need to examine the letters that immediately precede Louis XIV's death, where Usbek provides a thorough analysis of France's existing honour cultures. In Letter 89 of *Persian Letters* he writes, 'A desire for glory is no different from that instinct that all creatures have for their own preservation.'[88] It could be moulded in myriad ways, since 'imagination and education modify it in a thousand ways'.[89] This malleability provides the basis for Montesquieu's qualified defence of the nobility. Yet, in a less sanguine passage, Usbek identifies an uneasy tension between liberty and justice. 'If one follows the laws of honour, one perishes upon the scaffold; if one follows the laws of justice, one is forever banished from the society of men.'[90] Usbek's reflections on French honour reach a crescendo in Letter 92, which juxtaposes a brief, pedestrian account of the Sun King's death with a meditation on the fledgling *parlements*. The latter

> resemble those ruins which we tread under foot, but which always recall to our mind the idea of some temple famous for the ancient religion of the people. They seldom now interfere in anything more

than in affairs of justice; and their authority will continue to decline, unless that some unforeseen event should arrive to restore life, and to strengthen it. These great bodies have followed the course of human affairs; they yielded to time, which destroys everything, to the corruption of manners, which hath weakened everything, to the supreme, which hath overturned all things. But the regent, who wished to render himself agreeable to the people, seemed at first to respect this shadow of public liberty.

Usbek's panegyric reads as a theoretical response to the innate tension between liberty, honour and justice that he leaves unresolved in Letter 90. France reached a crossroads with the Sun King's death. We have seen how the Parlement de Paris's quid pro quo agreement with the duc d'Orléans made the institution politically relevant again, allowing it to immediately seize the opportunity to exercise their newly endowed power of remonstrance against Law's System at its inception.[91] More importantly, with the Parlement's 'points of honour' reinvigorated, it now had a unique capacity to harmonise the otherwise natural tension that existed between liberty and justice. The institution maintained a higher sense of honour that motivated leading citizens to courageously challenge sovereign authority and sacrifice themselves for the common good, while concomitantly enlivening a spirit of moderation in commercial society, where laws alone cannot produce an innate sense of self-restraint. Here, Montesquieu points to the *parlements'* leading officeholders more broadly: the *noblesse de robe* whose bourgeois roots, education and civic honour made it best equipped to prevent France's political liberty from being sacrificed for the sake of economic expediency.[92]

Louis XIV's consolidation of power, and later John Law's System, weakened the *parlements* and threatened the intermediary bodies requisite for preserving liberty. Montesquieu was under no illusions. Clearly, power had already been centralised, and France's intermediary political bodies lost much of their influence while retaining a number of their privileges, as he details in *Persian Letters*.[93] While Law may have been hyperbolising when he stated that the entire country was governed by thirty intendants,[94] Montesquieu observed that modern finance, which predated Law's System, opened new avenues for the Crown to circumvent the natural restraints of intermediary powers in monarchical government, nudging France towards a spirit of base equality that corresponded more with despotic than moderate regimes.

In Letter 146 of *Persian Letters*, Usbek reflects on Law's personal moral failure, asking: 'What greater crime is there than the one a minister commits when he corrupts the morals of an entire nation, degrades the most generous souls, tarnishes the shine of high position, obscures virtue itself, and confounds the highest birth with universal scorn?'[95] We have seen with Law's System how new modes of finance may be used as instruments for wielding power over citizens and running roughshod over a nation's existing institutions of liberty. Yet, French citizens were already accustomed to Louis XIV's and the papacy's constant despotic encroachments. Montesquieu is alerting readers to how Law's personal corruption was even more insidious, threatening to tear apart France's social fabric. In a statement that further illuminates Montesquieu's personal attack against Law in *The Spirit of the Laws*, he writes that the worst crime was 'the bad example he [set]' for the whole of society; this eclipsed even his '[disservice to] his prince and [the financial ruin] of his people'.[96]

In our recent analysis of Letter 132,[97] which details the socioeconomic consequences of Law's levelling scheme, Emily Nacol and I explain why the Scottish financier's personal corruption was so worrisome to Montesquieu. We note how Rica overhears a man in a Parisian café bemoan the fact that most of his assets were tied up in land, only to return to the same café six months later and overhear another man complaining that he is financially 'ruined' because he no longer owns any land. Rica then witnesses another man who is hopeful that Law's System would put an end to his penury, that 'all the lackeys in Paris [will become] richer than their masters' as the value in Mississippi shares continue to rise.[98] Such reversals of fortune had already become commonplace in France. In a 1717 letter to his friend Ibben, Usbek writes, 'There is no country in the world where fortune is as inconstant as in this one. Every ten years a revolution takes place, which hurls the rich into extreme poverty and with rapid wings elevates the poor onto the summit of riches.'[99] Rica later confirms Usbek's ominous observation that Law's scheme disrupted France's social hierarchy, having 'turned the state like a second-hand dealer turns clothes; he appears to have placed on top what was beneath, and what was on top he reversed.'[100]

In *Letters from Xenocrates to Pheres*, written five years after the System's failure, Montesquieu will once again employ mythical Greek allegory to describe the Law debacle, but this time it will be from the duc d'Orléans' vantage point. The mythical allegory elegantly captures the full scope of Law's treachery – an agent of despotism who reintroduces the 'ills of Machiavellianism', and whose corruption permeates commercial society, sparing no one. It takes the form of five letters. The first letter explores the regent's psychology through the figure of Alcmenes, a tyrant who ruled over the Greek city-state Sicyon in the sixth century BCE. Alcmenes is a strikingly sympathetic figure with an admirable temperament, made for society. He governs with moderation and justice and has an impulse for exercising clemency, which Montesquieu would have admired.[101] His heart 'so dominates him that he is unable . . . to punish'.[102]

Notwithstanding Alcmenes' relatively healthy emotional constitution, he suffers from an insatiable spirit of commercial improvement. In an allusion to how Law enchanted the regent with his innovative designs, Xenocrates observes that Alcmenes' preference for 'the talents rather than the virtue of men' stunts his capacity to differentiate between 'the honest and the wicked man, and all the different degrees between these two extremes'. He 'constantly wants to go from good to best, and that he is always more struck by what is wrong than by the disadvantage involved in rectifying it'.[103] Finally, Alcmenes is a proto-Machiavellian figure for whom religion is nothing more than an instrument of statecraft – a reference to the regent who was known to appreciate religion for its political utility, recognising how it creates 'fear among ordinary minds and keeps peoples in submission'.[104]

The third letter provides an elegant mythical account of the Law debacle. Ironically, revelation is the primary cause of Alcmenes' failure. The story begins with Xenocrates explaining how the gods became angry with the inhabitants of Sicyon, and then decided to punish them by sending a 'dream one night to Alcmenes, making him believe he was master of all the treasures on earth. This dream was the cause of public misery.'[105] He then recounts how Themis, the goddess of justice and a stand-in for the Parlement de Paris, then notices to her horror that avaricious greed has firmly taken hold over the population. Their unchecked commerce produced a religiosity of sorts, with the people of Sicyon erecting temples to Pluto all over the city, eventually driving Themis from her temple.[106] The episode ends with Pluto's altars being overturned, alluding to the public's anger following the Mississippi Bubble's collapse.

Xenocrates' Letter to Pheres adds a fresh light for understanding Montesquieu's abiding preoccupation with Law. Despite embracing modern commerce for fostering a calculating quality that incentivised European princes to reconcile their individual interests with the public interest, the mythical allegory reveals how unchecked commerce may incite the unpredictable passions, sparing no one, including the moderate legislator. It powerfully illustrates the fate of modern commercial nations, shorn of a non-commercial pole of identification to enliven a general feeling of justice among citizens. Montesquieu's prescriptive maxim 'no monarch, no nobility: no nobility, no monarch' – his precondition for maintaining free, moderate monarchies in the modern commercial world – takes a slightly different, more encompassing meaning in his earlier writings, proving to be of paramount importance vis-à-vis 'the greatest monarch on earth'.

To recap, Montesquieu presents to his contemporary readers a more stable foundation for maintaining free, moderate government in the face of high finance. Usbek's nostalgia for the *parlements* in Letter 92 of *Persian Letters* is significant given the institution's decline as a beacon of liberty. Honour and justice may have corrupted the manners that made the ethical life possible, but 'this shadow of public liberty' continued to inspire the public mind in early eighteenth-century France, notwithstanding its fledgling status. In disrupting the already delicate balance between commercial life and France's remnant 'points of honour', Law removed the most reliable institutional counterpoise to an unhinged commercial ethos that tends towards instability and corruption.

Concluding Remarks

In *The Old Regime and the Revolution*, Alexis de Tocqueville writes: 'Let it be borne in mind that France was the only country in which the feudal system had preserved its injurious and irritating characteristics, while it had lost all those which were beneficial or useful.'[107] The Crown's assault on the nobility since the early days of the ancien régime and its failed economic policies that culminated in John Law's levelling scheme systematically debased the nobility socially and politically. By the turn of the eighteenth century commoners associated France's political and economic elites with poor fiscal and monetary management, special privileges and tax exemptions, while they shouldered most of France's economic burdens. The nobles' diminished role no longer justified the special status they continued to enjoy throughout the seventeenth and eighteenth centuries. By contrast, although England underwent similar transformations during this period, Tocqueville held that a harmonious spirit of inequality persisted as commoners there recognised the social, economic and political utility of the upper classes and therefore tolerated the nobility's special privileges. English commoners believed their relationship with the nobility corresponded with a natural order of things, whereas France found itself situated on the tip of providence's arrow of history, with its people increasingly viewing themselves as equals in a moral sense. Montesquieu would have disagreed with Tocqueville's account of England. As we shall see, he thought England had largely jettisoned its social and politically viable feudal structures, making its citizens vulnerable to becoming the most enslaved people on earth. Tocqueville nonetheless held that democratisation affected all nations, distinguished only by the manner of which they jettisoned their feudal structures. He writes: 'Had [the French Revolution] never taken place, the old edifice would nonetheless have fallen, though it would have given way piecemeal instead of breaking down with a crash.'[108]

Montesquieu's acerbic reaction to Law's System reveals his overall awareness that France was following a trajectory of equality and centralisation that was dangerously headed towards a crash. Yet his attempt to reconcile France's feudal vestiges with the exigencies of modern commerce shows that he would have opposed the Tocquevillian arc of history. He suggests the possibility of an alternative direction, accompanied by a genuine form of liberty that retains the salutary effects of commerce – that is, only if legislators rein in the elements of modern commerce that undermine political justice. Here, Montesquieu separates himself from French Enlightenment counterparts, such as Melon and Dutot, and Voltaire, who reconcile their respective notions of economic and literary liberty with a friendlier form of political despotism.[109] More specifically, Montesquieu's political vision imagines the possibility of moderate government that, on the one hand, steers clear of a friendly despotism reliant on positive law to maintain order and, on the other, safeguards against pathological forms of equality characteristic of modern commercial society. John Law's policies may have resolved France's economic policy in the short term, but, in Montesquieu's view, they threatened its political and individual liberty. Correspondingly, he sought to preserve France's delicate social and institutional arrangements, to safeguard against the excesses of eighteenth-century high finance.

Notes

1. *The South Sea Bubble, and the Numerous Fraudulent Projects to which it gave rise in 1720, Historically Detailed as a Beacon to the Unwary against Modern Schemes* (London: for Thomas Boys, Ludgate Hill, 1825), 6.

2. A number of Montesquieu's readers emphasise the importance of John Law's System in his political thought; it is the 'secret chain' that links modern commerce with despotism. To support this reading, Agnès Raymond emphasises the intentional ordering of the later letters of Montesquieu's satire, which juxtaposes John Law's System (Letter 146) with the collapse of Usbek's Seraglio (Letter 147). Cited in Jonathan Walsh, 'A Cultural Numismatics: The "Chain" of Economics in Montesquieu's *Lettres persanes*', *Australian Journal of French Studies* 46 (2009), 140. Cf. Theodore Braun, '*La chaîne secrète*: A Decade of Interpretations', *French Studies* 42.3 (1988): 278–91.

3. Antoin E. Murphy, *John Law: Economic Theorist and Policy-maker* (Oxford: Clarendon Press, 1997), 5.

4. Paul Cheney, 'Montesquieu and the Scottish Enlightenment', *A Montesquieu Dictionary*, ed. Catherine Volpilhac-Auger (Lyon: ENS Lyon, September 2013), 22.

5. John Brewer, *The Sinews of Power: War, Money and the English State, 1688–1783* (New York: Routledge, 1989), 5.

6. Ibid., 42.

7. Murphy, *John Law*, 107.

8. Here Brewer explains that, unlike England, France had only consolidated its territory by the end of the fifteenth century. Therefore, local administrators held greater authority over France's provinces and were generally more defiant towards Crown authority than their English counterparts. Gradually, the Crown systematically expanded its offices to dilute regional power, but France nevertheless remained 'less centralized . . . and much more administratively encumbered than its counterpart across the Channel due to its relatively greater regionalism.' Brewer, *The Sinews of Power*, 6.

9. Paul Cheney, *Revolutionary Commerce: Globalization and the French Monarchy* (Cambridge, MA: Harvard University Press, 2010), 22.

10. Brewer, *The Sinews of Power*, 128.

11. This is in contrast to England, where elected representatives in Parliament determined all imposts.

12. Brewer, *The Sinews of Power*, 130.

13. Here, Brewer identifies another important advantage England had over France: its 'acceptance of institutions of central government . . . meant that when kings, lords and commons acted in unison, they were an overwhelming force'. Ibid., 22.

14. Patrick O'Brien, 'The Political Economy of British Taxation', *Economic History Review* 41.1 (1988): 1–32.

15. Edward Andrew. 'Locke on Consent, Taxation, and Representation', *Theoria* 62.2 (2015): 15–32.

16. Guy Rowlands, *The Financial Decline of a Great Power: War, Influence, and Money in Louis XIV's France* (Oxford: Oxford University Press, 2013), 1.

17. Brewer, *The Sinews of Power,* 139.
18. Rowlands, *The Financial Decline of a Great Power,* 15.
19. Ibid., 9.
20. Ibid., 13.
21. Philip T. Hoffman, 'Early Modern France, 1450–1700', in *Fiscal Crises, Liberty, and Representative Government,* ed. Philip T. Hoffman and Kathryn Norberg (Stanford: Stanford University Press, 1994), 226.
22. Jean-François Melon, *A Political Essay upon Commerce,* trans. David Bindon (Dublin: Printed for Philip Crampton Bookseller at Addison's Head, 1738), 267. This translation was based on the first edition from 1734; Melon published a second edition in 1736.
23. Thomas E. Kaiser, 'Money, Despotism, and Public Opinion in Early Eighteenth-Century France: John Law and the Debate on Royal Credit', *The Journal of Modern History* 63.1 (March 1991), 12.
24. 'Le moyen pour remettre l'ordre et la confiance est d'établir des affaires sur de vrais principes qui doivent necessairement estre nouveau, car en matière de Crédit, la France n'a pas encore eu le Bonheur d'en avoir' (English translation my own). John Law, 'Réponse de Law aux objections présentées à sa proposition [19 Oct. 1715]', in *Œuvres complètes Vol. 2,* ed. Paul Harsi (Paris: Sirey, 1934), 260.
25. Ibid., 261.
26. Murphy, *John Law,* 7.
27. Franklin L. Ford, *Robe and Sword: The Regrouping of the French Aristocracy after Louis XIV* (Cambridge, MA: Harvard University Press, 1962), 6.
28. Ibid., 23.
29. Brewer, *The Sinews of Power,* 16.
30. Prior to the social transformations of the late sixteenth and seventeenth centuries that resulted from the expansion of France's 'commerce de luxe', the common austere dress attire among the bourgeoisie and the *noblesse de robe* symbolised their deeper affinities. Régine Pernoud, *Histoire de la bourgeoisie en France: Les temps modernes* (Paris: Éditions du Seuil, 1962), 17.
31. 'For the great lords, for the nobility in general, for the *parlements,* for the Gallican enemies of the late ruler's Jesuit advisers, for the increasingly powerful business class, even for the peasantry, hopeful of a lightened tax load and fewer troops swarming over the countryside, long suppressed ambitions were at last able to emerge onto the surface of public life.' Cf. Ford, *Robe and Sword,* 6.
32. Murphy, *John Law,* 126.
33. Lettres patentes du Roy, 'Portant privilege en faveur du Sr. Law & sa compagnie, d'éstablir une banque generale', in *Actes Royaux 1716 Avril–Juillet,* 2 and 20 May 1716 (Paris: Imprimerie royale, 1716), 3 [Article 1].

34. Lettres patentes du Roy, 'Portant privilege en faveur du Sr. Law & sa compagnie, d'établir une banque générale', 2.

35. John Law, 'Idée générale du nouveau Système des finances. Vol. 2', in *Œuvres complètes*, ed. Paul Harsin (Paris: Sirev, 1934), 92.

36. John Law, 'Réponse de Law aux objections présentées à sa proposition [19 octobre 1715]', in *Œuvres complètes*, ed. Paul Harsin (Paris: Sirev 1934), 131.

37. Ford, *Robe and Sword*, 84.

38. Murphy, *John Law*, 252.

39. Law, 'Idée générale du nouveau Système des finance', *Œuvres complètes*, 77.

40. Murphy, *John Law*, 180.

41. Ibid., 182.

42. Law, 'Idée générale du nouveau Système des finance', *Œuvres complètes*, 96.

43. Nicolas Dutot, *Réflexions politiques sur les finances, et le commerce. Tome II* (The Hague: Les Frères Vaillant & Nicolas Prevost, 1754), 327.

44. Here, Dutot is making reference to l'Ordonnance du Roy of 15 October 1719, which facilitated the return of French citizens who had previously left the country to seek employment. Dutot, *Réflexions politiques sur les finances, et le commerce. Tome II*, 331.

45. 'que le crédit & la confiance avoient fait naître au profit de l'État' (English translation my own). Dutot, *Réflexions politiques sur les finances, et le commerce. Tome II*, 328.

46. Cited in Antoin E. Murphy, Introduction to Dutot's *Histoire du Système de John Law* (Paris: L'Institut national d'études démographiques, 2000), lxvi.

47. Ibid., lxvi.

48. Ibid., lxviii.

49. 'Cet Arrêt souleva le Public: le cri universel frappa le Régent, qui consentit avec regret à la révocation, mais le crédit & la confiance se trouverent entierement perdu. Il semblait depuis ce tems là qu tout étoit conduit par le seul hazard: ce qui se faisoit un jour, se détruisoit le lendemain, & l'inégalité des Billets avec l'argent, causoit un désordre continuel, qui ne finit que par le retour à l'argent seul, le premier novembre 1720' (English translation my own). Jean-François Melon, *Essai politique sur le commerce*, ed. Francine Markovits (Caen: Presses universitaires de Caen, 2014), 317.

50. Ibid., 383.

51. Céline Spector cited in Jonathan Walsh, 'A Cultural Numismatics: The "Chain" of Economics in Montesquieu's *Lettres persanes*', *Australian Journal of French Studies* 46.1–2 (2009), 147.

52. Ibid.
53. Montesquieu, *The Spirit of the Laws*, ed. and trans. Anne M. Cohler, Basia C. Miller and Harold S. Stone (Cambridge: Cambridge University Press, 1989), 2.4, 19.
54. Ibid., 20.4, 340.
55. Ibid., 23.10, 344.
56. Andrew Scott Bibby, *Montesquieu's Political Economy* (New York: Palgrave MacMillan), 57.
57. For a more comprehensive analysis, see Emily Nacol's treatment of the 'Myth of Aeolus' in Emily Nacol and Constantine Christos Vassiliou, 'The Plague of High Finance in Montesquieu's *Persian Letters*', in *The Spirit of Montesquieu's* Persian Letters, ed. Jeffrey Church, Alin Fumurescu and Constantine Christos Vassiliou (Lanham: Lexington Books, 2023 [forthcoming]).
58. Montesquieu, *Persian Letters*, trans. and ed. Stéphane Douard and Stuart Warner (South Bend: St. Augustine's Press, 2017), 18.241.
59. Ibid.
60. Ibid., 242.
61. '[il] empesche le gain qui proviendroit de leur circulation est un mauvais citoyen, qu'en ces cas, un souverain peut les obliger d'en donner l'usage à l'État' (English translation my own). Law, 'Idée générale du nouveau Système des finance', in *Œuvres complètes*, 91.
62. Kaiser, 'Money, Despotism, and Public Opinion', 17.
63. Law, 'Idée générale du nouveau Système des finance', 86.
64. 'Quand il n'y a qu'un seul intérêt, un seul crédit, une seul puissance dans un Royaume étendu, fécond, bien situé et bien peuplé, tout marche par le mesme ressort; l'intérêt commun devient l'intérêt de chacun en particulier; l'intérêt du chef est inséparable de celuy des membres et l'un ne peut subsister dans l'autre' (English translation my own). Ibid., 80.
65. However, the India Company would later reimburse most of these families for their financial losses as a result of the stock market crash. Melon, *Political Essay upon Commerce*, 112.
66. Ibid., 112.
67. Ibid., 274.
68. Ibid., 31.
69. 'C'est un homme captieux, qui a du raisonnement, & dont toute la force est de tâcher de tourner votre réponse contre vous, en y trouvant quelque inconvénient; d'ailleurs, plus amoureux de ses idées que de son argent.' Montesquieu to Berwick Venice, 15 Sept. 1728, *Œuvres complètes*, 1007.
70. Montesquieu, *The Spirit of the Laws*, 21.21, 390.
71. Ibid., 21.21, 390.
72. Ibid., 20.4, 340.

73. Ibid.
74. Ibid., 21.20, 389.
75. Ibid.
76. Ibid.
77. Ibid.
78. Here Montesquieu writes: 'And, happily, men are in a situation such that, though their passions inspire in them the thought of being wicked, the nevertheless have an interest in not being so.' Montesquieu, *The Spirit of they Laws*, 21.21, 390.
79. Michael Mosher, '"Empires of Imagination": Montesquieu, the Financial Crisis of 1720 and the Future of Inequality', paper presented at the 14th Congress of the International Society for Eighteenth-Century Studies, Rotterdam, The Netherlands, 28 July 2015, 11.
80. Montesquieu here refers to Solon's and Tullius's institutional reforms that divided Rome and Athens into six and four classes, respectively. Montesquieu, *The Spirit of the Laws*, 2.2, 12.
81. Ibid., 8.2, 112.
82. Ibid., 8.2, 113.
83. Lee Ward provides an excellent discussion concerning Montesquieu's debt to Mandeville, in 'Female Modesty and Commerce in *Persian Letters*', in *The Spirit of Montesquieu's* Persian Letters, ed. Constantine Christos Vassiliou, Alin Fumurescu and Jeffrey Church (Lanham: Lexington Books, 2023 [forthcoming]).
84. Montesquieu, *Persian Letters*, Letter 106, 173.
85. Ibid., Letter 30, 51; Letter 50, 81; Letter 54, 87.
86. Bibby, *Montesquieu's Political Economy*, 57.
87. Cf. Chapter 6 for an in-depth treatment of Montesquieu's pluralistic conception of honour.
88. Montesquieu, *Persian Letters*, Letter 89, 144.
89. Ibid.
90. Ibid., Letter 90, 146.
91. Céline Spector cited in Walsh, 'A Cultural Numismatics', 147.
92. Cf. Chapter 1, 30.
93. Céline Spector cited in Walsh, 'A Cultural Numismatics', 147.
94. 'The Marquis d'Argenson tells us in his Memoirs that one day Law said to him, "I never could have believed beforehand what I saw when I was comptroller of finances. Let me tell you that this kingdom of France is governed by thirty intendants. You have neither Parliament, nor estates, nor governors; nothing but thirty masters of requests, on whom, so far as the provinces are concerned, welfare or misery, plenty or want, entirely depend."' Alexis de Tocqueville, *The Old Regime and the Revolution*, trans. and ed. John Bonner (New York: Harper & Brothers, 1856), 54.
95. Montesquieu, *Persian Letters*, Letter 146, 256.
96. Ibid., Letter 146, 255.

97. For a more comprehensive account of Letter 132 and some of the earlier letters which anticipate Usbek's clinical account of the Mississippi Bubble's collapse in Letter 146, see Emily Nacol and Constantine Christos Vassiliou, 'The Plague of High Finance in Montesquieu's *Persian Letters*', in *The Spirit of Montesquieu's* Persian Letters, ed. Constantine Christos Vassiliou, Alin Fumurescu and Jeffrey Church (Lanham: Lexington Books, 2023 [forthcoming]).
98. Montesquieu, *Persian Letters*, Letter 132, 219.
99. Ibid., Letter 98, 158.
100. Ibid., Letter 138, 228.
101. Montesquieu, 'Letters from Xenocrates to Pheres', in *Montesquieu: Discourses, Dissertations and Dialogues, on Politics, Science, and Religion*, 156.
102. Ibid., 157.
103. Ibid., Montesquieu captures Alcmenes' principal flaw as a statesman in the following passage from his Preface to *The Spirit of the Laws*, 'in an enlightened age, one trembles even while doing the greatest goods. One feels the old abuses and sees their correction, but one also sees the abuses of the correction as well.' Montesquieu, *The Spirit of the Laws*, Preface, xliv.
104. Louis de Rouvroy, duc de Saint-Simon, cited in 'Letters from Xenocrates to Pheres', fn. 157.
105. Ibid., 158.
106. This is an allusion to when the Parlement de Paris was exiled to Pontoise between July and December 1720 for its remonstrances against Law's System. David W. Carrithers and Phillip Stewart, 'Letters from Xenocrates to Pheres', 158n.
107. Tocqueville, *The Old Regime and the Revolution*, 246.
108. Ibid., 36.
109. Ibid., 192.

Chapter 2

'Real Wealth' versus 'Fictional Wealth' in an Age of High Finance: Montesquieu, Hume and Smith

> What pity Lycurgus did not think of paper-credit, when he wanted to banish gold and silver from Sparta! It would have served his purpose better than the lumps of iron he made use of as money; and would also have prevented more effectually all commerce with strangers, as being of so much less real and intrinsic value.
>
> David Hume, 'Of the Balance of Trade'[1]

This chapter examines how Montesquieu, Hume and Smith adapted and theoretically responded to the gradual financialisation of government that was taking place on both sides of the Channel. First, it considers Montesquieu's response to the fiscal and monetary crises that plagued France between the time of Louis XIVs death in September 1715 and the collapse of John Law's System in November 1720. Correspondingly, Montesquieu sought to preserve France's delicate social and institutional arrangements, to safeguard against the excesses associated with new forms of high finance. His concern was that Louis XIV's territorial wars and the Crown's ministers responsible for its fiscal and monetary management were transforming France into an empire of conquest, anchored by a culture of odious luxury, reminiscent of the Later Roman Empire and, more recently, contemporary Spain. It then examines David Hume's essays on political economy, which echo Montesquieu's concerns about the gradual financialisation of free, European governments. Hume observed how innovations in high finance engendered a culture of odious luxury that atrophied the population's industrious character. Echoing Montesquieu, he feared that the paper money economy would disturb European nations' social distinctions, whose maintenance he deemed necessary for preserving free, moderate government in the modern commercial world. Finally, I compare Adam Smith's response to the collapse of the South Sea Bubble in England to Montesquieu's response. Despite Montesquieu's abiding preoccupation with England throughout his writings, he is conspicuously silent in the face of a touchstone event in British economic history, which coincided with the failure of Law's System. In juxtaposing Montesquieu's preoccupation with France's *noblesse de robe* – a symbol of aristocratic valour in the modern commercial age – with Hume's and Smith's preoccupation with Britain's gentry – a symbol of commercial meritocracy – this chapter highlights a moderate perspective in the eighteenth-century commerce and virtue debates, which embraces commerce but harnesses existing honour-yielding institutions to produce a civic republican counterpoise to its excesses.

Montesquieu's Political Economy

Montesquieu's unpublished *Reflections on Universal Monarchy in Europe*, an intended companion to his *Considerations on the Causes of the Greatness of the Romans and their Decline*,[2] critically reflects upon Louis XIV's reign, and the subsequent economic and social disorder that resulted therefrom. He attributes Europe's great transformation since the fall of the Roman Empire to important marriages, treaties, edicts and various civil dispositions, in contradistinction to the naked conquests that conferred power in previous ages.[3] He cites two principal factors that increasingly rendered territorial conquest obsolete: commercial progress and 'gothic liberty', which Montesquieu associates with the nobility's critical role in checking the Crown's sovereign power.[4] On the question of commercial progress, he argues in the *Considerations* that innovations such as the postal service had rendered it strategically impossible to keep conspiracies under wraps, whereas successful conquests in the past had demanded secrecy first and foremost.[5] On a more fundamental level, Montesquieu held that modern imperial ambitions pursued through territorial conquest did not correspond with the spirit of liberty that thrived among modern European nations. Commercial progress incited innumerable passions among citizens and soldiers, making it inefficient and impractical to plan long-term conquests and pillage neighbouring countries.[6] What was more, territorial wars in the modern age would lead to mass borrowing and high tax burdens to service the more complex needs of fighting soldiers. Such imperial ambitions stifled manufacturing, trade and employment. In sum, conquest ultimately weakened the state's ability to produce natural wealth, commensurate with the individual passions, as contemporary Spain's example in the Americas demonstrated.[7]

Montesquieu argues that empires in the modern age needed to establish free trading partnerships abroad to stimulate domestic growth and prosperity. In his *Reflections*, he writes: 'That which has taken shape, from age to age and over the centuries, is a genius of liberty, which makes it difficult to subjugate any part [of the country] to an external force, other than by the utility of its trade [that it has to offer].'[8] Europe's historical arc since the fall of the Roman Empire had turned away from territorial conquest and now bent towards a spirit of commercial and 'gothic liberty', forcing the continent to divide into multiple nations, so that the laws could have greater authority over their citizens. He invokes contemporary Spain's experience in the Americas as a cautionary tale against imperial expansion, warning that this form of empire in the modern age ultimately produced idleness and poverty. And once again alluding to Louis XIV's own ambitions, he states that modern-day empires of conquest were foolishly pouring their resources into conquered nations, which in turn enriched them, while enervating the conquering country's law and economy.[9] Here, Montesquieu further elaborates his distinction between fictional and real, or natural, wealth. He writes: 'It is a bad type of wealth . . . which depends neither on the nation's industry, nor the number of its inhabitants, nor on the culture of its lands.'[10] Imperial conquest transformed Spain into a nation based on gold and silver, rather than the natural wealth that comes from the cultivation of wine and wheat and the manufacturing of luxuries, the last motivating labour among a vibrant population and circulating economic wealth.[11]

Spain's importation of precious metals had an inflationary impact on Europe; that is, as more gold and silver flooded the European market, it became proportionately less valuable. It in fact operated at a loss, since, over and above having to deal with inflationary consequences, it had to inject further resources into extraction and transportation from the Americas.[12] On a more fundamental level, the wealth was fictional because it failed to stimulate the passions that motivate joyful labour domestically. The citizenry grew increasingly indolent, manufacturing declined, and despite Spain's ascendancy as Europe's major colonial power during the sixteenth and seventeenth centuries, only one twenty-fifth of European exports to the Americas arrived from Spain, with no imports besides gold and silver returning from the Americas.[13]

Montesquieu bases his diagnosis on the premise that 'the effect of the wealth of a country is to fill all hearts with ambition; the effect of poverty is to bring it to despair. Ambition is excited by work; poverty is consoled by laziness.'[14] He concludes that in the modern world it is more advantageous to establish free trade with the colonies without assuming the burdens of conquest, since exposure to foreign exotic luxuries provides incentive for the domestic economy to manufacture local goods for export.[15] In modern European society a spirit of commercial honour constantly drives citizens to distinguish themselves through various modes of ornamentation.

In *The Spirit of the Laws*, Montesquieu reiterates his anxieties concerning the vicious circle in contemporary European politics that preoccupied him in his earlier writings. He writes: 'A new disease has spread across Europe; it has afflicted our princes and made them keep an inordinate number of troops. It redoubles in strength and necessarily becomes contagious; for, as soon as one state increases what it calls its troops, the others suddenly increase theirs, so that nothing is gained thereby but the common ruin.'[16] The end result is that excess taxes stifle trade and manufacturing, and produce indolence among local populations who would otherwise suffer greater toil to achieve greater rewards.[17] The spirit of indolence leaves states with no choice but to promote commercial models anchored by imaginary wealth, which in turn further stifles the incentive to labour throughout the population. Spain pursued this path willingly in its obsession with extracting precious metals from Mexico and Peru. Meanwhile, Louis XIV's imperial ambitions in Europe crushed France's real wealth, leaving the country vulnerable to commercial schemes far more pernicious to liberty than what Spain had created following its colonisation of the Americas.

Hume's Political Economy

In 'Of Commerce', David Hume similarly distinguished between productive and odious luxury, and shared Montesquieu's anxieties over how European nations were trending towards Spain's economic model of 'fictional wealth'. Hume states that good luxury motivates individuals to work and creates the sufficient conditions for happiness.[18] He distinctively argued that economic models anchored by real wealth and *good luxury* produced a delicate balance between industry and repose that maximised pleasure for citizens who enjoy their liberty under both these conditions.[19] In Hume's view, this balance permits individuals to optimally 'cultivate the pleasures of the mind as well as those of the body'.[20]

By contrast, *vicious luxury* stems from the economic growth models that plagued France during and following the War of the Spanish Succession. It spoils the balance between labour and repose, yielding excess sloth and restless indolence across the population. Hume again echoes Montesquieu, arguing that free trade abroad harmonises industry and leisure domestically. He writes: 'And this perhaps is the chief advantage which arises from a commerce with strangers. It rouses men from their indolence; and presenting the gayer and more opulent part of the nation with objects of luxury, which they never before dreamed of, raises in them a desire of a more splendid way of life than what their ancestors enjoyed.'[21] Montesquieu and Hume both held that access to vibrant foreign markets in the Americas offered new opportunities for citizens to distinguish themselves and to rise above a stultifying state of anonymity. Moreover, they held that European nations could realise this potential if they exported a spirit of liberty abroad, which would safeguard against public debt domestically – the ultimate driver of 'fictional wealth' and despotism.

Unlike today, where greater sovereign debt typically reflects higher infrastructure and social spending, in the eighteenth century state debt exclusively reflected the depth and breadth of the fiscal-military state apparatus. Louis XIV and his ministers fuelled this phenomenon, and European states wary of the French king's imperial ambitions had no choice but to emulate France's fiscal and monetary regime.[22] This deeply troubled both Montesquieu and Hume. It is for this reason that Montesquieu's earlier writings were preoccupied with France's monetary and fiscal challenges.

Montesquieu clearly envied England's central administrative efficiency, while fretting over the frivolous offices Louis XIV created when he expanded his Court with yes-men and flatterers. He nonetheless held that France could continue to modernise its state apparatus while preserving some of its feudal remnants – namely, the titled nobility and their offices – that he deemed indispensable for preserving liberty. This is the principle that underpinned Montesquieu's prescriptions to France's new regent who had solicited public intellectuals for solutions to the economic crisis. In his 1715 work 'Lettre sur les dettes de l'État', Montesquieu offers a number of prescriptions for restoring France's public credit, without causing disruption to individual families and to the prevailing institutional and social order.[23] Rather than replacing the *rentes*, *billets d'États*, pensions and venality, which in their current state created more liabilities than assets for the French Crown, Montesquieu instead prescribed that each be reduced proportionately,[24] via lower interest rates, and a reduction of pensions and venality appointments. These measures would allow for an overall reduction in taxes allocated to all subjects proportionately according to their wealth. Here, Montesquieu argues that lower government revenues would provide states with a greater strategic military advantage since a decrease in tax burdens on the populace left greater room for future tax hikes in case of war.[25] Moreover, Montesquieu acknowledged that private financiers were 'a necessary cog in the existing machinery of state finance'.[26] But he observed that although France's elites were indispensable for preserving the social, political and economic order, they did not pay their fair share of taxes vis-à-vis the commoners, nor did they proportionately shoulder the economic burdens they themselves were largely responsible for creating.[27] His prescriptions aimed to placate commoners who grew increasingly resentful towards government and economic elites, without undermining the titled nobility.

Despite Hume's distaste for the old aristocracy in his native Scotland, he shared Montesquieu's concern for preserving social distinctions that reflected the new commercial order. It is for this reason that he perceived John Law's System, a practical consequence of the public credit economy, as a harbinger for future threats to European liberty. Alluding to John Law and his notorious System, Hume explains that France's post-war debt situation made room for 'a daring projector with some visionary schemes for their discharge'.[28] He playfully evokes memories of Lycurgus,

> [who] did not think of paper-credit, when he wanted to banish gold and silver from Sparta! It would have served his purpose better than the lumps of iron he made use of as money; and would also have prevented more effectually all commerce with strangers, as being of so much less real and intrinsic value.[29]

Hume understood the utility of carrying some public debt, but nonetheless held that it left desperate governments vulnerable to John Law–type schemes, which replaced specie with paper money as the standard currency in France, retaining all the disadvantages of gold and silver as a medium of exchange without any of its advantages.[30]

Hume thought public credit was intrinsically bad for France or any European nation including Great Britain. He writes that 'it must, indeed, be one of these two events; either the nation must destroy public credit, or public credit will destroy the nation.'[31] By contrast, Montesquieu was more sanguine about England's capacity to support its public debt. Its constitution enabled it to carry larger debt sustainably, without posing a threat to its liberty. He believed that England's love of liberty could be harnessed to raise taxes and imposts that support a vast debt-load during times of war, in a manner that preserves the nation's real wealth, thus obviating the need for innovative schemes to manage public finances. Whereas large debt produces fictional wealth in monarchical regimes like France, England's ability to raise taxes with relative ease means that its credit would remain secure, since a greater proportion of the nation would be borrowing from itself rather than from foreign investors.[32] Its flexibility in taxation counterbalances the instruments of high finance that nudge other European monarchies towards becoming fictional wealth-based economies. As Montesquieu writes, in England, 'It could happen that it would undertake something beyond the forces natural to it and would assert against its enemies an immense fictional wealth that the trust and the nature of its government would make real'.[33]

Hume categorically opposed public debt, regardless of regime type. He held that it ought to only be considered in cases of national emergency, and that magistrates should avoid the temptation to leverage debt for the purpose of expanding the nation economy.[34] Nor did he share Montesquieu's confidence that Britain could continually support large debt through higher taxes. He warned that 'as public credit will begin, by that time, to be a little frail, the least touch will destroy it, as happened in France during the regency . . .'[35] Mirroring France, Britain will cross a threshold where the population will resist higher taxation. Hume feared that public credit would yield unpredictable socially disruptive wealth streams in Britain.

Indeed, the feudal remnants that Montesquieu perceived as sources for maintaining social harmony in France were sources of disorder, instability and toxic factionalism for Hume. Yet, he shared Montesquieu's sensitivity to how new modes of commerce may destroy a nation's social distinctions, as evidenced by Hume's expressed anxiety about how paper money schemes will inevitably produce a 'lethargy of a stupid and pampered luxury, *without spirit, ambition, or enjoyment*' (emphasis added). One may say '[a]dieu to all ideas of nobility, gentry, and family'. Those social orders which enjoy magistracy over the state will be completely lost. He predicts that, as the financialisation of government destroys the natural middle power between the king and the people, 'a grievous despotism must infallibly prevail. The landholders, despised for their poverty, and hated for their oppressions, will be utterly unable to make any opposition to it.'[36] Overall, Hume had a more reactionary attitude towards the paper money economy than Montesquieu, fearing that it threatened a nation's social order, irrespective of constitution.

Although Montesquieu had serious concerns about the political economy of European nations, he held that the excesses associated with public credit were manageable under favourable circumstances. Montesquieu's concerns were more specific to monarchical France's institutional context. 'Republics' such as England and Holland could raise debt and introduce schemes in public and private finance without corrupting their constitutions. However, 'progressive' schemes such as Law's System in France fuelled an international politics of 'territorial conquest' and yielded a domestic culture ripe for despotism, producing conditions found in harsher non-European climates less conducive to liberty, as we shall see.

The Double Edge of Commercial Progress in *The Spirit of the Laws*

In Book 14 of *The Spirit of the Laws*, Montesquieu first accentuates the disharmony between human nature and physical nature,[37] stating that physical nature – that is, climate and terrain – shapes the individual dispositions of men. It follows that individuals are subject to innumerable passions, and in certain climates physical nature emboldens the passions conducive to liberty – industry, labour, courage, virtue – while in other climates '[n]ature . . . has given these peoples a weakness that makes them timid, [and] has also given them such a lively imagination that everything strikes them to excess'.[38] Human nature is malleable to physical nature. Therefore, the laws should accommodate the differences that climate and terrain have bestowed on citizens. Montesquieu illustrates this point in Book 15 where he prevaricates on the question of slavery. He writes: 'There are countries where the heat enervates the body and weakens the courage so much that men come to perform an arduous duty only from fear of chastisement; slavery there runs *less* counter to reason, and as a master is as cowardly before his prince as his slave is before him, civil slavery there is again accompanied by political slavery.'[39] He then states that, even though all men are born equal, slavery does not run counter to natural reason, which justifies civil slavery in a climate where people would otherwise be unwilling to do the labour society requires.[40] Finally, at the end of 15.8 Montesquieu further qualifies his defence of slavery, suggesting that perhaps there is no climate on earth where good political laws cannot induce free individuals to work.[41]

Here, Montesquieu is responding to Aristotle, who distinguishes between the artificial slave, that is, the enslavement of a man 'who is undeserving of being a slave',[42] and the natural slave, who does not have the psychological wherewithal to be an independent citizen, and whose bondage with his master is mutually beneficial. Indeed, there is a subversive element implicit in Aristotle's reflections on slavery, in so far as most Athenian slaves at the time were acquired by conquest, and thus undeserving of their plight. Yet, Aristotle cannot conceive a flourishing Greek *polis* in the absence of slavery. Slavery secured the material conditions that afforded leisure for political association and made the 'good life' possible. By contrast, Montesquieu begins with the premise 'that [since] all men are born equal, one must say that slavery is against nature, although in certain countries it may be founded on a natural reason, and these countries must be distinguished from those in which even natural reason rejects it, as in countries of Europe where it has so fortunately been abolished.'[43] It is the constraints of physical nature, rather than differences in human nature, that make slavery 'reasonable' according to Montesquieu's account. Yet, he optimistically held that commercial innovation provided the impetus (at the *minimum* for European peoples) to overcome aspects of physical nature that justified slavery in past ages. Steady commercial progress over the century made a world free of slavery and despotism conceivable, since 'with the convenience of machines invented or applied by art, one can replace the forced labour that elsewhere is to be done by slaves'.[44] Commercial progress allows human beings to counteract the various constraints imposed by climate, and in fact shapes physical nature so that it favours the needs of human beings. Thanks to human ingenuity, 'we [now] see rivers flowing where there were lakes and marshes'.[45] Innovation in shipping made navigation more efficient, as narrower, deeper hulls permitted ships to sail on longer voyages.[46] The invention of the compass led European commerce to the Americas.[47] Montesquieu's account of the commercial revolution emphasises not only the contribution of knowledgeable craftsmen to public life, but also the merits of various modes of financial engineering developed in the banking sector, which helped raise capital and facilitate the circular flow of money. That is, private stock exchanges and debenture markets allowed manufacturing and industry to expand, which in turn increased employment and wealth.

Montesquieu held that politics must give way to commercial exigencies as they do in contemporary England. As Paul Rahe recently explains, the 'viability of polities has come to depend to a very considerable extent on the extent to which they can accommodate and even promote commerce'.[48] To be sure, Montesquieu celebrates contemporary Europe's commercial dynamism, and in it he sees a vehicle for overcoming some of the physical constraints imposed by nature on individual and political liberty, enabling human beings to overcome their destructive prejudices. Yet in Book 21 of *The Spirit of the Laws*, he highlights the odious side of these same innovations that transformed human society.

That is, the arts could reinforce physical nature's constraints, and embolden the same passions across Europe that physical nature emboldens in regions where people are indolent, exclusively preoccupied with base necessity, and where despotism reigns. In contemporary France, John Law's System promoted political despotism at the top and odious luxury among citizens. It overturned the political institutions that moderated the passions of the king, while destroying France's 'real wealth' with greater efficiency than Spain or any other 'empire of conquest'. Montesquieu in fact juxtaposes the Spanish example with the emerging fiscal and monetary regime that inspired John Law's System.[49] He warns that, although 'paper money' commercial models open new avenues for liberty, they may in fact destroy natural wealth, and like Spain, have exhibited their capacity to embolden the passions that thrive under naturally despotic conditions.[50] Indeed, commercial progress bestowed innumerable benefits on people as it found new means to harmonise human nature with physical nature, yet it had the capacity to fuel despotism, as John Law made evident in France.[51] While Montesquieu increasingly appreciated the merits of new modes of financial capital, he feared that the 'monied class' and government actors would exploit these new innovations for their own ends at the expense of the public interest.

The Case of England and the South Sea Bubble: Montesquieu and Adam Smith

It may seem curious to Montesquieu's interpreters that he lauds England's monetary regime and conspicuously demurs from engaging in polarising debates over England's South Sea crisis, while labelling John Law as 'the greatest promoter of despotism' for importing an idealised version of English finance to France.[52] The following historical and textual considerations may help explain his silence on this question. The South Sea Bubble's collapse generated a great deal of scathing satire and propaganda throughout England that continued well after its collapse, alongside John Trenchard and Thomas Gordon's sharp theoretical response to the crisis in their pseudonymously written *Cato's Letters* (1720–3). In reality, the collapse of the South Sea Bubble had a negligible impact on England's economy. Overseas trade persisted as usual, the excise tax – a principal source of English revenue – remained unchanged throughout the crisis, individual bankruptcy rates held steady, and social mobility remained constant after the South Sea shares plummeted.[53] By contrast, across the Channel, Law's policies directly undermined the economic lifeline of France's aristocracy, whose wealth historically relied on consistent interest-bearing government debt-holdings and tax-farming operations. For Montesquieu, such concerns would not have factored into his considerations on England because, from his perspective, its aristocracy had already been economically and politically undermined well before the Financial Revolution.[54]

Montesquieu's economic pluralism may further explain his diverging positions on England and France. His famous distinction between 'economic commerce' and 'commerce of luxury' in Book 20 of *The Spirit of the Laws* directly responds to those proponents of Law's System who presumed that commerce could be theorised independently of political considerations.[55] We learn that monarchies are better suited for engaging in luxury-based commerce because their 'principal object is to procure for the nation engaging in it all that serves its arrogance, its delights and its fancies'.[56] Yet, he warns monarchies against forming 'great commercial enterprises'. In 'government by one alone' such institutions could become a source of despotic power, as Law's System demonstrates.[57] In monarchical France, commercial and political interests must always remain separate, even with the *parlements*' political powers fully restored.[58] In England, power is diffused among many, where a vigilant representative parliamentary body checks the affairs of government and economic actors. Its constitution – which he famously describes as a republic that 'hides under the form of monarchy'[59] – in fact favours large enterprises like the South Sea Company.

While Montesquieu feared the Crown's ability to wield power through its control of commerce, he did not ideologically oppose joint-stock companies. Otherwise, it would have been a clumsy omission to remain silent on the often-debated South Sea Bubble – across the Channel.[60] Given the centrality of the English constitution in *The Spirit of the Laws*, Montesquieu's conspicuous silence on this issue suggests that his emphasis on freedom of trade does not imply that he championed a wholesale absence of political control. Rather, mobile capital had to remain free from the capricious whims of the *absolute* sovereign. We saw that in France the king was the source of sovereign authority, and Law's System exposed the flow of mobile capital to potential abuses from the Crown. By contrast, political power distribution in England left commerce less susceptible to abuse than if it were under the control of one king and his submissive royal council. This explains why Montesquieu does not engage nor intimate any affinity with Trenchard and Gordon, despite sharing a republican aversion to the corrupting features of high finance. 'Cato's' opening letters exhibit a temper that betrays the spirit of Montesquieu's moderate legislator. They call for severe and immediate retribution towards stockjobbers for their malfeasance,[61] an exercise of cruelty that Montesquieu would have deemed antithetical to England's liberty, and to the principles of free, moderate government, more generally. He would have opposed the imperialist impulse underlying Cato's republicanism as well. Mirroring Montesquieu, Cato differentiates between 'empires of commerce' and 'empires of conquest' to present Spain as a cautionary model of conquest that modern commercial nations ought to avoid. However, his distinction is not as sharp as the Bordeaux aristocrat's. For instance, in Letter 106, Cato suggests that colonies must be subjected until they otherwise prove themselves independent:

> I would not suggest so distant a thought, as that any of our colonies, when they grow stronger, should ever attempt to wean themselves from us; however, I think too much care cannot be taken to preserve their dependences upon their mother country . . . Nor will any country continue their subjection to another only because their great-grandmothers were acquainted.[62]

We saw that, for Montesquieu, 'empires of commerce' needed to export a spirit of liberty abroad to maintain their strength, whereas Cato remains wedded to imperial Rome as a pedagogical framework for forging a political system that approximates a 'Roman province' rather than a 'Greek colony'.[63] From Cato's vantage point, the South Sea's failure presented an immediate threat to

England's imperial prospects. Conversely, Montesquieu perceived John Law's System as a vehicle for imperial expansion that had to be contained. In sum, both Montesquieu and Cato exhibit their republican sensibilities in the face of eighteenth-century high finance, but their ends differed greatly. Cato provides a civic republican remedy to the South Sea debacle to combat corruption and restore Britain's imperial glory, whereas Montesquieu prescribes a civic republican response to the Law debacle, but to combat corruption and contain the prince's imperial ambitions.

Adam Smith – who also considered the two contexts *sui generis* – did not share Montesquieu's confidence in the British Parliament. Even though Law's immediate success with the Mississippi Company provoked the South Sea directors to initiate their debt conversion scheme, Smith deemed the two cases materially incomparable. First, few ordinary citizens owned South Sea shares in Britain, whereas a greater proportion of French citizens owned Mississippi shares.[64] Second, the British government had no direct involvement in the conversion scheme beyond approving a partial debt transfer to the South Sea Company.[65] By contrast, the Mississippi debt-to-equity conversion took place under Law's direct stewardship. Finally, British citizens kept a small portion of their wealth in notes,[66] whereas by 1720 French citizens held most of their wealth in newly issued paper money whose value was tied to the Mississippi Company's fortunes. The Mississippi collapse had a more destructive impact in France than its analogue did in Britain.

Moreover, Smith held that the *sociological* origins of the two crises differed, and that the underlying causes of the South Sea Bubble posed a greater threat to the modern commercial order in the long term. Notwithstanding his cursory treatment of the Mississippi and South Sea cases throughout his two most famous works, his psychological description of the 'man of system' in the *Theory of Moral Sentiments* and his unflattering description of monopolistic corporate culture in *The Wealth of Nations* offer useful lenses for understanding his forensic analyses of the two financial crises.

In Part 6.2.2 of *The Theory of Moral Sentiments*, Smith distinguishes the moderate legislator from the 'man of system'. Echoing Jean-François Melon (1675–1738) and Montesquieu, [67] he explains that the moderate legislator grounds his vision of politics in historicity. He accommodates himself to the nation's customs, its prejudices and its citizens. By contrast, 'the "man of system" is often so enamoured with the supposed beauty of his own ideal plan of government that he cannot suffer the smallest deviation from any part of it. He goes on to establish it completely and in all its parts, without any regard either to the great interests or to the strong prejudices which may oppose it.'[68] The 'man of system' betrays the core principles of political moderation when he uncompromisingly imposes his vision of politics on the population. He 'remove[s] those obstructions – to reduce the authority of nobility – to take away the privileges of cities and provinces, and to render both the great individuals and orders of the state as incapable of opposing their commands as the weakest and most significant'.[69] In recalling his disregard for France's longstanding intermediary institutions, namely the cumbersome *parlements*, readers may reasonably extrapolate that John Law himself may have embodied Smith's unfortunate 'man of system', notwithstanding Smith's actual cursory treatment of the Scottish financier.[70]

Smith's account of Law in his *Lectures on Justice, Police, Revenue, and Arms* might suggest as much. He writes that Law genuinely 'believed in [his scheme] and was a dupe of it himself'.[71] Law erringly thought that paper money could entirely replace specie, which would in turn benefit the Crown, giving it greater flexibility in raising the public revenue it desperately needed. Smith's sympathy towards Law becomes more apparent when we consider the 'man of system's' psychological motivations. Smith writes: '[A]midst the turbulence and disorder of faction, a certain spirit of system is apt to mix itself with that public spirit which is founded upon the love of humanity, upon a real fellow-feeling with the inconveniences and distresses to which some of our fellow-citizens may be exposed.'[72] As such, it was France's political and economic turmoil following the War of the Spanish Succession that may have fuelled Law's impulse for 'humanity'. Law's untamed beneficence made him an inadvertent promoter of despotism, who betrayed the fundamental maxims of moderate legislation.

Smith clearly has less sympathy for the South Sea Company directors. In Smith's view, the crisis resulted from distinct ills endemic to commercial society. The South Sea directors' malfeasance illustrates how monopolies produce a dangerous nexus between economic and government actors, antithetical to free, moderate government. Their impropriety reflects the grave threat monopolies and mercantile commerce pose to the modern order. He echoes John Trenchard, whose polemic essays in response to the South Sea scheme anticipate Hume's warning that high finance threatened Britain's 'real wealth'.[73] Observing how financial speculation 'debauches the Morals and Manners of Mankind', turning people away 'from pursuing their proper Business and Callings, whereby they might maintain and enrich themselves and their Families'.[74] Financial speculation gives people the hope of becoming rich quickly, disincentivising them from cultivating the virtues that provide the modern order with its moral bearings. The South Sea scheme was epiphenomenal to Britain's monopolistic corporate culture at the time, which undermined prudence, moderation and creditworthiness – the commercial virtues that constitute the bedrock of free, moderate government. Moreover, corporate monopolies socialise risk. Joint-stock owners may easily transfer their shares when the underlying company faces adversity, and neither shareholders nor directors assume personal liability for any incurred debts.[75] Subsequently, directors become less vigilant in their decision-making. Smith writes: 'It was naturally to be expected, therefore, that folly, negligence, and profusion should prevail in the management of their affairs.'[76] By their very nature monopolies are poorly managed. Yet, their privileged status enables them to compete in foreign markets, despite their underperformance. The South Sea scheme – which led to the prosecution of company directors and British parliamentarians – was emblematic of how large enterprises co-opt state power.[77] It moreover demonstrates how seamlessly monopolistic ventures funnel corruption into the public sphere in an age of high finance.

To recap, for Smith the Mississippi and South Sea's failures grew out of distinct pathologies endemic to the modern commercial order. In the case of the South Sea debacle, we learn how monopolistic joint-stock ventures create avenues for new modes of public corruption. Montesquieu, by contrast, did not oppose monopolies. He would have likely attributed the South Sea directors' corruption to the absence of *direct* government control over the company's operations, but he would have rejected Cato's imperial republican response to the problem. Joint-stock ventures undoubtedly posed a danger to monarchical France, whose sovereignty wholly lies in the Crown. However, England's more 'republican' political culture necessitated large state-run monopolies. Montesquieu would have agreed that large enterprises could undermine the commercial virtues salutary to modern political life, but he would not have shared Smith's view that monopolies themselves were the source of degeneracy. He thought 'the ill comes when an excess wealth destroys the spirit of commerce; one sees the sudden rise of the disorders of inequality which had not made themselves felt before.'[78] Economic inequality undermines the virtues in a commercial republic such as England, which 'hides under the form of monarchy'.[79] Inequalities may be tolerated in honour-loving, luxury-driven nations such as monarchical France, but they are antithetical to Britain's constitution. As such, state-run monopolies should remain under direct political control in Britain, where political power diffuses across Crown and Parliament.

Concluding Remarks

Montesquieu's responsiveness to England's and France's distinct political cultures reflects his divergent views on questions concerning new modes of finance and the role of the nobility in commercial society. He shows that multiple constitutional mixtures could successfully harmonise political and commercial ends. That is, free, moderate government does not take one ideal institutional form; its structures correspond with the nation's political culture. He refused to separate commerce from politics in his theorising.[80]

John Law's policies may have resolved France's economic challenges in the short term, but in Montesquieu's view they threatened its political and individual liberty. Law promoted a fictional wealth model akin to what Spain had established in the Americas in the previous centuries, which forged conditions commonly prevalent under 'the tyranny of climate'. In this context, Montesquieu had two core objectives in his earlier writings concerning public credit and taxation: to preserve France's delicate social and institutional arrangements, and to safeguard against dysfunctional economic models that produced the material conditions for despotism.

Practical economic concerns related to the 1720 financial crises in Europe informed Montesquieu's, Hume's and Smith's political arguments. They each witnessed how financial innovation may intensify the pathological features of modern commerce. Montesquieu shared Hume's contempt towards fictional wealth economies for rendering the population indolent and stifling a nation's industry and labour. He shared Smith's sensitivity towards large enterprises that undermined the virtues associated with commercial exchange relations. However, the objects of their concerns differed. Hume bemoaned public credit in general, and Smith categorically opposed monopolistic, joint-stock ventures, whereas Montesquieu's assessment of these institutions varied according to the political context. In Hume's and Smith's view, the commercial mores, which form the bedrock of their respective visions of politics, flourish in well-ordered economies that either avoid incurring national debt or prevent the formation of large state enterprises. Alternatively, Montesquieu sought a republican antidote to the ills associated with eighteenth-century commercial innovation, which carves a civic space for aristocratic virtue to flourish. These meaningful points of discontinuity between Montesquieu and his Scottish counterparts illuminate the divergent philosophical arguments that informed their respective understandings of free, moderate government. Paul Cheney has noted that in Montesquieu the Scots found 'the genetic material for modern liberty ... which was congenial to [their] fundamental bourgeois outlook'.[81] Montesquieu, Hume, Ferguson and Smith indeed recognised that commerce opened new avenues for liberty. However, as Istvan Hont convincingly explains, Smith's and Hume's conceptions of modern liberty more closely aligned with James Harrington, who associated the institutional forms and structures of modern liberty with wealth distribution.[82] On this point, Montesquieu would have profoundly disagreed with his Scottish counterparts. The next chapter considers Montesquieu's response to the political thought of James Harrington whose philosophy deeply informed Hume's and Smith's conceptions of political liberty. In exploring why Montesquieu rejects Harrington's republican project, readers will discern a distinct conception of liberty premised on Montesquieu's abiding concerns about the modern commercial world.

Notes

1. David Hume, 'Of the Balance of Trade', in *Essays Moral, Political, Literary*, ed. Eugene F. Miller (Indianapolis: Liberty Fund, 1987), 318, available at http://oll.libertyfund.org/titles/704. All other parts of Essays Moral refer to this edition.
2. Paul Rahe, *Montesquieu and the Logic of Liberty: War, Religion, Commerce, Climate, Terrain, Technology, Uneasiness of Mind, the Spirit of Political Vigilance, and the Foundations of the Modern Republic* (New Haven: Yale University Press, 2009), 21.
3. Montesquieu, 'Réflexions sur la monarchie universelle', in *Œuvres complètes*, vol. 2 (Paris: Gallimard, 1951), 21.
4. Ibid., 24.
5. Montesquieu, *Considerations on the Causes of the Greatness of the Romans and Their Decline*, trans. David Lowenthal (Indianapolis: Hackett Publishing Company, 1999), 199.
6. Montesquieu, 'Réflexions sur la monarchie universelle', 22.

7. 'The unhappiness of the Spanish was that by the conquest of Mexico & Peru, they gave up natural wealth for symbolic wealth that degraded by itself' ('Le malheur des Espagnols fut que par la conquête du Mexique & du Pérou, ils abandonnèrent les richesses naturelles pour avoir des richesses de signe qui s'avilissoient par elles-mêmes'; English translation my own). Montesquieu, 'Réflexions sur la monarchie universelle', 31.

8. 'C'est ce qui forme, d'âge en âge et dans la perpétuité des siècles, un genie de liberté qui rend chaque partie très difficile à être subjuguée et soumise à une force étrangère autrement que par les lois et l'utilité de son commerce' (English translation my own). Ibid., 24.

9. Ibid., 19.

10. 'C'est une mauvaise espèce de richesses qu'un tribut d'accident et qui ne depend ni de l'industrie de la Nation, ni du nombre des ses habitants, ni de la culture de ses Terres' (English translation my own). Ibid., 33.

11. Montesquieu, 'Considérations sur les richesses de l'Espagne', in Œuvres complètes, vol. 2 (Paris: Gallimard, 1951), 10.

12. Ibid., 12.

13. Ibid., 15.

14. Montesquieu, The Spirit of the Laws, , ed. and trans. Anne M. Cohler, Basia C. Miller and Harold S. Stone (Cambridge: Cambridge University Press, 1989), 13.2, 214.

15. 'nos richesses seront plus solide, parce qu'une abondance toujours nouvelle viendra pour des besoins toujours nouveau.' Montesquieu, 'Considérations sur les richesses de l'Espagne', 18.

16. Montesquieu, The Spirit of the Laws, 13.17, 224.

17. Ibid., 13.2, 214.

18. David Hume, 'Of Commerce', in Essays Moral, Political, Literary, 255.

19. David Hume, 'Of the Refinement in the Arts', in Essays Moral, Political, Literary, 270.

20. Ibid., 271.

21. Hume, 'Of Commerce', 264.

22. Michael Sonenscher, Before the Deluge: Public Debt, Inequality, and the Intellectual Origins of the French Revolution (Princeton: Princeton University Press, 2007), 1.

23. Montesquieu, 'Lettre sur les dettes de l'État', Œuvres complètes, vol. 2 (Paris: Gallimard, 1949), 66.

24. Ibid.

25. Ibid.

26. David W. Carrithers, 'Montesquieu and the Spirit of French Finance: An Analysis of his Mémoire sur les dettes de l'état (1715)', in Montesquieu and the Spirit of Modernity, ed. David W. Carrithers and Patrick Coleman (Oxford: Voltaire Foundation, 2002), 172.

27. Ibid., 176.

28. David Hume, 'Of Public Credit', in *Essays Moral, Political, Literary*, 361.
29. David Hume, 'Of the Balance of Trade', in *Essays Moral, Political, Literary*, 318.
30. Ibid., 317.
31. Hume, 'Of Public Credit', 361.
32. Montesquieu, *The Spirit of the Laws*, 19.27, 327.
33. Ibid.
34. Hume, 'Of Public Credit', 351.
35. Ibid., 361.
36. Ibid., 358.
37. Cf. Paul Rahe's excellent analysis which interrogates the relationship between liberty and physical nature in Part III of Montesquieu's *Spirit of the Laws. Montesquieu and the Logic of Liberty*, 170.
38. Montesquieu, *The Spirit of the Laws*, 14.3, 235.
39. Ibid., 15.7, 251.
40. Ibid., 252.
41. Ibid., 15.9, 253.
42. Aristotle, 'The Politics', in *A New Aristotle Reader*, ed. J. L. Ackrill (Princeton: Princeton University Press, 1988), 514.
43. Montesquieu, *The Spirit of the Laws*, 15.7, 252.
44. Ibid., 15.8, 252.
45. Ibid., 18.7, 289.
46. Ibid., 21.6, 361.
47. Ibid., 21.21, 390.
48. Paul Rahe, *Montesquieu and the Logic of Liberty*, 179.
49. 'When they conquered Mexico and Peru, the Spanish abandoned natural wealth in order to have a sign which gradually debased.' Montesquieu, *The Spirit of the Laws*, 21.22, 393.
50. Ibid., 395.
51. In fact, Law's System threatened the entire continent since, after observing its early success in resolving France's most pressing economic challenges, countries across Europe were provoked by jealousy to adopt similar schemes. This in fact made France more vulnerable since investors quickly moved their capital to other joint-stock companies once they sensed that the Mississippi Company had been overvalued. Antoin E. Murphy, *John Law: Economic Theorist and Policy-maker* (Oxford: Clarendon Press, 1997), 265.
52. Montesquieu, *The Spirit of the Laws*, Book 2.4, 19.
53. Julian Hoppit, 'The Myths of the South Sea Bubble', *Transactions of the Royal Historical Society*, 6th series, vol. 12 (2002), 153.
54. Cf. Chapter 3, 73–6.
55. Cf. Catherine Larrère, 'Montesquieu économiste? Une lecture paradoxale', in *Montesquieu en 2005: Studies on Voltaire and the*

Eighteenth Century, ed. Catherine Volpilhac-Auger (Oxford: Voltaire Foundation, 2005), 260.

56. Montesquieu, *The Spirit of the Laws*, 20.4, 340.
57. Here, Montesquieu again echoes Defoe, who observed how England's institutions restrain the government's ability to wield its power through high finance. By contrast, '[Law] plainly saw also, how easie it was to push those things there, which he could not so much as think of in *England*, without apprehensions of being pull'd in pieces by the Rabble. Daniel Defoe, *The chimera: or, the French way of paying national debts* (London: Printed for T. Warner, 1720), 10.
58. Montesquieu, *The Spirit of the Laws*, 20.4, 340.
59. Ibid., 5.19, 70.
60. Stefano Condorelli, 'The 1720 Bubble: A European Perspective', ISECS Conference, Rotterdam, 27 July 2015. In a recent talk, Stefano Condorelli explains that, although the South Sea Bubble, and its effects, paled compared to the Mississippi Bubble, the latter received relatively little public attention.
61. Cf. J. G. A. Pocock, who situates 'Cato' among the neo-Harringtonian republican tradition in Augustan-era British political thought. *The Machiavellian Moment: Florentine Political Thought and the Atlantic Republican Tradition* (Princeton: Princeton University Press, 2003), 468.
62. Ibid., 749.
63. In 10.14 of *The Spirit of the Laws*, Montesquieu praises Alexander for fostering a spirit of liberty in his 'Greek colonies'. He writes: 'The Romans conquered all in order to destroy all, [whereas] in every country [Alexander] entered, his first ideas, his first designs were always to do something to increase its prosperity and power' (150).
64. Adam Smith, *Lectures on Justice, Police, Revenue and Arms, delivered in the University of Glasgow* (Oxford: Clarendon Press, 1869), 218, available at https://oll.libertyfund.org/titles/2621.
65. Ibid., 219.
66. Ibid., 218.
67. Cf. Chapter 1, 35–6.
68. Adam Smith, *Theory of Moral Sentiments* (London: Henry G. Bohn, 1853), 363.
69. Ibid., 344.
70. Pia Paganelli, 'Vanity and the Daedalian Wings of Paper Money in Adam Smith', in *New Voices of Adam Smith*, ed. Leonidas Montes and Eric Schliesser (London: Routledge, 2006), 278.
71. Smith, *Lectures on Justice, Police, Revenue, and Arms*, 218.
72. Smith, *Theory of Moral Sentiments*, 341.
73. 'The people's protection will be squandered away to support Laziness, Prodigality and Vice, and the Bread of the children will be thrown to Dogs.' John Trenchard, *Some Considerations Upon the*

STATE of our Publick Debts in General, and Of the Civil List in Particular (London: Printed, and sold by J. Roberts, 1720), 30.

74. John Trenchard, *An examination and an explanation of the South-Sea Company's scheme, for taking in publick debts* (London: Printed, and sold by J. Roberts, 1720), 17.

75. Adam Smith, *An Inquiry into the Nature and Causes of the Wealth of Nations, Vol. 2* (London: Methuen, 1904), 232.

76. Ibid., 233.

77. Cf. Emily Nacol, who astutely associates Smith's account of how joint-stock venture operations socialise risk with his broader critique of political corruption in the modern world. *An Age of Risk: Politics and Economy in Early Modern Britain* (Princeton: Princeton University Press, 2016), 109.

78. Montesquieu, *The Spirit of the Laws*, 5.6, 48.

79. Ibid., 5.19, 70.

80. In Catherine Larrère's view, Book 20 responds directly to the principles underlying Law's System, which Montesquieu held 'would open the way to despotism, putting merchants at the mercy of one person's or the few's capricious will' (my translation). See Larrère, 'Montesquieu économiste?', 260.

81. Paul Cheney, 'Montesquieu and the Scottish Enlightenment', in *A Montesquieu Dictionary* [online], ed. Catherine Volpilhac-Auger (Lyon: ENS Lyon, September 2013), http://dictionnaire-montesquieu.ens-lyon.fr/en/article/1376427088/en

82. Istvan Hont, *Politics and Commercial Society: Jean-Jacques Rousseau and Adam Smith*, ed. Béla Kapossy and Michael Sonenscher (Cambridge, MA: Harvard University Press, 2015), 80.

Chapter 3

'Ancient Prudence' versus 'Modern Prudence': Montesquieu's Response to Harrington

Harrington, in his *Oceana*, has also examined the furthest point of liberty to which the constitution of a state can be carried. But of him it can be said that he sought this liberty only after misunderstanding it, and that he built Chalcedon with the coast of Byzantium before his eyes.[1]

Montesquieu, *The Spirit of the Laws*

In 29.19 of *The Spirit of the Laws*, Montesquieu situates James Harrington (1611–77) among the utopian thinkers in the history of political thought. He writes: 'Thomas More, who spoke rather of what he had read than of what he thought, wanted to govern all states with the simplicity of a Greek town. Harrington saw only the republic of England, while a crowd of writers found disorder wherever they did not see a crown.'[2] Harrington attempted to establish the best regime beyond human realisation rather than the most practical regime in *The Commonwealth of Oceana* (1656). Montesquieu doubted the possibility of modelling a modern commonwealth after ancient republican principles for two reasons. First, Harrington's vision of politics inadvertently demanded an impractical degree of self-denying virtue out of citizens. Second, Harrington's republicanism insufficiently addressed the particularities of modern commercial life, whose challenges only became amplified following Europe's financial revolutions. Montesquieu's criticisms reflect his broader warning to moderate legislators that they ought to avoid rationalist system-building approaches towards attaining political goods. Ironically, his counsel echoes Harrington's *own* insistence that politics must be grounded in historicity, in prudent empiricism rather than rational design or 'geometry'. This begs the question: what shrouded Harrington's perception of England's liberty?

With these considerations, one might defend Harrington's so-called 'utopianism' on two fronts. First, his republican vision corresponded with a unique historical situation. Henry VII's assault on the feudal peerage in late fifteenth-century England kick-started a socioeconomic transition where the balance of property shifted in 'the people's' favour. In addition, the beheading of Charles I in 1649 turned England into a de facto republic to the extent that re-establishing a monarchy appeared as the less likely alternative at the time. For Harrington, these events brought forth an opportunity to do away with 'modern prudence', which he associated with the early medieval/feudal tradition, and to establish a commonwealth based on 'ancient prudence', which he associated with Sparta, Rome, Athens, the Hebrew Republic, *and* with contemporary commercial republics such as Switzerland and Holland. Harrington found the material conditions on the ground ripe for making his republican vision practicable in England.

Second, England's Financial Revolution in the 1690s and its subsequent impact on eighteenth-century political thought might further temper the view concerning Harrington's utopianism. Following the establishment of the Bank of England, public debt ascended as the new means for waging wars of imperial expansion, which in turn yielded an increasingly interdependent and toxic relationship between government and private economic actors, or the so-called 'monied' interest.[3] This new speculative class posed a viable challenge to the gentry that previously anchored the political community. Harrington could not have anticipated the Financial Revolution and its reverberations across Western Europe, nor that mobile property would ever challenge England's abundance of landed wealth. A political society based on the independent gentry still seemed within the realm of possibility from Harrington's vantage point.

This chapter argues that, despite Montesquieu's sympathies for Harrington's republican project, new social historical circumstances meant he had to reject his political model. Harrington naively held that the new gentry could participate in financial capitalism while providing sufficient leadership in the Commonwealth's Senate. For Montesquieu, this vision was too ambitious and dangerous in an eighteenth-century context and had to be dismissed. Harrington believed in a reconciliation of commerce and 'ancient prudence', whereas Montesquieu held that prevailing commercial circumstances by the mid-eighteenth century, namely the emergence of mobile capital and new modes of high finance, demanded an alternative basis for free, moderate government, whose roots he traced to Europe's gothic (feudal) tradition. In examining his unflattering references to Harrington in *The Spirit of the Laws*, the chapter distinguishes Montesquieu's 'modern prudence', which, I argue, acknowledges the ineluctable role of raw emotion not only among 'officeholders within the various bodies of the state'[4] and their citizens, but also in the moral and political reasoning of philosophical 'legislators'.[5]

Moreover, the chapter examines why Harrington's enthusiasm exceeded Montesquieu's more qualified appreciation for commerce, emphasising how their constitutional prescriptions reflect this fundamental divide between them. First, I will compare Montesquieu's and Harrington's constitutional prescriptions with respect to commerce, liberty, and their perceived role of religion in market society to evaluate Harrington's so-called utopianism. Second, I explain how exchange relations and new modes of capital accumulation challenged traditional notions of political morality and led to new, yet still lofty, principles that could undergird the political community.[6] In Montesquieu's estimation, eighteenth-century material conditions demanded an alternative to Harrington's republican project.

Montesquieu's Moderate Response to Harrington's 'Ancient Prudence'

Montesquieu cites Harrington only twice in *The Spirit of the Laws*, but his critique of the English republican mirrors his ambiguity towards England. For instance, Montesquieu criticises England for removing its intermediary powers, subsequently making its people vulnerable to becoming 'the most enslaved peoples on earth'.[7] One recalls that, for Harrington, the nobility's defanging had a salutary historical effect on England, paving the way for popular government and ancient prudence, whereas Montesquieu held that popular government dangerously relying on selfless civic virtue is a utopian dream, antithetical to a naturally gothic nation whose origins lie in the German forests.[8]

In a passage where Montesquieu must have had Harrington and his republican contemporaries in mind, he mockingly writes: '[I]t was a fine spectacle in the last century to see the impotent attempts of the English to establish democracy among themselves.'[9] He then disparagingly writes: 'Harrington, in his *Oceana*, has also examined the furthest point of liberty to which the constitution of a state can be carried. But of him it can be said that he sought this liberty only after misunderstanding it, and that he built Chalcedon with the coast of Byzantium before his eyes.'[10] Harrington conflated power with liberty, whereas Montesquieu held that power concentrated in the people unchecked inevitably leads to despotism. Rather, government must reflect the inequalities of wealth, distinction and honours that naturally arise in a society and lead to factions that have no interest in defending the common liberty.[11] Harrington prescribes one popular legislative body for his Oceana, divided into those who debate and those who resolve according to capacity.[12] In Montesquieu's estimation, such arrangements inevitably lead to corruption. Liberty could be procured only when distinct legislative bodies representing the different tiers in society *each* have the capacity for debate *and* resolution, while concomitantly serving as institutional checks on one another. In short, for Harrington liberty is possible only when competing interests are unified under one civic body, while for Montesquieu liberty exists only when 'power [checks] power by the arrangement of things'.[13]

The weakness in Harrington's republican regime is that its health unintentionally relies on human beings' self-denying virtue. Power divided within one legislative body yields corruption, not a spirit of compromise between competing interests as Harrington erringly presumed. Montesquieu held that the so-called gothic constitution Harrington had before his eyes in England offered a more stable model for balancing competing interests. That is, its erstwhile institutional checks and balances more effectively forged a sense of civic unity. Despite these fundamental differences, the following discussion concerning Harrington's and Montesquieu's perceived role of religion in market society will compare the two thinkers' temperaments, examining whether historical circumstances or deep theoretical divisions informed their diverging constitutional prescriptions.

Both Harrington and Montesquieu held that a national religion serving political ends was compatible with the principle of religious toleration.[14] Moreover, they both emphasised the interdependent relationship between liberty of conscience and civil liberty in their works. However, Harrington doubted the practicality of sustaining liberty with a constitution that divides power among the king, nobility and commons. Such arrangements place the nobility in conflict with the king,[15] who in turn relies on a powerful, oppressive clergy to secure the Crown.[16] Rather, only in a commonwealth can man follow 'the free exercise of his religion and also enjoy preferment and employment by the state'.[17] Moreover, Harrington held that to sustain a free commonwealth, politics had to *fully* subordinate religion.

By contrast, Montesquieu held that religion and politics may work towards similar just ends, albeit independently,[18] rejecting the dichotomy that church and state needed to be kept separate or that religion needed to be fully subordinated to politics. And although the clergy poses a danger in both despotic regimes *and popular regimes*,[19] a monarchical government's separation of powers between the different levels of jurisdiction safeguards against the clergy pursuing nefarious ends. As he explains in an elegant metaphor describing the various subordinate powers that constitute well-ordered monarchies, 'Just as the sea, which seems to want to cover the whole earth, is checked by the grasses and the smallest bits of gravel on the shore, so monarchs, whose power seems boundless, are checked by the slightest obstacles and submit their natural pride to supplication and prayer.'[20] Even though Montesquieu goes through great efforts to circumscribe clerical power, he held that certain constitutional forms of free, moderate government may channel religion to check the despotic tendencies of monarchical power. Montesquieu most likely sympathised with Harrington's anxieties over the clergy, considering the Englishman's constitutional prescriptions tended towards popular government, with his acknowledgement that clerical power corrupts republics. However, Harrington did not share Montesquieu's confidence that a separation of powers could circumscribe the independent clergy's power. Power ultimately corresponds with property distribution for Harrington;[21] therefore, institutional checks in themselves fail to safeguard against oppression.

In sum, for Montesquieu, religious institutions may reinforce the principles of free, moderate government only when power sufficiently checks power. Moreover, whereas Harrington sees the clergy as a fundamental threat incompatible with popular government, for Montesquieu the clergy 'is suitable in monarchies'[22] along with the nobility and lords, which make up the intermediary powers that keep the monarch in check. In the absence of a clergy with an independent jurisdiction 'in a monarchical regime, you will soon have a popular state [the practicality of which Montesquieu doubted in the modern era] or else a despotic state'.[23]

Despite these differences between Harrington and Montesquieu, some argue that Montesquieu remained committed to Harrington's republican vision, albeit responding to a different historical context.[24]

Indeed, both thinkers express a common principle that privileges an 'empire of laws'[25] over an 'empire of men' in so far as proper constitutional arrangements procure free, moderate government. However, Montesquieu feared that Harrington's more democratic vision allowed men to trump the laws that were supposed to hold them in check. For Montesquieu, the degeneracy lies in the classical republican model itself, whose form necessarily demands self-denying virtue – an unreliable principle for a commercial world of 'small souls'.

Would a greater sensitivity to Harrington's historical context have made Montesquieu more sympathetic to the republican thinker's vision of politics? Harington responded to an English constitution under Charles I that approximated despotism, whereas Montesquieu responded to a freer, more moderate post-1688 English constitution, when clerical power had lost its sting.[26] But Montesquieu had deep reservations concerning the practicality of Harrington's republicanism in post–Financial Revolution Europe. Ecclesiastical authority was the handmaid of despotism in the seventeenth century; however, financial innovation yielded new forms of despotism in the eighteenth century, as we have seen in the previous chapter,[27] rendering Harrington's republican vision impractical under material and social circumstances that favoured 'modern prudence'. Montesquieu's evocation of the ancients in *The Spirit of the Laws* indeed generates a deep nostalgia and appreciation for 'the things [that] were done in those governments that we no longer see and that astonish our small souls'.[28] However, the change in circumstances rendered a society grounded in republican virtue, or 'ancient prudence', obsolete. Politics needed to rest on a new foundation commensurate with the exigencies of modern commerce.

Harrington's Republicanism in the Face of Modern Commerce

Scholars disagree over the degree to which market society figured into Harrington's republican vision. Here, I will show how J. G. A. Pocock's and C. B. Macpherson's classic commentaries both provide textual evidence that corroborates their diverging interpretations of Harrington, which suggests tensions in Harrington's own view on this question. According to Pocock, Harrington did not have the wherewithal to anticipate the commodification of land in the eighteenth century,[29] which is significant since landed property was the fulcrum upon which Oceana was based.[30] By contrast, Macpherson held that Harrington supported a bourgeois commonwealth, where the new nobility – namely, the landed gentry – actually supported and actively participated in market society.[31] Moreover, Harrington thought the gentry's involvement in financial capitalism (specifically, moneylending) had a stabilising effect on the republic, protecting the balance of power between gentry and yeomanry, regardless of any subsequent unequal balance of landed property in the gentry's favour.[32] Specifically, their involvement in moneylending promoted industry and conferred equality of opportunity to accumulate greater wealth among the freemen and yeomanry more efficiently than broader agrarian distributions would have provided.[33]

The textual evidence in Harrington's post-*Oceana* works corroborates Macpherson's interpretation that his commercial republicanism was compatible with stable *or* mobile property. In opposition to his 'neo-Harringtonian' descendants, who associated new finance and the modern economic order with pre–Financial Revolution patronage and corruption,[34] Harrington optimistically held that commercial man could still meet his citizen obligations. The following passages from his post-*Oceana* works demonstrate the wholly anodyne nature of modern commercial activity, in the English republican's estimation.

In 'Pour Enclouer le Canon' (1659)[35] and again in 'A discourse upon this saying . . .' (1659),[36] Harrington refers to commercial republics as the most tranquil and freest of nations. He argues that Venice, Holland and Switzerland were less prone to civil war, strife and sedition than monarchical states such as Germany, France, England and Spain. And in Book I of *The Prerogative of Popular Government* (1658), he repeatedly refers to contemporary Holland along with Israel and Rome as the nations that are most difficult to conquer and to hold.[37] It is again in *The Prerogative of Popular Government* where Harrington suggests that commercial republics based on mobile property may even be more desirable than republics based on landed property. He writes: 'The Balance in money may be as good or better than that of land. For example, [in] cities of small territory and great trade, as Holland and Genoa, the land, not being able to feed the people, who must live upon traffic, is overbalanced by the means of traffic; which is money.'[38] Indeed, mobile capital society concerned Harrington, but he simply thought republics such as Holland required stricter laws against usury and general financial commerce than larger territorial republics such as England.[39]

Yet, multiple passages present the Dutch republic as an inferior republican model to avoid, suggesting a qualified view towards market society.[40] For instance, Harrington argues that, despite a few exceptions, a republic based on land conferred greater stability than one based on money. Moreover, he privileges Rome over Holland as the ideal *expansionary* republic.[41] Despite these weaknesses, one should not disregard Holland as an equally (if not more) relevant model for Harrington's Oceana. The following passage in *The Commonwealth of Oceana* helps explain some of the glaring contradictions with respect to the Dutch republic. It reveals a moderate approach to politics and a conscious attempt to prevent utopianism from shaping his constitutionalism. Moreover, it raises the question whether Harrington would have remained as committed to his republicanism as some of his neo-Harringtonian descendants in the eighteenth century:

> Lycurgus, as I said, by being a traveller became a legislator; but in times when prudence was another thing. Nevertheless, we may not shut out this part of education, in a commonwealth which will be herself a traveller, for those of this make have seen the world; especially because this (though it be not regarded in our times, when things being left to take their chance, it fares with us accordingly) is certain: *no man can be a politician, except he be first an historian or a traveler* for except he can see what must be, or what may be, he is no politician. Now, if he have no knowledge in story, he cannot tell what hath been; and if he hath not been a traveler, he cannot tell what is; but he that neither knoweth what hath been, nor what is, can never tell what must be or what may be.[42] (emphasis added)

Plutarch's 'Life of Lycurgus' seemingly inspired Harrington's approach for constructing his political vision.[43] Political education requires one to follow the Spartan legislator's example by becoming a historian and a traveller. Contemporary and past regimes informed Lycurgus's constitution for Sparta, and similarly Harrington draws from past and contemporary republics for his Oceana. As a historian, Harrington invokes Israel, Athens, Sparta and Rome as the superlative models for ancient prudence. As a 'traveller', he draws from Holland, Switzerland and Venice. While these republics each exercise ancient prudence, the wise legislator must remain attuned to their defects to avoid their importation to Oceana. Rome is the paragon of increase,[44] yet its failure to uphold agrarian laws, which produced inequality, strife and ultimately ruin, must be avoided.[45] Holland and Switzerland are useless and dangerous models for propagation, yet 'the Switz for valour have no superior, the Hollander for industry no equal'.[46] Again, while the

wise legislator avoids Holland's confederate model, its otherwise
internal tranquillity, inherent agrarianism and commerce inform
Harrington's vision for England. Most importantly, Harrington's
inclusion of the more contemporary commercial republics as paragons of 'ancient prudence' suggests that the classical republican
form is indeed compatible with self-interested commerce.

A 'historian' and 'traveller' himself, Montesquieu's evaluation
of past and contemporary regimes shaped his idea of free, moderate
government. How then, should interpreters differentiate Montesquieu's perceived moderation from Harrington's so-called utopianism? Is his inclusion of Harrington rhetorical, to reject a vision
of politics that simply cannot meet the exigencies of the modern
commercial world? Or is Harrington's empiricism as prone to utopianism as the ancients' idealism and the fashionable geometric
political reasoning of Harrington's contemporaries? The following
passage will enable us to work through this apparent ambiguity in
The Spirit of the Laws:

> Aristotle sometimes wanted to satisfy his jealousy of Plato, some-
> times his passion for Alexander. Plato was indignant at the tyranny
> of the people of Athens. Machiavelli was full of his idol, Duke
> Valentino. Thomas More, who spoke rather of what he had read
> than of what he had thought, wanted to govern all states with
> the simplicity of a Greek town. Harrington saw only the repub-
> lic of England, while a crowd of writers found disorder wherever
> they did not see a crown. The laws always meet the passions and
> prejudices of the legislator. Sometimes they pass through and are
> coloured; sometimes they remain there and are incorporated.[47]

In *Montesquieu and the Despotic Ideas of Europe*, Vickie Sullivan
explains how this critical passage encapsulates the combat
Montesquieu has taken throughout *The Spirit of the Laws* against
Europe's despotic ideas and practices.[48] She argues that Plato's
inclusion among those whose ideas inadvertently promulgated
despotism confirm what others have noted, that Montesquieu
categorically aligns himself with contemporary men of commerce
vis-à-vis the political men of Greece. In her interpretation,
'the political men of Greece' are a stand-in for Plato as part of
Montesquieu's attempt to subvert the political philosopher's
ideas, which purportedly had a despotic quality and continued to
shape the character of modern European nations.[49] By contrast,
Montesquieu observed that commerce inadvertently produced
good outcomes. This is why, according to Sullivan, Alexander the

Great emerges as a 'wise prophet of commerce' in *The Spirit of the Laws*.[50] If Montesquieu aligns himself with the political men of today wholesale, how then did Harrington – a prophet of modern commerce in his own right, who adapts its most innovative features to his republican project – earn himself a place alongside Plato, Aristotle, Machiavelli and More in 29.19?

Montesquieu's inclusion of Machiavelli, Harrington's republican hero, among his immoderate philosophical legislators should give readers pause. By relativising Machiavelli with Plato and Aristotle, Montesquieu alerts his readers that political moderation does not simply mean that Machiavellian realism trumps Platonic idealism. Machiavelli's realism did not prevent a clash between his laws and his passions and prejudices. Our unknown prejudices may corrupt our political designs irrespective of our ontological or methodological commitments. It is by the dint of their humanity that the political truth claims of Plato, Machiavelli et al. may lead us astray. What appears as a reified principle of justice is often coloured by the legislator's passions and prejudices.

Montesquieu intentionally inserts his repudiation of Plato et al. after providing a careful history of institutional life in France, to distinguish his own moderate approach to 'legislation'. He warns his readers that enlightenment does not inoculate us against our despotic passions and prejudices. As he states in the Preface to *The Spirit of the Laws*, 'In a time of ignorance, one has no doubts even while doing the greatest evils; in an enlightened age, one trembles even while doing the greatest goods.'[51] Montesquieu shared his Enlightenment contemporaries' view that philosophy can liberate human beings from the shrouds of mysticism. However, he took it for granted that certain inheritances from the pre-modern period were inescapable. His work differentiates our cultural inheritances that we could jettison, by the careful institution of political and civil laws, from our biological inheritances – encoded passions that we cannot transcend through philosophy. No one is immune to the siren calls of affect. Political philosophers cannot free themselves from the human experience. Their utopian projects are a manifestation of the pen's natural intemperance.

Montesquieu's Preface reveals to readers that *The Spirit of the Laws* concerns both the emotional constitution of citizens and the emotional constitution of legislators. He intimates that neither philosophers nor political actors can arrive at justice and happiness through unaided reason. The spirit of Montesquieu's legislation transcends the is/ought distinction commentators often employ to differentiate classical and modern republican political thought. The book's opening paragraph states: 'Plato thanked heaven that he was born in Socrates' time, as for me, I am grateful that heaven had me born in the government in which I live and that it wanted me to obey those whom it had me love.'[52] Plato's laws are coloured by his passions and prejudices, whereas Montesquieu's 'principles' did not stem from his prejudices, but 'from the nature of things'. In Plato's *Republic*, the structure of the dialogue itself provides the model for breaking out of the exigencies of 'doxa' and achieving intellectual clarity over questions concerning justice. Conversely, for Montesquieu, it is a love of country, its institutions and laws, that enables him 'to feel the certainty of the principles'. The architecture of his book serves as a model for achieving intellectual clarity. In a key passage that serves as a guidepost for political understanding, he writes: 'Man, that flexible being who adapts himself in society to the thoughts and impressions of others, is equally capable of knowing his own nature when it is shown to him, and of losing even the feeling of it when it is concealed from him.'[53] Admittedly, our experience may send us awry, but it may reliably direct our political and moral reasoning, if properly channelled by our prudent evaluation of past and present regimes. Montesquieu's Preface adumbrates the 'legislator's' emotional education, which will take place throughout the 31 books, an inoculation of sorts that the author develops against the destructive prejudices that led his predecessors awry. Mirroring Harrington, Montesquieu is a historian, as we observe with his deliberately nostalgic account of past republics (Rome/Athens), and an astute traveller, identifying the institutional/cultural sources of moderation in neighbouring England, continental Europe, China and so on. Yet, the following passage explains why his cosmopolitan journey did not lead him awry: 'When I turned to antiquity, I sought to capture its spirit in order not to consider as similar those cases with real differences or to overlook differences in those that appear similar.' He immediately follows this with: 'I did not draw my principles from my prejudices but from the nature of things.'[54] Our prudent empiricism equips us to follow the logic of liberty, order and justice particular to our constitution, confirmed by a *feeling* of justice that blunts the negative passions incited by 'the thoughts and impressions of others'. The Bordeaux aristocrat is merely a citizen of France without any formal prescriptions to offer his readers. Rather, his book aims to impart the spirit of the moderate 'legislator'. Anticipating his rejection of Harrington's Oceana, a modern republic that combines the 'greatest hits' of past and contemporary republics, Montesquieu invites readers to critically evaluate past and present regimes, to attune themselves to the best possibilities concealed within their *own* nations. One recalls his candid statement: 'If I could make it so that everyone had new reasons for loving his duties, his prince, his homeland and his laws and that each could better feel his happiness in his own country, government, and position, I would consider myself the happiest of mortals.'[55] He will consider himself the happiest of mortals if he incites contemporary and future readers to unearth poles of meaning that exist *within* their nations. Montesquieu's cosmopolitan journey naturally ends in France, where he is now equipped to employ the aid of emotion to identify the good contained within its vestigial institutions.

In sum, both Harrington and Montesquieu grounded their respective visions of politics in historicity. Harrington's propensity for ancient prudence and Montesquieu's propensity for modern prudence reflect a shared sensitivity to the particularities of their own contexts. Harrington's deeper suspicion towards clerical power and unqualified enthusiasm for commerce correspond with his preferred regime which contains features of both ancient republics and contemporary commercial republics. However, in abstracting away from the modern prudence of England's existing institutions, his sense for the harmonics and levellers that enabled free, moderate government at home atrophied. Harrington's inclusion in 29.19 points to a more ambiguous relationship between commerce and liberty that mirrors Montesquieu's deliberately neutral opposition between the political men of Greece and their contemporary counterparts in 3.3. Montesquieu's nostalgic accounts of Europe's republican past and his admiration of England do not aim to supplant France's gothic foundations, but rather to identify the means available for approximating virtue within France's particular context. This explains Montesquieu's purposeful ambivalence towards commerce and religion, spheres of human activity that European nations needed to temper and regulate to avoid despotism.

The Promise and Limits of Eighteenth-century Commerce

In his classic commentary, Thomas Pangle argues that Montesquieu nostalgically invokes the classical republic – whose lofty ideals had become obsolete in the modern age – and promotes commerce to defang and enervate religious belief, the chief companion of despotism.[56] He cites a key passage in 25.12, the most important statement on religion in *The Spirit of the Laws*, which expounds the depth of Montesquieu's commercial republicanism:

> Therefore, one does not succeed in detaching soul from religion by filling it with this great object, by bringing it closer to the moment when it should find religion of greater importance; a more certain way to attack religion is by favor, by the comforts of life, by the hope of fortune, not by what reminds one of it, but by what makes one forget it; not by what makes one indignant, but by what leads one to indifference when other passions act on our souls and when those that religion inspires are silent.[57]

Rather than attack religion outright, the passage suggests that it could be done gradually, and more peacefully, through commerce, since the relentless pursuit of wealth redirects the passions towards material comforts, vitiating people's reverence for God and his splendour.[58] Commerce replaces religion and becomes the new, more worldly foundation for ethical guidance.

Indeed, Montesquieu appreciated the merits of eighteenth-century commerce. Commerce conferred peace between nations,[59] and new exchange relations had a pacifying effect on the mores.[60] However, the following considerations demonstrate he had a more qualified appreciation for commerce. First, Montesquieu's earlier cited distinction between 'empires of conquest' and 'empires of commerce' suggests that realpolitik, rather than his anxieties concerning Christianity, at least partly drove his obsession with commerce. In contrast to Harrington, whose Oceana drew lessons from Rome's superlative expansionary model, Montesquieu held that the modern age demanded an alternative basis for imperial growth. France – a country itself on the verge of bankruptcy due to its costly foreign wars – had to keep pace with *England's* commercial growth and prosperity.

Second, although commerce safeguards against despotism, and religion acts as a companion to despotism, the reverse may also hold true for Montesquieu: if religion is the companion of despotism, it may also aid in procuring liberty, and if commerce confers liberty, it may also undergird despotism. Indeed, Montesquieu associates despotism with religion, and this is most evident when he writes about the papacy and the vizier interchangeably in his discussion concerning despotic regimes.[61] Monotheistic faiths perfectly suit this type of regime since their otherworldliness provides consolation for individuals who live under wretched despotic conditions.[62] Alternatively, readers learn how commercial innovations have imposed natural restraints on the prince, offering an antidote to the ills of Machiavellianism.[63]

However, unfettered commerce may equally serve as a handmaid of despotism for Montesquieu.[64] In 20.21, Montesquieu forbids trade among the nobility, citing their involvement in commerce as one of the main factors that undermined the English constitution.[65] Moreover, in the previous chapters we saw how John Law preoccupied Montesquieu, with the latter witnessing how innovations in high finance enabled a form of Court capitalism that created new revenue streams to fight costly territorial wars, while yielding a fictional wealth economy that enervated the public spirit requisite for preserving liberty. Law's System demonstrates how modern forms of commerce may accommodate despotism *or* civil liberty.

Finally, Montesquieu observes how religion itself may restrain the dangerous excesses associated with commerce.[66] Recent scholars have rejected the monist premise that Montesquieu unqualifiedly boosted commerce as the new religion for eighteenth-century Europe, since it ignores the possibility that religiosity may be desirable under certain forms of free, moderate government.[67] In Joshua Bandoch's interpretation, it is acceptable to weaponise commerce against religion only under circumstances when ecclesiastical authority undermines the principles of free, moderate government.[68] Keegan Callanan's recent commentary explains that, in reality, Montesquieu admires how religious faith had a salutary effect on England, by fostering a sense of moral restraint among an increasingly inward-looking people.[69]

Montesquieu's earlier works were indeed anti-clerical in temperament, expressing contempt for the clergy while arguing for a standard of religious toleration.[70] However, in his later works, Montesquieu parts from his English predecessors by privileging Christianity over the other religions for its softening effects on the mores and its capacity to harness self-restraint.[71] Perhaps this change in temperament relates to his overall concerns about the shadow side of commerce that he witnessed following the John Law debacle that took place around the same time *Persian Letters* was published. Montesquieu's chapters on religion in *The Spirit of the Laws* intimate a complementary relationship between religion and commerce, both of which can work towards just ends.

Montesquieu credits Christianity for its moderating, restraining effect on tyrants in despotic regimes, as the Christian religion 'makes princes less timid and consequently less cruel'.[72] However, his response to Pierre Bayle's atheism in 24.2 suggests that religious faith may play a complementary role in free political societies. He writes:

> To say that religion gives no motive for restraint because it does not always restrain is to say that the civil laws are not a motive for restraint either. It is to reason incorrectly against religion to collect in a large work a long enumeration of the evils it has produced, without also making one of the good things it has done.[73]

Further building his case against atheism, Montesquieu reminds readers in Book 26 that civil laws alone were an insufficient source for restraint, demarcating the boundaries between the different sources that govern human conduct.[74] That is, certain actions are best regulated through the fear of law, while others through the belief in God.[75] In fact, 'It is necessary in society for something to be fixed, and religion is that fixed thing.'[76] Religious belief is indispensable in society as a whole, since it is 'made to speak to the heart'[77] when the civil laws are silent. Chaos ensues only when the 'different orders of laws' overstep their boundaries.

In 24.14, Montesquieu shifts his focus from the despot to the people to explain how religion may support the principles of civil liberty. He writes: 'As religion and the civil laws should aim principally to make good citizens of men, one sees that when either of these departs from this end, the other should aim more toward it; the less repressive religion is, the more the civil laws should repress.'[78] Religion and politics may be harnessed to produce good citizens, while both spheres act as a check on each other in case they depart from their common ends. In the paragraph that follows he explains that Japan, consistently cited as the most despotic regime throughout *The Spirit of the Laws*, has little dogmas to follow, and lacks a conception of hell or paradise.[79] Such an agnostic nation requires more oppressive laws than a nation whose citizens feel bound to universal religious principles. Therefore, the *more* repressive religion is, the *less* the civil laws should repress. As such, if properly harnessed, religion may support the principles of liberty.

Concluding Remarks

Montesquieu may have been more sympathetic towards Harrington's republican sensibilities than the two unfavourable references in *The Spirit of the Laws* suggest, but the material conditions had changed. The Financial Revolution challenged the landed aristocracy and generated new possibilities for corruption inconceivable to Harrington. Rather than adapting Harrington's republican thought to accord with current conditions, Montesquieu dismisses the Commonwealth Englishman's so-called 'utopianism' to safeguard against attempts at engineering ancient republican virtue in post–Financial Revolution Europe. Given Harrington's penchant for being 'a historian' and 'a traveller', would he have shared a similar view in the eighteenth century?

Although Montesquieu promoted commerce, its hazards concerned him. On the one hand commerce could not produce the virtues necessary for civic restraint, and on the other the laws were insufficient for safeguarding against corruption. Realising that motivation for self-restraint had to come from elsewhere, Montesquieu prescribes institutional arrangements that include a circumscribed clergy nudged towards just political ends. However, he doubted that clerical presence yielded sufficient cultural supports, and instead he pointed to the nobility as the 'most natural intermediate, subordinating power'. His fundamental maxim, *no monarch, no nobility: no nobility, no monarch*, suggests that honour is a more reliable 'principle', commensurate with the exigencies of the modern commercial world. Montesquieu rejected Harrington's republican project because it failed to recognise that commerce was *both* a source of liberty and despotism in the modern world. The Bordeaux aristocrat favoured the feudal model of government because it contained institutional features that counteracted the excesses of modern commercial life.

The next chapter compares Montesquieu's and David Hume's understandings of liberty. We have already seen that both thinkers were sensitive to how commercial innovation threatened their respective nations' distinctions of rank, although Hume did not share Montesquieu's propensity for formal titles that distinguished non-commercial from commercial elites. This subtle disagreement explains their divergent conceptions of free, moderate government.

Notes

1. For an insightful interpretation, which explains Montesquieu's allusion to Herodotus in this passage, see Céline Spector, 'James Harrington', in *A Montesquieu Dictionary* [online], directed by Catherine Volpilhac-Auger (Lyon: ENS Lyon, September 2013), http://

dictionnaire-montesquieu.ens-lyon.fr/en/article/1376427088/en.
Montesquieu, *The Spirit of the Laws*, ed. and trans. Anne M. Cohler,
Basia C. Miller and Harold S. Stone (Cambridge: Cambridge University Press, 1989), 11.6, 166.

2. Ibid., 29.19, 618.

3. J. G. A. Pocock, 'Historical Introduction', in *The Political Works of James Harrington, Part I*, ed. J. G. A. Pocock (Cambridge: Cambridge University Press, 1977), 137.

4. Ibid., Part 6, 28.41.

5. In 29.19, Montesquieu employs the term 'legislator' to illustrate how, even in the careful reasoning of political philosophy the 'laws always meet the passions and prejudices of the legislator'. Montesquieu, *The Spirit of the Laws*, Part 6, 29.19, 618. Cf. Chapter 2.

6. Here, Pocock distinguishes Montesquieu, Hume, Hamilton and Smith as the most important thinkers of the eighteenth century who realised that under these new circumstances 'alternative social values had to be found'. J. G. A. Pocock, *Virtue, Commerce, and History* (Cambridge: Cambridge University Press, 1985), 79.

7. Montesquieu, *The Spirit of the Laws*, 2.4, 19.

8. Ibid., 11.6, 166.

9. Ibid., 3.3, 22.

10. Spector, 'James Harrington'; Montesquieu, *The Spirit of the Laws*, 11.6, 166.

11. Montesquieu, *The Spirit of the Laws*, 11.6, 160.

12. James Harrington, 'The Commonwealth of Oceana', in *The Political Works of James Harrington Vol. 1*, ed. J. G. A. Pocock (Cambridge: Cambridge University Press, 1977), 172.

13. Ibid., 155.

14. Keegan Callanan argues that Montesquieu tolerates religion because he thought that, in an age of self-interested commerce, religious faith was a critical source for preserving free, moderate regimes. '*Une infinité de biens*: Montesquieu on Religion and Free Government', *History of Political Thought* 35.4 (2014): 739–67. Cf. Ronald Beiner for an insightful discussion on how Harrington draws inspiration from the ancient republican tradition to reconcile his anti-clericalism with his civil religion project; 'Civil Religion and Anti-Clericalism in James Harrington', *European Journal of Political Theory* 13.4 (2014): 388–407. Recent scholarship on Montesquieu reveals how, despite their divergent political visions, he and Harrington were close intellectual allies on the question of civil religion. Montesquieu considered the role of religion in relation to *both* politics and commerce. On how Montesquieu drives inspiration from the Roman republican tradition to instrumentalise religion for just political ends; cf. Walter Seitter, 'Montesquieu, Pléthon: Politique et religion dans l'Empire byzantine et dans un projet de réforme tardo-byzantin', in

Montesquieu, l'état et la religion (Sofia: Éditions Iztok-Zapad, 2007), 125–40. In the same volume, cf. Catherine Larrère, 'Montesquieu: tolérance et liberté religieuse', 153–71. Larrère discusses how, for Montesquieu, toleration and religious pluralism best corresponded with the emerging cosmopolitan spirit of commerce that modern European nations needed to adapt to ensure their survival.

15. Harrington, 'The Commonwealth of Oceana', 196.

16. James Harrington, 'The Prerogative of Popular Government', in *The Political Works of James Harrington Vol. 1*, ed. J. G. A. Pocock (Cambridge: Cambridge University Press 1977), 563.

17. James Harrington, 'A System of Politics', in *The Political Works of James Harrington Vol. 2*, ed. J. G. A. Pocock (Cambridge: Cambridge University Press, 1977), 844.

18. Rebecca Kingston, 'Montesquieu on Religion and on the Question of Toleration', in *Montesquieu's Science of Politics*, ed. David W. Carrithers, Michael A. Mosher and Paul A. Rahe (New York: Rowman & Littlefield, 2001), 397.

19. Montesquieu, *The Spirit of the Laws*, 2.4, 18.

20. Ibid.

21. Harrington, 'The Commonwealth of Oceana', 163.

22. Montesquieu, *The Spirit of the Laws*, 2.4, 18.

23. Ibid.

24. Along these lines, Rachel Hammersley suggests Montesquieu's few and disparaging references to Harrington in *The Spirit of the Laws* veil the Frenchman's affinities with the English republican's commonwealth project. Like his neo-Harringtonian counterparts, Montesquieu had to transform Harrington's thought to correspond with France's eighteenth-century context, while hiding his controversial republican convictions. *The English Republican Tradition and Eighteenth Century France* (New York, Manchester University Press, 2010), 74.

25. '. . . for a commonwealth . . . trusteth not herself to the faith of men but launcheth immediately forth into the empire of laws and, being set straight, bringeth the manner of her citizens unto her rule . . .'. Harrington, 'The Commonwealth of Oceana', 207.

26. Rachel Hammersley, *The English Republican Tradition and Eighteenth Century France* (New York: Manchester University Press, 2010), 77.

27. Cf. Chapter 1.

28. Montesquieu, *The Spirit of the Laws*, 4.4, 35.

29. Pocock, 'Historical Introduction', 61.

30. Ibid., 61.

31. C. B. Macpherson, *The Political Theory of Possessive Individualism* (Oxford: Oxford University Press, 1962), 162.

32. Ibid., 190.

33. Harrington allows individuals to possess lands generating revenue up to £2,000 a year. 'Commonwealth of Oceana', 231. Here, Macpherson illustrates that this would allow land 'to fall into the hands of 5000 men, leaving the rest of the 500,000 citizens with no land at all'. Macpherson, *The Political Theory of Possessive Individualism*, 185.

34. J. G. A. Pocock, *The Machiavellian Moment: Florentine Political Thought and the Atlantic Republican Tradition* (Princeton: Princeton University Press, 1975), 426.

35. James Harrington, 'Pour Enclouer le Canon', in *The Political Works of James Harrington*, vol. 2, ed. J. G. A. Pocock (Cambridge: Cambridge University Press 1977), 728.

36. James Harrington, 'A Discourse upon this Saying', in *The Political Works of James Harrington*, vol. 2, ed. J. G. A. Pocock (Cambridge: Cambridge University Press, 1977), 737.

37. Harrington, 'The Prerogative of Popular Government', 441, 452.

38. Ibid., 406.

39. Ibid., 407.

40. Pocock, 'Historical Introduction', 60.

41. Harrington, 'The Commonwealth of Oceana', 324.

42. Ibid., 310.

43. Ibid., 75–6, and cf. 'The Life of Lycurgus', where Plutarch describes how Lycurgus travelled to different city states and 'of some things he heartily approved, and adopted some of their laws, that he might carry them home with him and put them in use; for some things he had only contempt'. Plutarch, 'The Life of Lycurgus', in *The Parallel Lives*, vol. 1, trans. Bernadotte Perrin (Cambridge, MA: Loeb Classical Library, 1914), 4.1.

44. Harrington, 'The Commonwealth of Oceana', 325.

45. Ibid., 328.

46. Ibid., 324.

47. Montesquieu, *The Spirit of the Laws*, 29.19, 618.

48. Vickie B. Sullivan, *Montesquieu and the Despotic Ideas of Europe: An Interpretation of 'The Spirit of the Laws'* (Chicago: University of Chicago Press, 2017), 205.

49. Ibid., 141.

50. Ibid., 159.

51. Montesquieu, *The Spirit of the Laws*. Preface, xliv.

52. Ibid., xliii.

53. Ibid., xlv.

54. Ibid., xliv.

55. Ibid.

56. Thomas Pangle, *The Theological Basis of Liberal Modernity in Montesquieu's Spirit of the Laws* (Chicago: The University of Chicago Press, 2010), 70, 103.

57. Montesquieu, *The Spirit of the Laws*, 25.12, 489.

58. For a further discussion of this key passage, see Ian McEwan in Ronald Beiner, *Civil Religion: A Dialogue in the History of Political Philosophy* (Cambridge: Cambridge University Press, 2011), p. 4, n. 8.
59. Montesquieu, *The Spirit of the Laws*, 20.2, 338.
60. Ibid.
61. Pangle, *The Theological Basis of Liberal Modernity in Montesquieu*, 31.
62. Ibid., 47.
63. Ibid., 111.
64. Cf. Roger Boesche's discussion about Montesquieu's concerns that commerce produced cultural conditions for corruption in both monarchies and republics. 'Fearing Monarchs and Merchants: Montesquieu's Two Theories of Despotism', *The Western Political Quarterly* 43.4 (1990), 741–67, 759.
65. Montesquieu, *The Spirit of the Laws*, 20.21, 350.
66. Callanan, '*Une infinité de biens*', 741.
67. Joshua Bandoch, 'Montesquieu's Selective Religious Intolerance in *Of the Spirit of the Laws*', *Political Studies* 64.2 (2016), 353.
68. Ibid., 361.
69. Callanan, '*Une infinité de biens*', 741.
70. Rebecca Kingston, 'Religion', in *A Montesquieu Dictionary* [online], ed. Catherine Volpilhac-Auger (Lyon: ENS Lyon, September 2013), http://dictionnaire-montesquieu.ens-lyon.fr/en/article/1376427088/en
71. In 24.4, Montesquieu privileges Christianity over Islam for its softening effects on the mores. Montesquieu, *The Spirit of the Laws*, 24.4, 462.
72. Ibid., 24.3, 461.
73. Ibid., 24.2, 460.
74. Ibid., 26.1, 494.
75. Ibid., 26.2, 495.
76. Ibid.
77. Ibid., 24.7, 464.
78. Ibid., 24.14, 468.
79. Ibid.

Chapter 4

Montesquieu and Hume's English and French Affinities

The commonalities between David Hume and Montesquieu are striking when one considers their biographical and intellectual trajectories. They both inherited considerable wealth and belonged to the lower branches of the elite class in their respective societies. Moreover, they shared a distaste for legal scholars in spite of family circumstances which nudged both Hume and Montesquieu towards careers in law.[1] Their shared scepticism concerning the legal profession accords with their deeper philosophical resentment towards contractual reasoning in politics. This is most discernible in their respective understandings of modern liberty, each of which hinges on the interrelationship of institutions that emerged from historical evolution.[2] Yet, their analyses lead them to different understandings. Montesquieu formalises 'principles' (honour and virtue) as active springs to explain how liberty and political order arose in aristocracies, democracies and monarchies, whereas Hume interprets these outcomes as fortunate products of historical actors fighting over interests.

Moreover, both thinkers shared a vision of politics that rejected their republican contemporaries' appeals to emulate ancient polities. They instead emphasised the need to adapt politics to a modern, more humane, commercial world, although on a different basis in the two cases. Whereas Montesquieu frequents the halcyon days of France's feudal past to illustrate the nobility's indispensable role for checking the despotic tendencies of the Bourbon Crown and checking commercial activity, Hume viewed such feudal remnants as hindrances to liberty and social stability. He instead shared Harrington's admiration of the gentry, observing its salutary role in political and economic life. Despite Montesquieu and Hume's disagreements over what they deemed the most viable intermediary bodies for anchoring the political community, both shared the belief that contemporary England led its European neighbours in adapting to the modern commercial order.

Hume's and Montesquieu's respective analyses of Britain's constitution are constitutive of their broader political visions, but in neither of their works should their reflections on the island nation be considered *sui generis*. Both thinkers were constitutional pluralists. They observed that liberty, order and the impartial administration of law and justice – that is, free, moderate government – emerged in multiple European contexts. France itself, despite its shortcomings, was moderate, and offered distinct helpful lessons for sustaining liberty and political order in contemporary commercial Europe. In fact, for each thinker, it was only natural to look beyond his borders for practices that could be adapted to remedy his own nation's ills. In 'Of the Rise and Progress of the Arts,' Hume explains that increased international trade and modern commerce have produced a spirit of 'cosmopolitanism' in Europe akin to the 'cosmopolitanism' of ancient Greece, where a natural transmission of cultural and political norms took place between neighbouring city-states.[3] In contemporary Europe, modern commercial society physically expanded the possible size of a dynamic cosmopolitan community.[4] It permitted the people of Edinburgh to adopt the manners, mores, and literary and political ideas of Bordeaux and vice versa without fully emulating each other. Hume and Montesquieu's own writings embody a tradition of cultural exchange between their respective nations, which corresponds with the commercialisation of Europe since the Middle Ages.[5]

Each thinker admired his nation's cross-Channel rival. For Montesquieu, England successfully adapted its feudal institutions to the exigencies of modern commercial society. Yet, his praise is more measured relative to his Scottish counterpart's, who, following the Hanoverian takeover, viewed Great Britain as the world's most politically advanced nation. Nevertheless, the potential for toxic factionalism at home deeply troubled Hume, and mirroring Montesquieu, he looked across the Channel to France, where he thought French politesse and civility were antidotal to Britain's own pathologies. Montesquieu shared Hume's view that commerce produced a sense of fellow feeling among citizens, which he deemed important for maintaining the modern order. Their shared enthusiasm for commerce corresponds with a mutual understanding of free, moderate government, which relies on modulated sentiment for supporting good positive laws and procedural institutions. However, Montesquieu's ambiguity towards England reflects an abiding concern that commerce alone could not produce the public spiritedness necessary for preserving liberty and order, as we saw in the previous chapter. In comparing Hume's and Montesquieu's respective understandings of modern liberty, this chapter develops Montesquieu's conception of political moderation, which is premised on the notion that honour and virtue are the two principles requisite for free, moderate government to flourish.

In the first part I explain how both thinkers ground their theories of free, moderate government on the social passions they deemed necessary for providing vigour and stability to their nation's laws. Hume observed how the French salons created a tactile sociability mechanism that permitted various classes of society to congregate and engage in delightful, polite conversations about philosophy, history, politics and the various issues of the day. The pleasure derived from the commercial transmission of ideas and values that took place in the salons tempered the political factionalism, which, in Hume's view, posed the greatest threat to European nations. Montesquieu equally appreciated France's culture of commercial sociability. Yet, he would not have shared Hume's optimism that commerce alone yielded the public passions necessary for supporting free, moderate government. On this point, the chapter explains how Montesquieu's analysis of England led him towards a more robust conception of political moderation, which emphasises the importance of channelling non-commercial sources of public sentiment to preserve free, moderate government.

Montesquieu's Idea of Liberty

Montesquieu had a pervasive preoccupation with England throughout his life. Following the War of the Spanish Succession and the subsequent financial crises, England surpassed France in military strength and finances.[6] Culturally, early eighteenth-century French travelogs portray a more open, tolerant society across the Channel, with a greater literary liberty that impressed Montesquieu during his intellectually formative years.[7] By contrast, France became increasingly intolerant and suppressed literary and religious freedoms, culminating in the formal expulsion of the Huguenots with Louis XIV's Edict of Fontainebleau in 1685.[8] It is in this context that Montesquieu invokes England in *Persian Letters*, disabusing

French readers of common prejudices towards the English, who had until then been perceived as unstable, savage and anarchic.[9] During the intervening years between *Persian Letters* and *The Spirit of the Laws*, Montesquieu observed that England's constitution increasingly produced social mores and ideas salutary to commerce and thereby offered valuable lessons for France. He praised England for adapting to the modern commercial world in a way that an economically struggling, degenerative France was failing to.[10] England served as a pedagogical model for understanding liberty in the modern commercial world, but his deliberately ambiguous theoretical assessment of the island nation stops short of presenting it as a constitutional blueprint for free, moderate government. What is more, Montesquieu intimates a preference for the tempered liberty he identifies in its continental European neighbours, as we shall presently see.

Montesquieu begins his famous chapter on England's constitution by defining political liberty as that 'tranquility of spirit which comes from the opinion each one has of his security'.[11] We have seen that to best ensure one's subjective sense of liberty power needs to be divided between the legislative, executive and judicial powers of government.[12] Moreover, we learned that government needs to reflect the plurality of interests which naturally arise in a political community. It is why Montesquieu drew attention to how England's legislature is divided into a lower and upper chamber, the latter of which appeases those 'people who are distinguished by birth, wealth, or honours'.[13] The legislature must then convene regularly, where the commons exercise their faculty of enacting while the nobles retain a right to veto their legislation. The nation's executive should then have a further right of veto over the legislature to prevent it from becoming too powerful. Otherwise, the legislature would eventually 'wipe out other powers, since it will be able to give to itself all the power it can imagine'.[14] Interestingly, Montesquieu prioritises the division of judicial powers over the executive and legislative, which, even if united, may still confer a subjective sense of liberty among citizens or subjects.[15] As he incrementally revises his barometer for measuring liberty throughout 11.6 and 11.7, it becomes increasingly discernible to readers that the civilised monarchies of continental Europe sufficiently provide conditions for free, moderate government to flourish.[16]

Montesquieu's emphasis on judicial autonomy corresponds with a broader narrative throughout his political writings, which repeatedly reminds readers that the *subjective* experience of liberty may not always correspond with the actual degree of constitutional or formal liberty one finds in a given nation. In a less than romantic recurring metaphor from Montesquieu's *Pensées*, he describes the *feeling* of liberty as akin to what fish experience, when swimming freely in the water, without realising that they are trapped in wide nets.[17] When he expands the metaphor to situate England along his 'spectrum' of liberty, one finds that the island nation falls short of his criterion for 'free government':

> The men who enjoy the government I have spoken of [England] are like fish who swim in the sea without restraint. Those who live in a prudent and moderate monarchy or aristocracy seem to be in large nets, in which they are caught, though they think themselves free. But those who live in purely despotic states are in such tight nets that they feel themselves to be caught right at the outset.[18]

Here, readers learn that liberty and independence are incongruent at the level of individual psychology. Liberty is an internal mental disposition – a *sense* of security rather than an external fact alone. If citizens do not *feel* liberty, then they do not have it regardless of their independence.

These personal reflections from his *Pensées* adumbrate a second facet of political liberty that Montesquieu develops in Book 12 of *The Spirit of the Laws*, entitled 'Political Liberty in Relation to the Citizen'. He again emphasises the subjective nature of political liberty, with the added qualifier that security *extends beyond one's physical wellbeing*. He writes:

> I have said that, in the former instance, liberty is formed by a certain distribution of the three powers, but in the latter it must be considered with a different idea in view. It consists in security, or in one's opinion of security. It can happen that the constitution is free and that the citizen is not. The citizen can be free and the constitution not. In these instances, the constitution will be free by right and not in fact; the citizen will be free in fact and not by right.
>
> Only the disposition of the laws, and especially of the fundamental laws, forms liberty in its relation to the constitution. But, in the relation to the citizen, mores, manners, and received examples can give rise to it and certain civil laws can favour it . . .[19]

Montesquieu's treatment of China at the end of Book 12, and later in Book 19 – which explores the spirit, mores and manners of various nations – reveals how fluidly he conceptualises regime types in relation to liberty. He writes: 'Though despotic government in its nature is everywhere the same, yet circumstances, a religious opinion, a prejudice, received examples, turn of mind, manners, mores, can leave considerable differences among them.'[20] Despite its constitutional structure, China is a less overt despotic regime than Russia or Japan, and even shares some features of European liberty, as evidenced by the relatively low severity of its penal system during the intervening years between revolutions.[21] Here, he credits early legislators, who successfully harmonised their laws with China's culture.[22] Laws in China are an affirmation of mores, manners and religious rites. As such, subjects do not constantly feel the boot on their necks as their Tartar neighbours do. Of course, China is not a paragon of liberty for Montesquieu. Its constant revolutions show readers that even friendlier, enlightened regimes, whose despots are congenial to European liberty, naturally tend towards instability and eventually become indistinguishable from the more severe regimes that he details throughout *The Spirit of the Laws*.

Certainly, from a bird's-eye view, England's people are the 'freest'. Yet, it is not clear whether their objective liberty is preferable to the *feeling* of liberty among those who are trapped in wide, permissive fishnets. These reflections correspond with the caveat that follows Montesquieu's praise for England's constitution in 11.6. He writes:

> I do not claim hereby to disparage other governments, or to say that this extreme political liberty should humble those who have only a moderate one. How could I say that, I who believe that the excess even of reason is not always desirable and that men almost always accommodate themselves better to middles than to extremities?[23]

Montesquieu's 'moderate' liberty thus appears as a mean of sorts, lying between the 'extreme' liberty one finds in England and the despotism of most other nations.

England's free constitution betrays Montesquieu's principles (honour and virtue) that motivate moral and political action in his two archetypal regimes of political moderation. Here, Hannah Arendt's famous distinction between political and philosophical freedom, which, by her own admission, builds on Montesquieu's distinction in *The Spirit of the Laws*, helps deepen our understanding of the paradoxes associated with England's liberty.[24] Even though Montesquieu held that so-called 'gothic' nations enjoyed greater liberty than the ancients, Arendt states that his idea of liberty, premised on acting rather than willing, better aligns conceptually with ancient understandings in the history of political thought.[25] She explains that Montesquieu's political liberty presupposes human sociability.[26] Honour and virtue are social 'principles', whose animating force depends on individuals' subjective sense of security to act in public with impunity. By contrast, Arendt explains that liberty defined as free will, or 'philosophical freedom', is antithetical to the political liberty that Montesquieu propounds. This sort of freedom – the genetic material of which is traceable to the theology of Saint Augustine – informs early modern republican *and non-republican* systems of politics, which associate freedom with independence or sovereignty.[27]

It is on this basis that Montesquieu criticises James Harrington's political system for conflating liberty, equality and sovereignty. Montesquieu feared that uniting the powers of the few and many[28] into one legislative body would have the effect of crippling the intermediary bodies' ability to check the power of the executive and the commons, as described in Chapter 3. In Montesquieu's view, Harrington's system dangerously promotes a culture of extreme equality, which inexorably leads to despotism, as witnessed in seventeenth-century England, where attempts to remove the nation's intermediary powers inevitably created the conditions for Oliver Cromwell's despotic reign.[29]

Some are tempted to align Montesquieu with Hobbes on the question of liberty since both thinkers reject Machiavellian/Harringtonian self-government in favour of moderate monarchical government, wholly grounded in personal security.[30] However, the 'moderate liberty' in Montesquieu's typology of civilised monarchy does not square with Hobbes' civil liberty, which privileges personal safety and material wellbeing over all other human needs. One recalls that in Montesquieu's monarchical regime liberty naturally lies with the nobility, whose demands for preferences and distinctions – that 'can oblige men to do all the difficult actions . . . which require force, with no reward other than the renown of these actions . . . ,'[31] – supersede material and personal security considerations. Here, 4.2 comes to mind, where Montesquieu describes the psychological motivations underlying the Viscount of Orte's refusal to follow Charles IX's orders to slaughter Huguenots. Orte is constitutionally incapable of killing 'good citizens and good soldiers' since such a cowardly act offends the aristocrat's sense of honour.[32] The Catholic protagonist risked his personal safety and material wellbeing, not out of consideration for next of kin, but for Huguenots – the most commonly persecuted subjects in France. Such acts of barbarism simply offended the dignity of this noble's rank. Montesquieu, like Hobbes, sought to defend monarchical government to his contemporaries. However, recalling Arendt's helpful heuristic, the nature of Montesquieu's archetypal monarchy and its animating principles intimate a broader, more social conception of civil liberty than one finds in Hobbes' *Leviathan*. On its face, Montesquieu's definition of liberty resembles Hobbes', the latter of which is premised on the notion that individuals enjoy their freedom where the laws are silent.[33] According to Montesquieu,

> In a state, that is, in a society where there are laws, liberty can consist only in having the power to do what one should want to do and in no way being constrained to do what one should not want to do ... One must put oneself in mind of what independence is and what liberty is. Liberty is the right to do everything the laws permit; and if one citizen could do what they forbid, he would no longer have liberty because the others would likewise have this same power.[34]

Both Hobbes's and Montesquieu's systems of liberty safeguard against the dangers associated with unrestrained freedom in politics; however, the basis of their respective positions differ. Hobbes's civil liberty is conceptually rooted in his idea of natural liberty, or the 'absence of impediments'.[35] The sovereign's positive laws, backed by the threat of force, permit individuals to exercise their individual freedom wherever their activity is left unimpeded. However, liberty as 'the right to do everything the laws permit' has different implications for Montesquieu than it does for Hobbes. For Montesquieu, 'the power to do what one should want to do' is not only regulated by the laws of the sovereign alone. In fact, one's actions, including the sovereign's, as illustrated in the fine act of honour discussed above, must accord with a broader range of inter-related physical (climate/terrain) and human (moral/civil/political) laws that reflect and support the nation's overall character. Positive laws, which constitute one out of a multitude of interrelated juris-dictions, are necessary conditions for liberty but ultimately insuf-ficient for conferring happiness, since they cannot possibly address the totality of human ends. Therefore, individuals cannot simply be forced to be free by a powerful sovereign; rather, the supports for liberty need to be cultural. As Montesquieu explains in his account of liberty in relation to the citizen, 'mores, manners, and received examples can give rise to [liberty] and certain civil laws can favour it . . .'[36] It is why honour and virtue distinguish free, moderate government from despotism. One's virtue, or honour in the case of the Viscount of Orte, animates individuals to do what they ought to do, according to a nation's established norms. By contrast, Hobbes regulates such public sentiments from above, as his political system relies on the unrestrained sovereign alone to secure the conditions requisite for civil liberty, alchemising human beings' fear of death.

To summarise, Montesquieu rejects Harrington's and Hobbes's systems of liberty. In erringly presuming the congruency of liberty and independence they each attempt to universalise pathologies inherent to England's political character. More specifically, both Harrington's extremely egalitarian and Hobbes's individualistic systems of liberty are conceptually rooted in 'philosophical freedom', which, in Montesquieu's view, makes them dangerously compatible with despotism.

Sharon Krause recently offered a subtler account of Montesquieu's conception of liberty. According to her interpretation, political and philosophical liberty are mutually reinforcing components.[37] She explains that, if one examines the logic of English liberty, one will discover that political liberty, simply defined as institutional restraint on arbitrary will, paradoxically leads to philosophical liberty, or individual agency, and vice versa. As such, Montesquieu's overall praise for England, 'the freest nation on earth', intimates a central place for philosophical liberty in his overall political vision. In its absence, there would be no room for individual agency,[38] and our political horizons would be confined to the limits imposed by strict determinism and social science in the crassest sense.[39] However, one's self-guided action does not have an entirely individualistic foundation in Montesquieu's thought.[40] The social principles (honour and virtue) inspire self-guided action, but they become attenuated under conditions of extreme liberty.

Montesquieu's account of England in 19.27 presupposes sociality rather than independence as a function of liberty. Montesquieu describes a culture of fear and inquietude among the English, where 'the people would be uneasy about their situation and would believe themselves in danger even at the safest moments'.[41] Moreover, one finds that the passions are undisciplined in England. As they 'are free there, hatred, envy, jealousy, and the ardour of enriching and distinguishing oneself would appear to their full extent'. Yet, 'if this were otherwise, the state would be like a man who, laid low by disease, has no passions because he has no strength'.[42] Finally, one observes that English liberty paradoxically produces a culture of atomisation that mirrors the atomisation one finds among subjected peoples in despotic regimes. It is the only nation whose direct object is liberty, yet for this very reason it phenotypically resembles despotic regimes. England ostensibly lacks the social fabric one typically finds in some of its neighbouring civilised monarchies.[43] This is why, if the English were to ever lose their liberty 'they would be one of the most enslaved peoples on earth'.[44]

Montesquieu's deliberately ambivalent theoretical assessment of England's constitution raises the following questions we need to work through to deepen our understanding of his moderate idea of liberty. On the one hand, how do we reconcile his ominous remarks concerning England's liberty amid his otherwise sanguine account of the island nation in 11.6 and 19.27 of *The Spirit of the Laws*? On the other, how do we account for the possibility of moral and political progress in Montesquieu's political thought, if by removing philosophical freedom from his overall system of liberty we are giving clinical behaviourism epistemic authority for preserving free, moderate government? The next section will address these questions by examining Book 19 of *The Spirit of the Laws*, which provokes readers to reflect on England and France dialectically. In this important book, Montesquieu explains how increased trade and the commercial traffic of ideas and norms fostered a cosmopolitan outlook among Europeans, and thereby opened new avenues for the peoples of England to *freely* adopt some salutary manners, mores, and literary and political ideas of France, and vice versa. More specifically, France's polite and civil national culture offers England instructive lessons for mitigating its pathologies, as the careful ordering of Montesquieu's chapters in Book 19 of *The Spirit of the Laws* intimates.

Montesquieu's France vis-à-vis England

In 19.10 Montesquieu articulates a meaningful incongruity in politics, premised on the notion that if political effect is the sole barometer for evaluating a constitution, then virtues may possibly produce less happy mixtures than vices in a nation. He observes that Spanish honesty turns commerce into a languid thing,[45] and that China has its own contradictions, which makes it untrustworthy in commerce.[46] This mode of argumentation opens the possibility for Montesquieu to praise both England and France, notwithstanding their vices. More broadly, it allows for the possibility of multiple constitutional 'mixtures' that permit flourishing in the modern world, in spite of their existing pathologies, which may oftentimes be sources of strength if considered within their own unique political contexts.

Montesquieu's juxtaposition of French happiness in 19.5–9 and English misery in the concluding remarks of 19.27 further develops this narrative. Without ever naming France, he states that its principal vice, namely vanity, produces a culture of politeness and civility, which confers a 'joy in life, a taste, and ease in communicating its thoughts; which was lively, pleasant, playful . . . a nation naturally full of gaiety . . . ', where it does 'frivolous things seriously and serious things gaily'.[47] Meanwhile, echoing his earlier remarks concerning English character,[48] Montesquieu states that individuals have greater freedom, but are always agitated, and 'would believe themselves in danger even at the safest moments'.[49] He then concludes: 'The majority who are witty would be tormented by that very wit; having disdain or disgust for everything, they would be unhappy while having so many grounds not to be so.'[50] Thus, again one finds in England a character of malaise where individuals are withdrawn and in desperation[51] – a disposition which is discernible in their scathing, irreverent and enthusiastically satirical political writings.[52]

Chapter 19.14 acts as the bridge that suggests the potential for a symbiotic relationship between England and France, where remedies to their respective degeneracies lie in one another. Montesquieu invokes Peter the Great – whose edict requiring Muscovites to shave their beards and shorten their robes was deemed tyrannical by the population – to develop his argument that positive laws alone cannot cure a nation's ills.[53] Here, Montesquieu follows a core theme in Enlightenment argumentation, which distinguishes between what can and cannot be controlled through legislation alone. He expands the argument and warns against enacting legislation which conflates laws and customs. Instead, it would be more prudent to introduce new manners and mores unnatural to the domestic laws of a neighbouring nation by first developing cross-border commercial exchange relations. In 19.8 he states: 'The more communicative peoples are, the more easily they change their manners, because each man is more a spectacle for another; one sees the singularities of individuals better.'[54] He restates this observation with greater normative conviction in 20.1: 'Commerce has spread knowledge of the mores of all nations everywhere; they have been compared to each other, and good things have resulted from this.'[55] Modern commerce permits nations to acquire new manners and mores without needing legislators to adopt laws that offend their nations' distinctive characters. Thus, commerce generates new avenues and opportunities for acquiring the habits commensurate with free, moderate government. In this context, France needs to incorporate elements of English toleration, dynamic trade and literary liberty, as Montesquieu and his French contemporaries urge their readers throughout their early eighteenth-century works. Conversely, England may look across the Channel to France for models of politeness and civility to manage the ills associated with its individualistic political culture – an idea one finds more fully developed in the *Essays* of David Hume.

Hume's Idea of Liberty

Montesquieu's and Hume's analyses of Britain's constitution reveal a shared commitment towards a moderate middle that steered clear of despotism on the one hand and extreme liberty on the other; although the bases of their conceptions of free, moderate government differed. Echoing Montesquieu, Hume deemed England the world's freest nation,[56] and in the same manner as his French counterpart, he pillories England's foolish attempts at establishing republican government during the seventeenth century:

> no expedient is more proper, *than to contain ourselves within the bounds of moderation*, and to consider, that all extremes, naturally and infallibly, beget each other. What madness, while everything is so happily settled under ancient forms and institutions, now more exactly poised and adjusted, to try the hazardous experiment of a new constitution, and renounce the mature wisdom of our ancestors to the crude whimsies of turbulent innovators. [emphasis added][57]

However, their immediate domestic preoccupations yielded important divergences between their respective understandings of liberty. Montesquieu – who observed that the Bourbon Crown had increasingly abused its power and nudged France towards despotism – articulates an idea of liberty in terms of 'security', as discussed in the previous section. By contrast, Hume, who observed that English liberty emerged out of a constellation of competing interests which gradually reconciled themselves over time,[58] did not preoccupy himself with the dangers of unchecked power in his account of liberty as much as his French counterpart did.

This divergence explains a fundamental difference in how Montesquieu and Hume perceived the relationship between authority and liberty within their respective political visions. For Montesquieu, liberty is a product of the general spirit, most felt when the 'laws' reflect the culture of the population. Therefore, at the very core of his political vision lies a naturally harmonious relationship between liberty and authority, underwritten by and only made possible through constant vigilance towards encroaching power(s). Inversely, for Hume the contingency and commercial character of England's constitution[59] produces a necessary tension, rather than harmony between authority and liberty, of which he aims to 'keep within the bounds of moderation'.

In 'Of the Origin of Government', Hume explains: 'In all governments, there is a perpetual intestine struggle, open or secret, between Authority and Liberty; and neither of them can ever absolutely prevail in the contest.'[60] British liberty and authority arose out of a unique historical evolution where Crown and Commons checked each other, and where rigid laws developed to restrain all individuals.[61] Both are necessary, but each taken sui generis to its logical extreme leads to either anarchy or despotism. Echoing Montesquieu, Hume did not consider liberty as an unalloyed good that needed to be maximised. However, he thought that Britain, not continental Europe's advanced monarchical regimes, most embodied the moderated liberty that they both espoused. The balance between liberty and authority is more stable in Hume's contemporary Britain, in spite of itself, than in any other country. As he explains in 'Of the Parties of Great Britain', 'A Tory, therefore, since the *revolution*, may be defined in a few words, to be *a lover of monarchy, though without abandoning liberty; and a partisan of the family of Stuart.* As a WHIG may be defined to be *a lover of liberty though without renouncing monarchy; and a friend to the settlement in* the PROTESTANT *LINE.*'[62] Hume took aim at the Court and Country parties, each of which increasingly held a moral claim to Britain's liberty and authority and viewed themselves as the sole originators of England's greatness. For this reason, one finds a number of conciliatory statements in this essay that deliberately blur the distinction between Britain's two dominant factions:

> The Tories, as men, were enemies to oppression; and also as Englishmen, they were enemies to arbitrary power. Their zeal for

liberty, was, perhaps, less fervent than that of their antagonists; but was sufficient to make them forget all their general principles, when they saw themselves openly threatened with a subversion of the ancient government. From these sentiments arose the *revolution; an* event of mighty consequence, and the firmest foundation of British liberty . . .[63]

Hume urges parties to be more moderate and modest about political claims, in light of the fact that *neither* is wholly responsible for Britain's greatness. Parties would have more self-restraint with their political projects if they did not associate their own faction with England's foundations. However, he feared that contemporary Britain's factionalism – fuelled by a debased press that fervently undermined the shared Whig/Tory narrative – threatened to spoil the existing salutary balance between liberty and authority.

Hume's 'Of Liberty of the Press' articulates eighteenth-century Britain's promise and danger to the modern order. He describes Britain's constitution as a mixture of despotism and liberty 'where the liberty predominates'.[64] He writes: '[A]s the republican part of the government prevails in England, though with a great mixture of monarchy, it is obliged, for its own preservation, to maintain a watchful *jealousy* over the magistrates, to remove all discretionary powers, and to secure ever one's life and fortune by general and inflexible laws.'[65] In a mixed monarchy such as Britain, Parliament and Crown are jealous of each other's power and constantly check the other's encroachment. One finds a situation where parliamentarians are afraid of royalists, and there is always a sense that the peace is maintained because of their confidence in the fact that, if the Crown encroaches on liberty, someone will sound the alarm, and the news will quickly spread throughout the population. Hume concludes: 'The spirit of the people must frequently be roused, in order to curb the ambition of the court.'[66] In the absence of a free, vigilant press, he warns that England would follow ancient Rome's trajectory and fall into tyranny since, although the latter had both free and tyrannical elements, no one there kept a vigilant eye on its frightful tyrants. Interestingly, it is not only England's representative government that makes it freer and more stable than ancient Rome, but also its culture of vigilance, vivified by a free and partisan press.

Yet how does one square Hume's fear of factionalism, a theme which runs throughout his political essays, with his overall defence of a partisan press that slanders political opponents and incites tumult and rebellion? Hume partly addresses this question in 'Of the Rise and Progress of the Arts and Sciences', where he identifies features of Britain's mixed constitution that prevent its literary liberty from spoiling the nation's civic culture. He writes: '[I]n a republic, the candidates for office must look downwards, to gain the suffrages of the people; in a monarchy, they must turn their attention upwards, to court the good graces and favour the great.'[67] He distinguishes between monarchies, whose subjects' gaze is turned upwards towards the king, and republics, where the chief magistrate is merely a servant of the people. In the struggle between liberty and authority the playing field in England, like Holland, is tilted in favour of liberty. England's republican features give it greater immunity to attacks on authority since its chief magistrates do not possess the same mystique as their counterparts did in absolute monarchies. An equally free press in France would have more jarring effects on subjects who have greater reverence for political authority.

Moreover, Hume observed that it was possible for the press to play an instrumental role in defanging Britain's factions. He writes: 'A man reads a book or pamphlet alone or cooly. There is none present from whom he can catch the passion by contagion.'[68] The spectator reads news alone and may soberly reflect on events of the day, insulated from outlets that encourage him to react in an immoderately partisan and unreflectively vitriolic manner. One's relationship with print media may produce a period of calm individual reflection, which buffers and mediates any pernicious activity one may be roused to engage in. Simply stated, mobs do not form when people read newspapers in solitude. Yet, Hume modulates his position in a later iteration of this essay, where, in its conclusion, he replaces a much vaster meditation concerning the merits of a free partisan press, with an arbitrary statement that runs counter to the tenor of the entire piece. In the earlier version, Hume concludes:

> Since therefore that liberty is so essential to the support of our mixed government; this sufficiently decides the second question, *Whether such a liberty be advantageous or prejudicial;* there being nothing of greater importance in every state than the preservation of the ancient government, especially if it be a free one . . .[69]

By contrast, the 1771 edition ends with an ominous warning: 'It must however be allowed, that the unbounded liberty of the press, though it be difficult, perhaps impossible, to propose a suitable remedy for it, is one of the evils, attending those mixt forms of government.'[70]

However, the Wilkes riots of 1768, which were fomented by a number of inflammatory pamphlets, changed Hume's perspective on the liberty of the press.[71] Hume surmised that factional behaviour could not be eliminated, but rather needed to be accepted as something 'necessarily evil' which had to be endured.'[72] He feared that the liberty of the press posed a threat to the delicate balance between liberty and authority, which could only be preserved if individuals socialised themselves to liberty through polite discourse.[73] The ambiguity of this essay suggests that Hume was aware that the 'evils' of private reading may outweigh the goods associated with polite reflection, and here, he warns against the dangers associated with liberty in the absence of polite discourse. His updated conclusion calls for quality in printed media, grounded in politeness.[74] Accordingly, Hume sought remedies to Britain's factionalism within its own tradition, where polite philosophical pamphlets comprised the majority of primary reading materials during earlier generations. Political writers such as Joseph Addison and Anthony Ashley Cooper, 3rd Earl Shaftesbury, exercised their liberty while displaying a modicum of politeness and civility.[75] Hume nonetheless observed that England's hyper-partisan culture existed well prior to the Wilkes affair, suggesting an overall awareness that there were natural limits and impediments to polite discourse contained within Britain's political culture.

Indeed, the balance between an Enlightened Hanoverian Crown and a vigilant House of Commons permitted England to burgeon into the world's most enviable government. However, we learn from Hume's arc of history that the world is still young. As such, he turns to contemporary France, which, in his view, offered Britain sources for self-reflection and improvement that were lacking in its own political tradition. Hume invokes Bourbon France – whose constitution he perceives as increasingly tantamount to an empire of laws rather than an empire of men[76] – to spread further scepticism of self-understanding among the two dominant parties in British politics. France demonstrates that the balance between liberty and authority manifests itself under various institutional structures.

Hume's England vis-à-vis France

In 'Of Civil Liberty', Hume accentuates his admiration for the French constitution. He follows Harrington's line of argumentation which traces the historical arc of liberty to constitutional models that contain elements of 'ancient prudence', ranging from Athens and Carthage among the ancients, through Venice and Genoa during the Renaissance, to England and Holland in the present. Yet, he challenges the republican theories of Shaftesbury and Addison, who earlier in the eighteenth century posited that Harrington's political framework alone could permit commerce and liberty to flourish in contemporary Europe.[77] Hume writes that civilised monarchies 'seem to prove . . . this maxim is no more certain and infallible than the foregoing, and that the subjects of an absolute prince may become our rivals in commerce, as well as in learning'.[78] Like Montesquieu, Hume observed that civil liberty had emerged under a plurality of institutional arrangements throughout Europe. One finds in civilised monarchies a predictability of laws and security of property, where the arts flourish.[79] This again is most observable in France, whose political and economic flourishing stems from the security and liberty that Henry IV provided when he 'improv[ed] the realm's finances and administration' and extended religious toleration towards French Protestants.[80]

France's liberty may indeed lag behind England's, but it nonetheless contains the conditions requisite for free, moderate government. France is an unchecked monarchy with no jealous guarding of prerogative. Here, no one feels the need to defend liberty. The people simply exercise it. By contrast, in the Low Countries common people have undeniable rights to sovereignty, by which they do not hesitate to transfer dictatorial power to the magistrate. Therefore, whereas candidates for office must appear useful to the populace in a republic, in a monarchy a man must 'render himself agreeable'.[81] This spirit of independence in republics leads to industry, knowledge and strong genius, whereas the spirit of reverence one finds in civilised monarchies such as France produces a culture of 'wit, complaisance . . . civility', where individuals desire to please one another.[82] The English may lead Europe in philosophy, and the Italians may lead in their arts and music, but French politeness and civility reflects a commercial spirit[83] that made them 'the only people, except the Greeks, who have been at once philosophers, poets, orators, historians, painters, architects, sculptors, and musicians'.[84]

Hume accentuates his affinity for commercial 'passion' in his unpublished essay *Of Essay Writing*. He states that what differentiates human beings from animals is their ability to employ themselves in 'the operations of mind' that may be divided into the learned and the conversible.[85] The conversible life allows for a commercial traffic of innovative ideas and values; and our sociable nature demands that legislators fuse these two realms of human activity to form a symbiotic relationship of sorts between the philosopher and the ordinary citizen. He warns that the highest levels of human learning atrophies when it is 'shut up in Colleges and Cells, and secluded from the World and good Company'.[86] That is, independent thought relies on commercial sociability for its cultivation. Hume's own essays, which he deliberately made accessible to a wider audience, attempt to merge these worlds in Great Britain. He writes, ''Tis to be hop'd, that this League betwixt the learned and conversible Worlds, which is so happily begun, will be still farther improv'd to their mutual Advantage; and to that End, I know nothing more advantageous than such *Essays* as these with which I endeavour to entertain the Public.'[87] The traffic of thoughts and opinions on questions concerning history, politics and philosophy produces a sort of psychological satisfaction in human beings. This is why he had such deep admiration for France. Indeed, he considered Britain as the most politically advanced European nation. However, he observed that the French salons fused the learned and conversant worlds, which translated into a happier, less factional political culture.

Echoing Montesquieu, Hume held that our desire to please reflects the natural affection which exists between the sexes.[88] Court culture simply nourishes this disposition. He writes: 'Art and education, in the most elegant courts, make no more alteration on it, than on all the other laudable passions. They only turn the mind more towards it; they refine it; they polish it; and give it a proper grace and expression.'[89] Eighteenth-century France was a superlative model for politeness, in contradistinction to Britain's brashness. Political and historical circumstances determined which of these two natural dispositions had greater prominence in a nation.

In the appellation of his essay 'On Superstition and Enthusiasm', Hume articulates a Janus-faced cast of mind – observable in contemporary European Catholicism and Protestantism – related to human beings' interaction with the world. 'Superstition' and 'enthusiasm' predate Catholicism and Protestantism, the latter of which are merely two epiphenomenal manifestations of a human temper that seeks either *structure* or *mass elevation*. Human frailty produces a superstitious temper among individuals, while worldly success produces an 'enthusiastic' temper. In the case of superstition, human beings' natural proneness to error, inevitable ill health and psychological malaise, resulting from their faulty self-understanding, lead them to search for imaginary objects of terror, 'to whose power and malevolence it sets no limits'.[90] That is, their meekness and frailty leads them to search *externally* to order themselves. As a result, human beings commonly subjugate themselves to priestly authority.

Conversely, 'enthusiasm' is grounded in self-elevation. Hume writes that 'the mind of man is ... subject to an unaccountable elevation and presumption arising from prosperous success, from luxuriant health, from strong spirits, or from a bold and confused disposition.'[91] Worldly success confers a sense of empowerment and a sense of clarity in individuals, to the point that they consider themselves in direct interaction with the divine. 'In a little time, the inspired person comes to regard himself as a distinguished favourite of the Divinity.'[92] Such individuals gain a boldness of spirit and certainty that even trumps human reason and morality. Consequently, the faculty of enthusiasm produces a crass individualism among citizens and tends to be extremely disruptive of civil order. It yields a distrust towards convention and established authority, and it potentially leads to spontaneous outbursts of violence. Yet, it is a necessary disposition for preserving liberty. By contrast, superstition is necessary for maintaining civil order; but over time, it may erode liberty, since individuals would passively defer to authority on all matters.

Hume explains that, along with the existing European religions, constitutional laws amplify these two frames of thought, and produce a certain set of corresponding mores and manners. Generally, monarchies embolden a spirit of superstition and reverence for authority among the people, while republics embolden a spirit of enthusiasm and independence. Indeed, the forces of both tempers are at play in England and France, but at different magnitudes in each of the cases. England tends more towards liberty since it is largely Protestant and its constitution has more republican features.[93] Bourbon France tends more towards authority, although the existing French Jansenist order, which actually shares greater affinities with Protestantism than conventional Catholicism, became a bastion of French liberty following the Revocation of the Edict of Nantes. As Hume writes, '*Jansenists* are enthusiasts ... and preserve alive the small sparks of the love of liberty, which are to be found in the French nation.'[94]

Hume warns his readers that 'superstition', as an enemy of liberty, may lead to extreme authority, while enthusiasm, as an enemy of authority, may lead to extreme liberty. Yet, if one carefully observes the effects of these oppositional psychological dispositions, one finds that they each engender indispensable mores and manners in populations, requisite for preserving a delicate balance between liberty and authority. Here, like Montesquieu, Hume again points across the Channel to French politeness and civility to redress his own nation's shortcomings. More broadly, Hume pushes Britain towards a monarchical direction to accommodate the exigencies of modern commerce.

Concluding Remarks

Montesquieu and Hume both embraced cosmopolitan trade-based commerce, which, in their view, created new opportunities for moral and political progress. Their writings leverage this new reality to encourage their respective nations to adapt some of their cross-Channel rivals' practices, while steering clear of each other's degeneracies. Montesquieu's and Hume's respective analyses of England and France mirror one another. They would each agree that Protestantism, commerce and self-government enabled liberty. Yet, they both observed that liberty manifested itself in France, where Catholicism reigned under conditions of absolute sovereignty. Moreover, one finds that they seek to emulate the effects of each other's constitutions without emulating their causes.

Hume agreed with Montesquieu that a free constitution does not necessarily confer free, moderate government. That is, liberty is not an inherent property of political structures. It is rather a property that requires both material *and* cultural supports. For Hume, liberty emerged out of a constellation of historical factors that coincided with the commercialisation of Europe, whereas, for Montesquieu, liberty is part and parcel of a nation's general spirit, constituted by both commercial and non-commercial mores and practices. In the next chapter, I explore this divergence between Hume and Montesquieu to provide a more textured account of how their notions of honour and politeness cascade and integrate differently throughout their respective political writings.

Notes

1. In a brief autobiographical note, Hume described the legal profession as 'a laborious occupation', requiring the drudgery of a whole life . . . 'utterly incompatible with every other study or profession'. James A. Harris, *Hume: An Intellectual Biography* (Cambridge: Cambridge University Press, 2015), 35. Montesquieu expresses similar ennui for legal culture in his *Pensées* when he writes: '[a]s for my occupation

as president, I had a very correct heart, I understood the questions themselves well enough, but as for the legal procedure, I understood nothing. I applied myself to it, however. But what disgusted me the most was that I would see idiots with the very talent that eluded me, so to speak.' Montesquieu, *My Thoughts*, ed. and trans. Henry C. Clark (Indianapolis: Liberty Fund, 2012), 86.

2. James A. Harris aptly surmises that, for both Hume and Montesquieu, 'the study of politics meant the study of constitutions, not the study of princes and their ministers, and the ambition was to understand forms of government, and the laws that defined them, in terms of their relations with physical causes, with manners, with commerce, and with religion.' Harris, *Hume: An Intellectual Biography*, 250.

3. David Hume, 'Of the Rise and Progress of the Arts', in *Essays Moral, Political, Literary*, ed. Eugene F. Miller (Indianapolis: Liberty Fund, 1987), 120–1, available at http://oll.libertyfund.org/titles/704. All other parts of *Essays Moral* refer to this edition. 120–1.

4. Ibid., 121.

5. Cf. Broadie, *Agreeable Connexions*.

6. Cf. Chapter 1, 26–9.

7. Ursula Haskins Gonthier, *Montesquieu and England: Enlightened Exchanges, 1689–1755* (London and New York: Routledge, 2016), 23.

8. To clarify, historians often refer to this edict as the Revocation of the Edict of Nantes.

9. Gonthier, *Montesquieu and England*, 20.

10. Ibid., 118.

11. Montesquieu, *The Spirit of the Laws*, ed. and trans. Anne M. Cohler, Basia C. Miller and Harold S. Stone (Cambridge: Cambridge University Press, 1989), 11.6, 157.

12. Cf. Chapter 2, 74–6.

13. Montesquieu, *The Spirit of the Laws*, 11.6, 160.

14. Ibid., 162.

15. 'In most kingdoms in Europe, the government is moderate because the prince, who has the first two powers, leaves the exercise of the third to his subjects.' Ibid., 157.

16. His opening remarks in 11.7, which state that civilised monarchies 'produce equally great things and can perhaps contribute as much *happiness* as liberty itself', reinforce the idea that the correlation between liberty and happiness is never fully congruent. Ibid., 11.7, 167.

17. 'A free government can be compared to a big net in which fish move around without thinking they are caught.' Montesquieu, *My Thoughts*, 874. See also 434, 597, 943.

18. Ibid., 828.

19. Montesquieu, *The Spirit of the Laws*, 12.1, 187.

20. Ibid., 12.29, 211.

21. Ibid., 6.9, 82.

22. Ibid., 19.17, 318.
23. Ibid., 11.6, 166.
24. Hannah Arendt, 'What is Freedom?' in *Between Past and Future* (New York: The Viking Press, 1961), 161.
25. Ibid., 160.
26. Ibid., 153.
27. Ibid., 165.
28. Cf. Chapter 2, 73–4.
29. Montesquieu, *The Spirit of the Laws*, 2.4, 22.
30. Annelien de Dijn, 'On Political Liberty: Montesquieu's Missing Manuscript', *Political Theory* 39.2 (2011), 183.
31. Montesquieu, *The Spirit of the Laws*, 2.7, 27.
32. Ibid., 4.2, 33.
33. Thomas Hobbes, *Leviathan in The English Works of Thomas Hobbes of Malmesbury; Now First Collected and Edited by Sir William Molesworth, Bart.* (London: Bohn, 1839–45), vol. 3. http://oll.libertyfund.org/titles/585, 206.
34. Montesquieu, *The Spirit of the Laws*, 11.3, 155.
35. Hobbes, *Leviathan*, 196.
36. Montesquieu, *The Spirit of the Laws*, 12.1, 187.
37. Sharon Krause, 'Two Concepts of Liberty in Montesquieu', *Perspectives on Political Science* 34.2 (Spring 2005), 89.
38. Ibid., 94.
39. Ibid., 95.
40. Sharon Krause, *Liberalism with Honor* (Cambridge, MA: Harvard University Press, 2002).
41. Montesquieu, *The Spirit of the Laws*, 19.27, 326.
42. Ibid., 325.
43. The pathologies inherent to England's constitution had become apparent to Montesquieu by 1729, when he visited the island nation. In his *Notes on England*, he acerbically writes: 'It seems to me that a lot of extraordinary things are done in England; but all of them are done for the sake of money. Not only are there no honour and virtue here, but there is not even the idea of them: the aim of an exceptional deed, in France, is to spend money; here, it is to get it.' Montesquieu, *Notes on England*, trans. Iain Steward (Oxford University, 2002), https://ouclf.law.ox.ac.uk.
44. Montesquieu, *The Spirit of the Laws*, 2.4, 19.
45. Ibid., 19.10, 313.
46. Ibid.
47. Ibid., 19.5, 310.
48. '. . . are rich, they are free, but they are tormented by their minds. They despise or are disgusted by everything. They are really quite unhappy, so many reasons not to be.' Montesquieu, *My Thoughts*, 7[26].
49. Montesquieu, *The Spirit of the Laws*, 19.27, 326.

50. Ibid., 332.
51. Ibid.
52. Ibid., 333.
53. Ibid., 19.14, 315.
54. Ibid., 19.8, 311.
55. Ibid., 20.1, 338.
56. '[a]nd it may justly be affirmed, without any danger of exaggeration, that we, in this island, have ever since enjoyed, if not the best system of government, at least the most entire system of liberty, that ever was known amongst mankind.' Hume, *History of England*, vol. 6, 531.
57. David Hume, *History of England*, vol. 5, 355–6.
58. Here, Knud Haakonssen explains that, for Hume, freedom was simply the outcome of 'messy power politics . . . during which Crown and Parliament were forced into a mutual dependency that put limitations upon the power of both.' Knud Haakonssen, 'Introduction', in David Hume, *Political Essays*, ed. Knud Kaakonssen (Cambridge: Cambridge University Press, 1994), xx.
59. Cf. Andrew Sabl, who describes Hume's liberty as an emergent property stemming from a commercial bargaining process between Crown and commoners dating back to the Middle Ages. It is only when Crown or Commons resisted this persevering tradition of 'commercial bargaining' that instability and chaos broke out. Andrew Sabl, *Hume's Politics: Coordination and Crisis in the History of England* (Princeton: Princeton University Press, 2015), 191–2.
60. David Hume, 'Of the Origin of Government', 40.
61. Knud Haakonssen, 'The Structure of Hume's Political Theory', in *The Cambridge Companion to David Hume*, ed. David Fate Norton and Jacqueline Taylor (Cambridge: Cambridge University Press, 2008), 348.
62. David Hume, 'Of the Parties of Great Britain', in *Essays Moral, Political, and Literary* (Indianapolis: Liberty Fund, 1777), 71.
63. Ibid., 70.
64. David Hume, 'Of the Liberty of the Press', in *Essays Moral, Political, and Literary*, 12.
65. Ibid., 12.
66. Ibid., 13.
67. Hume, 'Of the Rise and Progress of the Arts and Sciences', 126.
68. Hume, 'Of the Liberty of the Press', 14d.
69. Ibid.
70. Ibid., 14.
71. Cf. Marc Hanvelt for a thorough account of how the riots altered Hume's thinking about the press. 'Politeness, A Plurality of Interests and the Public Realm: Hume on the Liberty of the Press', *History of Political Thought*, 33.4 (Winter 2012), 630.
72. Ibid., 629.

73. Hanvelt writes: 'In order for a free press to contribute positively to the development of knowledge and judgment amongst the citizenry, it would have to engage in a different style of public discourse, one that did not shut off debate or impede moral sympathy.' Ibid., 639.

74. Ibid., 642.

75. Ibid., 639.

76. Hume, 'Of the Rise and Progress of the Arts and Sciences', 125.

77. David Hume, 'Of Civil Liberty', in *Essays Moral, Political, and Literary*, 90.

78. Ibid., 92.

79. Ibid., 94.

80. David Hume, 'That Politics May be Reduced to a Science', in *Essays Moral, Political, and Literary*, 15 n3.

81. David Hume, 'Of the Rise and Progress of the Arts and Sciences', 126.

82. Ibid.

83. Cf. Pocock's discussion which emphasises the centrality of public sentiment in Hume's political thought, identifying commerce as the passion that best supports contemporary political life. Pocock, *The Machiavellian Moment*, 494.

84. Hume, 'Of Civil Liberty', 91.

85. David Hume, 'Of Essay Writing', in *Essays Moral, Political, and Literary*, 532.

86. Ibid., 534.

87. Ibid., 535.

88. Montesquieu, *The Spirit of the Laws*, 1.2, 7.

89. Hume, 'Of the Rise and Progress of the Arts and Sciences', 132.

90. David Hume, 'Of Superstition and Enthusiasm', in *Essays Moral, Political, and Literary*, 73.

91. Ibid., 74.

92. Ibid.

93. Of course, Hume would have classified Britain's Anglicanism as superstition since it shared greater affinities with Catholicism than other dissenting forms of Protestantism. The fact that many Roundheads during the Cromwell period were members of the Church of England may raise further scepticism concerning the plausibility of this distinction between England and France. However, Hume's schema makes greater sense if one considers how he differentiates 'factions of interest' and 'factions of principle' in his preceding essays concerning the nature of Britain's political parties. Factions of interest, made up of Roundhead parliamentarians for instance, were part and parcel of politics, and thus could be easily contained, according to Hume. It is rather factions of principle – in this case made up of Roundhead *supporters* – that did not directly wield political power, but enjoyed a pernicious increase in social power throughout Britain.

David Hume, 'Of Parties in General', 61. Such factions were overwhelmingly Presbyterian, and as such, more authentically Protestant. Hume explains the nature of their alliance more fully when he writes: 'The Cavaliers being the court party, and the Round-heads the country-party, the union was infallible between the established prelacy, *and between the latter and Presbyterian non-conformists*. The union was so natural, according to the general principles of politics, that it requires some very extraordinary situation of affairs to break it.' Hume, 'Of the Parties of Great Britain', 69–70, emphasis added.

94. Hume, 'Of Superstition and Enthusiasm', 79.

Chapter 5

Liberty and Honour in Britain and France

We have already seen that Montesquieu and Hume were sensitive to how commercial innovation threatened their respective nations' distinctions of rank.[1] However, Hume did not share Montesquieu's propensity for the formal titles that distinguished non-commercial from commercial elites – a subtle disagreement that reflects their historically divergent understandings of liberty. In interrogating Montesquieu and Hume's disagreement over the role of the nobility in the modern world, this chapter provides a more textured account of the place of honour and its function within their political philosophies. First, I compare Montesquieu's and Hume's genealogies of modern liberty to demonstrate the importance of honour in their works. I show how Montesquieu traces the origins of modern liberty in France to Saint Louis's judicial reforms, whereas Hume follows James Harrington, tracing the origins of modern liberty in Britain to Henry VII's property reforms. The discussion then points to how their historically grounded theories of politics distinctly pacify honour by channelling it within the commercial world. I argue that, in contrast to Hume, who categorically privileged commercial honour over ancient and feudal modes, Montesquieu had deeper reservations concerning a political culture whose 'principles' were borne via commerce alone.

A number of scholars have identified important ideological, epistemic, and philosophical affinities between Montesquieu and Hume, rightly shining a spotlight on how their assessments of England constitute the two philosophers' political visions. These discussions often focus on their disagreements concerning the impact of climate on human beings.[2] However, if climate was so central to

Hume in his critical reading of Montesquieu's *Spirit of the Laws*, why was this topic not mentioned among Hume's friendly 'quibbles' in their 1749 epistolary exchange?[3] Inversely, Montesquieu applauds Hume for his essay 'Of National Characters', which most directly refutes the former's theory of climatic determinism.[4] These considerations have given recent readers pause during their examinations of Montesquieu and Hume's affinities.[5]

Despite Montesquieu's penchant for considering physical factors that shape a nation's general spirit, both he and Hume agree that commerce, communication and moral laws, rather than climate, have a greater effect on European national characters. For Montesquieu, commercial dynamism coupled with sophisticated political and civil laws diminished the effects of physical nature on human nature, although climate still accounted for some existing variances among free European nations. By contrast, in Hume's estimation climate has a more negligible impact on peoples. It perhaps explains variances concerning innocuous issues such as Northerners' inclination towards strong liquors and Southerners' treatment of women, but even here Hume is dubious and suggests that cultural and historical factors alone may explain such temperamental differences among nations more fully.[6]

Hume develops his argument by examining the physical factors that corresponded with both Greece and China's manners and mores. Ancient Greek city-states had vastly different characters despite sharing a similar climate, while China's inhabitants shared similar manners and mores despite significant variance in its climate and terrain.[7] Moreover, national characters change from one epoch to the next under static climatic conditions. For instance, he argues that 'the ingenuity, industry, and activity of the ancient Greeks have nothing in common with the stupidity and indolence of the present inhabitants of those regions'.[8] Rather, it is easily transmissible customs under broader conditions of plurality that develop national characters for Hume. Hume explains that 'the human mind is of a very imitative nature; nor is it possible for any set of men to converse often together, without acquiring a similitude of manners, and communicating to each other their vices as well as virtues.'[9] Human beings emulate one another, and modern commerce permits the English to adopt French *politesse* and civility without absorbing the causes particular to that nation.[10]

Hume understood modern Europe as a macrocosm of ancient Greece, where a type of cosmopolitanism existed and peoples scrutinised each other's manners, mores, philosophy and arts, and perceived each other as objects for self-improvement.[11] He was particularly impressed by Montesquieu's own scrutiny of England's constitution in *The Spirit of the Laws*, particularly in 19.27, where his French counterpart downplays the determinant role of climate in forming national character.[12] Hume was in fact instrumental in publishing an English pamphlet containing two principal chapters from *The Spirit of the Laws* (11.6 and 19.27) that critically evaluate the constitution of England.[13] Yet, what makes the publication more 'Humean' is the fact that it omits important bridge chapters (14.9–13) which establish the relationship between England's climate and its liberty. Moreover, the omission permits Hume to de-emphasise a more fundamental disagreement between the two thinkers: their divergent perspectives on how to channel and pacify honour to preserve the gains of the liberal commercial world. The next section investigates this core disagreement by examining the biographical and intellectual contexts that shaped their thinking on this question. It first examines contemporary events in France and Great Britain that may have further shaped their ideas of modern honour. It then examines the works of Bernard Mandeville, whose reflections on honour echo throughout Hume's and Montesquieu's writings, to explain why each thinker had a penchant for his own nation's honour-yielding institutions.

Bordeaux and Edinburgh: A Peripheral View of Modern Liberty

Hume's 1749 letter to Montesquieu illustrates the centrality of their disagreements concerning the promise and limits of commercial and non-commercial honour. It intimates that his French counterpart may have arrived at a distorted understanding of Britain, since he observed its political culture through a French historical prism. He writes:

> Your remark on page 26, line 3, 4 is novel and striking. Perhaps you will not be unpleasantly surprised to learn that the English Parliament, having discovered in light of recent events that the Scottish nation was not sufficiently republican, concluded that this violent penchant for monarchical government came from the fact that the nobles preserved their gothic, feudal jurisdictions. This is why Parliament abolished them two years ago.[14]

Montesquieu's and Hume's sensitivity to the historical factors that shaped their respective nations' liberty explains their divergence on the question of Europe's feudal legacy, and their immediate bio-graphical contexts must have only corroborated their respective narratives. Both philosophers lived a considerable distance away from their nation's capital, giving them each a unique vantage point for observing how Bordeaux and Scotland interacted with Paris and London, respectively. If we were to compare Montesquieu and Hume on the question of the role of the nobility in monarchical society, we would discover that Montesquieu has less anxiety at the level of individual psychology than Hume. In France, the pre-ponderance of aristocratic power was so ensconced that encroach-ments by the Crown did not affect the constitutional order. The nobility had a long-standing tradition of preserving French liberty. However, since the Fronde uprisings, Montesquieu observed a per-petual decline in French liberty that he attributed to Louis XIV's undermining of France's intermediary power structures. The legacy of past nobles' self-respecting heroism may explain why Montes-quieu had a patrician's scorn towards political men of today who 'speak to us only of manufacturing commerce, finance, wealth, and even luxury'.[15]

Hume observed a steady rise in English liberty which correlated with the overall material decline of the nobility. The threat of famine loomed large for Hume during his formative years,[16] which he could have attributed to the remnants of Scotland's stultifying feudalism. In his immediate context, the remaining Scottish old nobility and the hereditary jurisdictions of the Highlands threatened liberty and were a constant source of violence and disorder, as Hume forcefully explains in a pamphlet that defends Archibald Stewart, a friend who had been placed on trial for failing to protect Edinburgh from the Jacobite occupation of 1745.[17] Here, Hume distinguishes Scotland's burgeoning commercial mores from the feudal mores of the past, which continue to be embodied by Highlander chiefs who led the Jacobite rebellions. He writes: 'The Highlanders are altogether as ignorant of Discipline as the Low-Country ploughmen, and know as little the Nature of encampments, Marches, Ranks, etc . . .'[18] By contrast, '[w]hen Men have fallen into a more civilised life, and have been allowed to addict themselves entirely to the Cultivation of the Arts and Manufactures',[19] their ambition is channelled to other, more civil areas of human interest. The barbarism of the Scottish Highlanders during the Jacobite rebellions confirmed Hume's sus-picion of non-commercial nobles who posed a broader threat to liberty. He thus had little nostalgia for the pre-commercial reign of the Scottish chieftains, and for their martial stoic glory which, from his perspective, was so out of keeping with the present reality, and served only to contribute towards Britain's factionalism. Their disagreement over the merits of maintaining a non-commercial nobility is discernible in their theoretical responses to Mandeville's genealogy of modern honour in Europe.

Hume and Montesquieu's Response to Mandeville

Indeed, Mandeville's importance is undeniable, given the striking similarities between his, Hume's and Montesquieu's patterns of argumentation when articulating their understandings of honour. Yet, they both had meaningful historical and normative disagreements with the Dutch philosopher, which yielded distinct trajectories in their own works when addressing questions concerning commercial honour. The following discussion examines both Hume's and Montesquieu's response to Mandeville to help unearth their own points of divergence and similarity on this theme.

Mandeville identifies the origins of modern honour with the 'most ignorant Ages of Christianity'.[20] Churchmen and leaders who needed to keep dangerous men and rivals in check cunningly appealed to their followers' pride and vanity by telling them they had a special place in God's overall plan.[21] He writes: 'The great Propensity we have in our Nature to flatter ourselfs, *makes us easy Casuists in our own Concerns*' (emphasis added).[22] Simply stated, human beings respond to demagoguery that elevates their sense of self-importance. As Mandeville explains, 'The most effectual Method to breed Men of Honour, is to inspire them with lofty and romantick Sentiments concerning the Excellency of their Nature, and the superlative Merit there is in being a Man of Honour. The Higher you can raise a Man's Pride, the more refin'd you may render his Notions of Honour.'[23] Accordingly, Christian piety is nothing more than a reflection of one's self-indulgence, whether one is aware of it or not. It is not out of true benevolence and genuine faith that one adheres to Christian principles. Rather, one wants to flaunt one's critical place in God's overall plan. Otherwise stated, Christian piety more reliably manifests out of pride and vanity than out of genuine faith, the latter of which is a fleeting, unreliable impulse, no less among society's most angelic wills. Mandeville explains that even disagreeable individuals could be convinced of their godliness by appealing to their vain impulses. The appearance of one's courage and valour in defence of their supposed godliness has greater impact on one's esteem than genuine moral conduct.[24]

For these reasons, the animating passions – self-interested pride and vanity – associated with modern honour provide a more reliable basis for moral and political action.

Accordingly, Mandeville explains that modern codes of honour have been infused with Christian principles that encourage forgiveness and compassion. Yet, European nations, namely England and France, have retained their courage in spite of their increasing softness. He calls this fusion artificial, since courage is no longer motivated by its natural underlying impulses: anger and vengeance.[25] Natural courage may lead to extraordinary words and deeds in the face of adversity, observable among the great civilisations of antiquity, but it is inferior to modern-day courage, since it often yields erratic and foolhardy behaviour. Indeed, 'man may certainly be as violently rous'd by his Vanity, as a Lion is by his Anger . . .',[26] but, out of our vanity we follow codes of behaviour that temper and direct our courageous actions. For this reason, Mandeville embraced duelling, an erstwhile feudal practice, even as eighteenth-century modern commerce spawned new, more humane codes of honour and manners that regulate human activity.[27] In Mandeville's view, the medieval duel was the ultimate manifestation of modern-day courage. In duelling cultures, human beings may put their lives at risk over a slight or an insult but would never dare violate the intricate rules of play in pursuit of their satisfaction. The potential shame of violating such codes of honour counterbalances the enthusiastic impulses associated with modern honour. Duelling reinforces contemporary manners and mores that he deemed indispensable for modern-day strategic warfare, where victory relies less on adolescent, individual battlefield glory, and more on soldiers' strict adherence to codes of behaviour. In sum, Mandeville embraces modern honour, since its underlying passions could be harnessed by wise legislators to rouse citizens to action when circumstances demand it, while concomitantly restraining their potentially unruly or seditious behaviour.

Recent scholars have carefully scaffolded Hume's *Essay on Chivalry and Modern Honour* and unearthed aspects of both Mandeville's and Frances Hutcheson's political thought that shaped his intellectual formation. J. P. Wright argues that, although Hume accepts Mandeville's genealogy of modern honour, the Scottish philosopher distinctly prefers ancient modes of courage.[28] Mikko Tolonen rejects this view. He more persuasively argues that, for Hume, feudal honour was a necessary precursor to the commercial honour of the eighteenth century.[29] Indeed, Hume venerated the natural courage of the ancients. However, his admiration for

England's and France's unprecedented greatness reveals that authenticity was not his barometer for assessing the various codes and structures of honour. In the same essay, Hume states that human beings' propensity to aggrandise their purpose in this world could be harnessed to inspire civic self-sacrifice.[30] He accepts Mandeville's conspiracy theory concerning how honour codes emerged during the Middle Ages, and moreover agrees that ancient forms of honour lack the discipline identifiable in advanced commercial societies such as England and France. However, he has less of a penchant for the 'gothic' institutions and manners that his Dutch counterpart remained wedded to. He does not share Mandeville's praise for duelling. He moreover bemoans the underlying pathology contained in the artificial nexus between pride and religiosity that emerged during pre-commercial ages.[31] In Hume's account, 'gothic' codes of behaviour throughout the medieval and early modern periods incited citizens' most enthusiastic impulses, culminating in the disorder and instability of the seventeenth-century civil wars.[32]

Interestingly, England and France, eighteenth-century Europe's leading commercial powers, demonstrate that modern commerce could be harnessed to discipline courage more effectively than in previous ages. Hume writes: 'and if anger, which is said to be the whetstone of courage, loses somewhat of its asperity, by politeness and refinement; a sense of honour, which is a stronger, more constant, and more governable principle, acquires fresh vigour by that elevation of genius which arises from knowledge and good education.'[33] During 'ages of knowledge and refinement' it is education, not duelling, which brings constancy, discipline and moderation for Hume. Emergent commercial points of honour fostered the soft humanity encouraged by the Gospels, but without the religious enthusiasm that underpinned pre-eighteenth-century honour codes and structures. The desire for praise and glory indeed drove industry, but, as Hume explains, with modern commerce 'good manners have been invented and have carried the matter somewhat farther'.[34] Individuals now needed to conceal their pride and moderate their vices, to make themselves agreeable in their social interactions.[35] As such, commerce yields greater social and political stability since its honours and distinctions may only be 'cashed in' if one learns to temper one's enthusiasm.

Hume elaborates the historical relationship between modern commerce and contemporary points of honour in Volume III of *The History of England*, where he praises Henry VII, whose reforms gave the nobility and gentry a means for alienating their large estates in order to pursue frivolous luxuries.[36] The measures produced a gentleman class of Englishmen with a 'more civilised species of emulation . . . [who] endeavoured to excel in the splendour and elegance of their equipage, houses and tables'.[37] Henry VII's measures did not eliminate honour. Rather, they changed its object away from destructive martial glory to wealth.[38] In Hume's view, these transformations lay the foundations for long-term peace[39] and human flourishing.[40]

We have seen that Montesquieu shared Hume's view that commercial sociability was a boon for Europe, translating into moral and political progress.[41] However, his response to Mandeville's genealogy of modern honour suggests the need for an alternative source of public sentiment to balance the commercial mores. Montesquieu correspondingly traces the origins of modern honour to Europe's feudal heritage, and he shared the Dutch philosopher's view that false honour more reliably regulates human relationships than genuine religious faith. However, he rejects Mandeville's aforementioned conspiracy theory that feudal leaders developed modern honour codes as a sort of trick for regulating their subjects' behaviour. Honour equally restrains the sovereign. His praise for the Viscount of Orte's refusal to slaughter Huguenots demonstrates a more sanguine account of the non-commercial sources of honour. Moreover, he did not share his Scottish counterpart's optimism that commerce could universally produce self-sufficient mores. Despite its salutary effects, a spirit of individualism and 'exact justice' emerged in commercial Europe, which threatened to atrophy citizens' other-regarding affections. Certainly, commerce more reliably softened individuals than religion, and opened new avenues for fostering social bonds, but, if left unchecked, it threatened to vitiate the sociable spirit that permitted honour and virtue to flourish.

England, an alarmingly individualistic commercial nation, had relative immunity to the ill-effects of commerce because of its unique circumstances. In 14.13 of *The Spirit of the Laws*, Montesquieu discusses features of English character that would be difficult to comprehend by simply examining the laws in 11.6 and their effects in 19.27. He states that England's miserable climate made its people 'carry the repugnance for all things to include that of life'.[42] Under such conditions, a government that promotes individualism and independence is most appropriate, since one 'could not be allowed to blame any one person for

causing their sorrows . . .'.[43] England's harsh climate has produced an impatience among its citizens, and a fickleness, 'which
makes one undertake things without purpose and abandon them
likewise'.[44] It is this restlessness that helps preserve English liberty,
since it makes people vigilant, naturally more resistant to power,
and thus 'apt to frustrate the projects of tyranny'.[45] The existing
political and civil laws in England accommodate a temper made
intelligible by its climate. Here, commerce alone may produce the
cultural supports requisite for preserving liberty. By contrast, in
more temperate climates like France, one finds less impatient and
fickle inhabitants. Such conditions demand commercial *and* non-
commercial sources of honour and virtue to support good laws.

Echoing Hume, Montesquieu's optimism concerning England's
prospects lie in the burgeoning middle class that arose from the
property-levelling policies Henry VII enacted a couple of centuries earlier.[46] They had the effect of transferring property from the
nobles to the commons, which in turn made the House of Commons
the locus of English political power. In a letter to William Domville
a year following the publication of his *Spirit of the Laws*, Montesquieu wrote: 'There could not be middling people, as with you,
nor a spirit of liberty, as with you.'[47] England's virtue is in its lower
bodies, which are least corrupted. The people 'have more virtue
than those who represent them'.[48] It is not England's representative government alone that ensures its freedom, since its boroughs
and frequent elections are often mired in widespread corruption,
forcing citizens to maintain their vigilance. As Montesquieu writes,
England does 'not cease to be unencumbered because [its com-
merce] has made it difficult to put a veil over it'.[49] These 'middling
people' can sniff out any machinations immediately. England is
unique in so far as political and economic crises reinvigorate rather
than weaken the principles that animate its commercially infused
civic body.

In fact, Montesquieu articulates a causal relationship between
commerce and certain virtues when he famously establishes his
principles in Part I of *The Spirit of the Laws*: 'the spirit of commerce brings with it the spirit of frugality, economy, moderation,
work, wisdom, tranquillity, order and rule.'[50] It is rather *excess
wealth* that threatens the commercial republic, which is why in
the paragraph that follows he states that large enterprises must
be under the control of magistrates rather than private individuals, to safeguard against the corrupting effects of excess wealth
on citizens.[51]

One even finds in Book 14 a mode of English honour, which in Montesquieu's view, should inspirit Southern European legislators. He writes: '[I]t [England] would be well to give prizes to the plowmen who had best cultivated their lands and to the workers who had been most industrious. This practice will succeed in every country'[52] (emphasis added). Yet, Montesquieu prevaricates on the question of commercial honour throughout his works. On the one hand, commercial merit and wealth distinctions propel the economy and inadvertently foster a civic ethos among citizens. On the other, he consistently worried about wealth becoming the only barometer of self-worth in societies bereft of non-commercial distinctions. The prejudices associated with commercial self-interest have devitalised the existing prejudices associated with martial glory, noble birth or public office in England. These institutions of course still existed in England, but, as Montesquieu states in *My Thoughts*,[53] its people value only wealth and personal merit *and are moving towards admiring the former exclusively*. It is why Montesquieu examined sources in France's *own* political tradition for balancing commercial ends with the public interest.

In the final two books of *The Spirit of the Laws*, Montesquieu weighs in on the prevailing historiography of France's feudal past. He writes:

> The Count of Boulainvilliers and the Abbé Dubos have each made a system, the one seeming to be a conspiracy against the third estate, and the other a conspiracy against the nobility. When the Sun gave his chariot to Phaeton to drive, he said to him: 'If you climb too high, you will burn the celestial residence; if you drop too low, you will reduce the earth to ashes. Do not go too far to the right, or you will fall into the constellation of the Serpent; do not go too far to the left, or you will go into that of the Altar: stay between the two.[54]

Dubos, who forges a direct lineage between Clovis and the Roman emperors, over-Romanises France's heritage. Boulainvilliers, who romanticises the French aristocracy, over-Germanises France's heritage. Yet, Montesquieu deliberately sympathises with Boulainvilliers's account, to illustrate how liberty, for *both* modern republics and monarchies, depends on the existence of a viable aristocratic elite. However, his unease with Boulainvilliers's romantic portrait of France's nobility suggests serious reservations concerning the elites of his own time. On the one hand, we saw that Montesquieu bemoaned Louis XIV's exploitation of France's institution of venality, which yield a debased class of titled officeholders, unwilling to challenge the monarch's incursions.[55] On the other, while Montesquieu pays fealty to France's traditional *noblesse d'epée*, he realised that its members were ill-equipped for facing the exigencies of eighteenth-century free, moderate government. He instead extolls the virtues of his own class, the *noblesse de robe*. Its members share a *noblesse oblige* with the higher nobility and have the polite manners of bourgeois society. Moreover, their 'bourgeois' education provides them with the expertise requisite for understanding the increasingly complex machinery of the state.[56]

Montesquieu unearths the logic of France's liberty from his study of Saint Louis's judicial reforms, which he credits for tempering the nobles' vainglorious mores. Saint Louis gradually put an end to duelling as a means for settling judicial disputes. Consequently, civil and legal offices increased in gravitas, generating new points of honour that inspired the public mind. It is on this historical basis that Montesquieu could consistently share Mandeville's penchant for feudal institutions, while aligning himself with Hume on issues such as duelling. Saint Louis and Henry VII's measures inadvertently generated more humane sources of constancy, discipline and self-restraint. Interestingly, in both Montesquieu's and Hume's accounts, modern education and refined manners became principal currencies for achieving recognition in modern commercial societies. What differentiates Montesquieu is that he sought to balance commercial mores with bona fide aristocratic mores to preserve free, moderate government in eighteenth-century Europe.

In the concluding remarks to Book 13 of *The Spirit of the Laws*, Montesquieu writes: 'glory and honour are for that nobility which knows, sees, and feels no real good except honour and glory. Respect and esteem are for those ministers and those magistrates who, finding only work upon work, watch day and night over the happiness of the empire.'[57] In the French monarchical context, where honour is the animating principle, there exists a civic space where individuals glory in public service above all other modes of recognition. Montesquieu later traces this civic ethos to France's 'false honour' system of venality. He states that venality gives traders 'the expectation of becoming noble without the drawback of being nobles',[58] and, most importantly, the system '*encourages traders to put themselves in a position to attain* . . . [non-commercial distinctions]' (emphasis added).[59] Despite its drawbacks, Montesquieu tolerates France's system of venality because it preserves a non-commercial class committed to civic ends while permitting commercial and non-commercial sources of honour to function compatibly alongside one another. By this standard, France did not need to look across the Channel to tame commerce, as Montesquieu may have believed fourteen years earlier. In France, one finds a hierarchy of value where subjects asymmetrically recognise commercial merit, public service and military achievement, all of which diffuse or countervail the prejudices associated with wealth alone, as exemplified by Montesquieu's own haughty remarks concerning English culture during his sojourn in the island nation.[60]

Montesquieu presages a 'horizontal' society developing in England, whose only prejudices/honours emerge from commerce alone, where parochial self-interest dominates the other human impulses. Yet, its commerce has inadvertently produced self-sufficient mores. It may lack the lofty virtue of the ancients and the *noblesse oblige* of its European neighbours, but its unique situation permits its attenuated principles to provide sufficient support for preserving its liberty. Indeed, England's example contained invaluable lessons for France, namely for its emergence as a dominant European commercial power and for having a free constitution that privileges judicial autonomy and tolerates hierarchical stratifications. However, the English people's 'impotent attempts to establish democracy among themselves'[61] in the seventeenth century and their broader tendency to honour wealth exclusively in the eighteenth century reflect the degeneracies associated with a general spirit that tends towards extreme equality on the one hand and individualism on the other.

Hume did not share Montesquieu's feudal penchant for non-commercial distinctions. Such hierarchies of value undermine commercial activity and weaken nations' overall prospects. In a meaningful passage from 'Of Civil Liberty', he writes:

> Commerce, therefore, in my opinion, is apt to decay in absolute governments, not because it is there less *secure*, but because it is less *honourable*. A subordination of ranks is absolutely necessary to the support of monarchy. Birth, titles, and place, must be honoured above industry and riches. And while these notions prevail, all the considerable traders will be tempted to throw up their commerce, in order to purchase some of those employments, to which privileges and honours are annexed.[62]

France's aristocratic institutions were a source of degeneracy that potentially undermined its commercial culture. In contrast to

Montesquieu, Hume warns against fostering a hierarchy of value where individuals privilege non-commercial distinctions over wealth. He agrees with Montesquieu; in an absolute monarchy, commercial honours must necessarily be subordinate to the honours associated with births and titles. However, under such institutional arrangements non-commercial titles would subvert the *higher* honours associated with industry and riches. French distinctions grounded in aristocracy produced a situation where people became indolent and commercially unproductive. By contrast, England's commercial culture gives it an advantage over France. In England – where the king is a less mythic figure and inspires less reverence than his Bourbon counterpart – subjects prefer to seek recognition through categorically superior distinctions to those associated with the king's splendour.

In sum, honour is part and parcel of free, moderate government for both Montesquieu and Hume. Yet whereas Montesquieu's vertical idea of honour includes more and less gripping forms, for Hume the same form shifts to areas that are more *or* less conducive to liberty and prosperity. It is rather the degree of factionalism in a civic culture that determines the hold honours have on individuals. Hume writes that factionalism 'tends much to remove those great restraints, honour and shame; when men find, that no iniquity can lose them the applause of their own party, and no innocence secure them against the calumnies of the opposite'.[63] Yet, he presupposes that factionalism cannot be eliminated; it can only be reduced and channelled in ways that do not subvert the honour and virtue of a nation's character.

In 'Idea of a Perfect Commonwealth', Hume offers a series of proposals which aim to preserve the positive aspects of factions while eliminating the negative aspects.[64] Reflections in politics need to instead assume a corruptibility in human nature which demands institutional restraints. The essay responds to James Harrington and his republican contemporaries, whose theories of politics manifest an 'empire of men', naively emboldening factionalism. In a modern commercial context, one cannot count on the more redeeming human qualities requisite for public office. Montesquieu seemed less concerned about England's burgeoning factionalism, and he did not presume it to be negatively correlated to its honour culture as Hume did. England's factionalism in fact compensated for its lack of honour and virtue. Internal strife and discord were essential conditions of its liberty.[65] In his view, it was precisely England's internal strife, reflected in its hyper-partisanship, that permitted it to become a dominant commercial power.[66] Its partisan culture produced the necessary conditions for liberty, notwithstanding its less gripping manifestations of honour.

Concluding Remarks

Montesquieu and Hume were sensitive to factors exogenous to politics which made commercial activity the locus of society, and they both understood that the modern world's values needed to reflect this reality. For this reason, they each accepted commerce as the organising principle of the world. That is, they embraced 'commercial honour' as a barometer of recognition and, more broadly, as a progenitor of moral activity in eighteenth-century Europe, although at different degrees. Commerce was co-equal with liberty for Hume, and he believed in its capacities for creating the material and cultural conditions necessary for keeping liberty 'within the bounds of moderation'. For Montesquieu, on the other hand, commerce indeed provided the conditions for liberty to flourish, but there existed a shadow side to it which needed to be restrained, or it could equally serve as a handmaid for despotism; *commerce itself needed to be moderated*. He thus aims to balance commercial mores with non-commercial mores, while respecting a modicum of commercial politeness. Having England in mind, he held that modern commerce enervated the honour associated with public-minded action. As such, he examined non-commercial cultural supports for keeping liberty 'within the bounds of moderation'. As I explain more fully in the next chapter, Montesquieu feared that the salutary distinctions associated with commerce could potentially collapse into wealth distinction alone, stifling other important barometers of value in a political community. This concern partly informed his sanguine account of England's factionalism, seeing that its principles were too attenuated to support its constitution. Conversely, Hume held that the sheer vitriol and pettiness of factionalism emasculated honour more generally, although he realised the impracticality of expunging factionalism, and instead sought ways to harness it in a functional body politic. Their concerns have continuing relevance today, if one considers the roots and causes of the Great Recession, for instance – that is, commercial honour's failure to regulate elite behaviour – and its reverberations, culminating in the petty factionalism one encounters in contemporary political discourse.

Notes

1. Cf. Chapter 2, 51–9.
2. Paul E. Chamley, 'The Conflict between Montesquieu and Hume: A Study of the Origins of Adam Smith's Universalism', in *Essays on Adam Smith*, ed. Andrew S. Skinner and Thomas Wilson (Oxford: Clarendon Press, 1975), 274–305; Jean-Pierre Cléro, 'Hume et Montesquieu: sur deux chapitres de *L'Esprit des lois* traduits en anglais', in *Débats et polémiques autour de L'Esprit des lois* (*Revue française d'histoire des idées politiques* 35.1, (2012)): 73–91, http://www.jstor.org/stable/24610793.
3. David Hume, 'Letter 65: To President de Montesquieu: Londres, 10 avril 1749', in *The Letters of David Hume: Vol. 1. 1727–1765*, ed. J. Y. T. Greig (Oxford: Oxford University Press, 1932).
4. 'J'aime mieux vous parler d'une belle dissertation où vous donnez une beaucoup plus grande influence aux causes morales qu'aux causes physiques – et il m'a paru, autant que je suis capable d'en juger, que ce sujet est traité à fond, quelque difficile qu'il soit à traiter, et écrit de main de maître, et rempli d'ideés et de réflexions très neuves.' Montesquieu 'Letter from Montesquieu to Hume: A Bordeaux, 19 May, 1749', in *Life and Correspondence of David Hume: Vol 1*, ed. John Hill Burton (Edinburgh: William Tate), MDCCCXLVI, Appendix B, 456, https://ia802607.us.archive.org/13/items/lifeandcorrespoo3burt-goog/lifeandcorrespoo3burtgoog.pdf
5. Recent scholars infer that, in 'Of National Characters', Hume targets Montesquieu's contemporaries such as abbé Jean-Baptiste Dubos (1670–1742) who had a more wholesale commitment to climatic determinism than the Bordeaux aristocrat. Moore, 'Montesquieu and the Scottish Enlightenment', 183; Dennis C. Rasmussen, *The Pragmatic Enlightenment: Recovering the Liberalism of Hume, Smith, Montesquieu, and Voltaire* (Cambridge: Cambridge University Press, 2014), 257.
6. David Hume, 'Of National Characters', in *Essays Moral, Political, Literary*, ed. Eugene F. Miller (Indianapolis: Liberty Fund, 1987), 213.
7. Ibid., 206.
8. Ibid., 207.
9. Ibid., 202.
10. Knud Haakonssen explains that 'This was the model of the modern civilised monarchy emerging in France, which Hume admired and about which he tried to enlighten his countrymen.' Haakonssen, 'The Structure of Hume's Political Theory', in *The Cambridge Companion to David Hume*, ed. David Fate Norton and Jacqueline Taylor (Cambridge: Cambridge University Press, 2008), 367.
11. In Europe, with the progress of the arts, 'the English are become sensible of the scandalous licentiousness of their stage, from the example

of French decency and morals. The FRENCH are convinced, that their theatre has become somewhat effeminate, by too much love and gallantry; and begin to approve of the more masculine taste of some neighbouring nations. David Hume, 'Of the Rise and Progress of the Arts', in *Essays Moral, Political, Literary*, 122.

12. 'I don't say that the climate has not, in a great measure, produced the laws, morals and manners of this nation: but I affirm that the morals and manners of this nation must have a great relation to their laws.' Montesquieu, *The Spirit of the Laws*, ed. and trans. Anne M. Cohler, Basia C. Miller and Harold S. Stone (Cambridge: Cambridge University Press, 1989), 19.27, 325.

13. Cléro, 'Hume et Montesquieu', 73.

14. 'La remarque de la page 26, ligne 3,4 est nouvelle et frappante. Peut-être ne serez-vous pas fâché de savoir que le Parlement d'Angleterre, trouvant par ce qui s'étoit passé en dernier lieu que la nation écossaise n'étoit pas suffisamment républicaine, conclut que ce penchant violent au gouvernement monarchique venoit de ce que la noblesse avoit conservé les juridictions gothiques féodales; c'est pourquoi le Parlement les abolit, il y a deux ans' (English translation my own). Hume, 'To President de Montesquieu', 134.

15. Montesquieu, *The Spirit of the Laws*, 2.3, 23.

16. James A. Harris, *Hume: An Intellectual Biography* (Cambridge: Cambridge University Press, 2015), 148.

17. He argues that Stewart did not have sufficient forces to resist the Highlanders' incursions. [14] Edinburgh was structurally too vulnerable to be feasibly defended. [20] Had he resisted, the rebels would have razed the city to the ground. David Hume, *A true account of the behaviour and conduct of Archibald Stewart, Esq: late Lord Provost of Edinburgh. In a letter to a friend. London, 1748*, Eighteenth-Century Collections Online, Gale, University of Toronto Libraries, <http://find. Galegroup. com.myaccess.library.utoronto.ca/ecco/infomark.do?&source=gale&p rodld=ECCO&userGroupName-utoronto_main&tabID=T001&docl d=CW104873800&type=multipage&contentSet=ECCOArticles&vers ion=1.0&docLevel=FASCIMILE

18. Ibid., 6.

19. Ibid., 7.

20. Bernard Mandeville, *An Enquiry into the Origin of Honour, and the Usefulness of Christianity* (London: Brotherton, 1732), 15.

21. Ibid., 172.

22. Ibid., 199.

23. Ibid., 86.

24. Mandeville, *An Enquiry into the Origin of Honour*, 150.

25. Bernard Mandeville, *The Fable of the Bees or Private Vices, Publick Benefits. Vol 1* (Indianapolis: Liberty Fund, 1988), 228.

26. Ibid., 239.

27. Ibid., 243.
28. J. P. Wright, 'Hume on the Origin of "Modern Honour"', in *Philosophy and Religion in Enlightenment Britain: New Case Studies* (Oxford: Oxford Scholarship Online, 2012), 13/39.
29. Mikko Tolonen, 'The Gothic Origin of Modern Civility: Mandeville and the Scots on Courage', *Journal of Scottish Philosophy* 12.1 (2014), 52.
30. David Hume, 'Essay on Chivalry', in *Essays Moral, Political, Literary*, 29.
31. Ibid., 24.
32. 'No Wonder so great a grasp & so small a reach; so great an Endeavor & so small Abilities, produc'd very fantastical Effects on their manners, & such as were difficult to moderate & reduce to Nature & a just Simplicity.' Hume, 'Essay on Chivalry', 29.
33. David Hume, 'Of the Refinement of the Arts', in *Essays Moral, Political, Literary*, 274.
34. Hume, 'On the Rise and Progress of the Arts', 132.
35. Ibid., 132.
36. David Hume, *The History of England from the Invasion of Julius Caesar to the Revolution in 1688*, Foreword by William B. Todd, vol III (Indianapolis: Liberty Fund, 1983), 77.
37. Hume, *The History of England*, vol. III, 76.
38. As Sabl explains, education increasingly became the principal currency for gaining honours and distinctions. Previously idle commoners needed to learn a craft and increase their industry to address the growing demand of luxuries among the wealthy. Their burgeoning commercial activity generated new means for earning distinctions. Moreover, gaining civil employments in law and public office earned one noble recognition as societies required greater literacy and technocratic expertise for dealing with the complexities of modern commerce and affairs of state. Andrew Sabl, *Hume's Politics: Coordination and Crisis in the History of England* (Princeton: Princeton University Press, 2015), 69.
39. Ibid., 59.
40. 'The same age, which produces great philosophers and politicians, renowned generals and poets, usually abounds with skilful weavers, and ship-carpenters.' Ibid., 86.
41. Cf. Chapter 4, 10051–92 and 10651–910.
42. Montesquieu, *The Spirit of the Laws*, 14.13, 242.
43. Ibid.
44. Ibid., 14.13, 243.
45. Montesquieu presciently observes the shortcomings of this disposition in international affairs, where Englishmen lack the coolness and sober-mindedness required in negotiations, and thus 'lose by their treaties what they had gained by their weapons'. Ibid.

46. Cf. Chapter 3, 72. Henry VII's policies had the effect of transferring property from the nobles to the commons, thereby making the House of Commons the locus of English political power.
47. Montesquieu, 'Letter to Domville', in *My Thoughts*, ed. Henry C. Clark (Indianapolis: Liberty Press, 2012), 595.
48. Ibid., 593.
49. Montesquieu, 'Letter to Domville', 594.
50. Cited from my article '*Le système de John Law* and the Spectre of Modern Despotism in the Political Thought of Montesquieu', *Lumen* 38 (2019): 161–78. Montesquieu, *The Spirit of the Laws*, 5.6, 48.
51. Ibid.
52. 'it [England] would be well to give prizes to the plowmen who had best cultivated their lands and to the workers who had been most industrious. *This practice will succeed in every country*' (emphasis added). Montesquieu, *The Spirit of the Laws*, 14.9, 238.
53. 'If I am asked which prejudices they have, I would in truth not know which to answer: neither war, nor birth, nor dignities, nor men who get lucky, nor the frenzy over ministerial favour . . . They respect only two things: wealth and personal merit', *My Thoughts*, 227–8.
54. Montesquieu, *The Spirit of the Laws*, 30.10, 627.
55. 'The principle of monarchy has been corrupted when the highest dignities are the marks of the greatest servitude, when one divests the important men of the people's respect and makes them into vile instruments of arbitrary power.' Ibid., 8.7, 117.
56. Cf. Chapter 6, 147–8.
57. Montesquieu, *The Spirit of the Laws*, 13.20, 227.
58. Ibid., 20.22, 350.
59. Ibid., 351.
60. Cf. Chapter 4, 112 (43n).
61. Montesquieu, *The Spirit of the Laws*, 3.3, 22.
62. David Hume, 'Of Civil Liberty', in *Essays Moral, Political, and Literary*, 93.
63. Hume, *History of England*, vol. 6, 438.
64. James Moore, 'Hume's Political Science and the Classical Republican Tradition', *Canadian Journal of Political Science* 10.4 (Dec. 1977), 810.
65. '[a]s all the passions are free there, hatred, envy, jealousy, and the ardor for enriching and distinguishing oneself would appear to their full extent, and if this were otherwise, the state would be like a man who, laid low by disease, has no passions because he has no strength.' Montesquieu, *The Spirit of the Laws*, 19.27, 325.
66. He writes: 'This nation, always heated . . .' makes it 'easy for those who governed it to make it undertake enterprises against its true interests.' Ibid., 327.

Chapter 6

Montesquieu's Honour

Civic spirit is the desire to see order in the state, to feel joy in public tranquility, in the strict administration of justice, in the security of the magistrates, in the prosperity of those who govern, in the respect paid to the laws, in the stability of the monarchy or the republic.

Montesquieu, *Treatise on Duties*[1]

But the line dividing good and evil cuts through the heart of every human being.

Alexander Solzhenitsyn, *The Gulag Archipelago, 1918–1956*

A meaningful tension lies throughout Montesquieu's works. In *The Spirit of the Laws*, he states that virtue, or the love of the laws and the homeland,[2] is a principle contrary to human nature,[3] which requires constant self-renunciation. As such, it is an unreliable passion for anchoring the political community. Yet, he bemoans contemporary citizens' smallness of stature compared to the ancients. He laments 'The things that were done in those governments that we no longer see and that astonish our small souls.'[4] In *My Thoughts*, Montesquieu more poignantly writes: 'When one thinks about the pettiness of our motives, the baseness of our means, the avarice with which we seek out vile rewards, the ambition – so different from love of glory – one is astonished at the difference in spectacles, and it seems that, ever since those two great peoples ceased to exist, men have lost a few inches in stature.'[5] Notwithstanding Montesquieu's nostalgia for the classical politics of Athens and Rome, his emphasis on stature reveals an important philosophical insight, which intimates the possibility of fulfilling greater human capacities that once flourished during antiquity. If Montesquieu rejects the classical republican vision of politics on both practical and theoretical grounds, as we have seen in his rejection of James Harrington's political project,[6] what are the more human qualities of past ages that could be revived? The following two chapters will examine Montesquieu's and his Scottish counterparts' response to this question.

Scholars have argued that Montesquieu doubted the practicality of loftier forms of honour and virtue in a world of small souls. They unearth a theory of honour which aims to approximate Mandevillean virtue, whereby individuals pursue their private interests, unwittingly serving the public interest. In *The Economy of Glory*, Robert Morrissey convincingly rejects this reading since it erringly presumes that Montesquieu collapses vanity with the desire for glory. The Bordeaux aristocrat shared the Jansenist/Mandevillean position that glory needed to be pacified, but he nonetheless maintained that vanity and honour needed to operate on different levels.[7] In the *Treatise on Duties*, an unfinished manuscript inspired by Cicero's *De Officiis*,[8] Montesquieu casts doubt that commercial mores alone can sufficiently anchor free, moderate government:

> one of the causes of the infirmity of our courage is our education in which we have not sufficiently distinguished greatness of soul from arrogance and from vanity, unsuited to any good use, which has no supporting motive: this means that we have weakened the principle of actions and the more we have removed motives from men, the more we have demanded of them.[9]

Commerce may enable the material conditions for liberty, as we have seen in a previous chapter. Yet, Montesquieu reminds us how the civic spirit requisite for preserving liberty will atrophy should commercial self-interest, or 'the greatest monarch on earth' as Usbek famously says to Rhedi in *Persian Letters*,[10] reign over the population unchecked. This chapter reconstructs a pluralistic conception of honour contained in Montesquieu's political thought, which *necessarily* includes quotidian and loftier forms. I show how Montesquieu channels *both* lower and higher forms of honour to stave off despotism. To support my analysis, I examine the legacy of Saint Louis, Montesquieu's paragon of moderate legislation in *The Spirit of the Laws*. I explain how the Capetian monarch's judicial reforms provide Montesquieu with the institutional groundwork for a theory of free, moderate government which emphasises the need to preserve a dignified civic space that enlarges citizens' sense of interpersonal magnanimity.[11]

Nature of Honour and Its Function

In his entry on 'honneur' in the *Encyclopédie*, Jean François de Saint-Lambert (1706–1803) distinguishes between 'true' honour, derived from an internal love of order, and 'false' honour, derived from the esteem of others.[12] He writes that 'the love of order is in all men',[13] and that this extends to men's natural love for political order. The argument follows, that under proper political laws, citizens would willingly sacrifice themselves and have 'the courage to be poor' out of a love for the institutional arrangements that maintain political order.[14] His essay criticises Montesquieu for untethering honour from virtue in his famous tripartite regime distinction in *The Spirit of the Laws*. Saint-Lambert infers that Montesquieu doubts the feasibility of any loftier forms of honour flourishing in modern commercial society. The Bordeaux aristocrat privileges a form of honour associated with lower forms of pride and ambition, where 'the agreeable is honored more than the beautiful, the useful, and the honest',[15] and where the indiscriminate desire to please animates individuals into action. Saint-Lambert then outlines his own monarchical political vision that seeks to realign honour and classical virtue, which 'does not reign in the secondary and lowest classes, as true honour does in the first'.[16]

Céline Spector's compelling commentary equally presumes an untethering of honour from virtue in Montesquieu's political thought, associating his idea of self-interested honour with a broader theory of moderation, which encompasses civic considerations. She explains that Montesquieu preferred a political culture where each person's pursuit of glory inadvertently contributes to the common good.[17] The advantage of such a regime is that 'contrary to virtue, honour requires neither the orientation of individual intentions towards the common good nor a moral compass imposed by the state'.[18] Self-interested honour replaces virtue.

In *Montesquieu: pouvoirs, richesses, et sociétés*, Céline Spector elaborates that commercial honour forms Montesquieu's basis for moral and political action in *The Spirit of the Laws*. That is, he favours the love of gain over the heroism and glory that characterises past ages.[19] Spector's analysis aligns Montesquieu with Bernard Mandeville, who famously argues in his *Fable of the Bees* that by seeking private material ends individuals in civil society pursue false honour for its utility in increasing one's standing and influence.[20] Honour is a useful currency for gratifying selfish ends, which confers public goods when it animates the wider citizen body. She explains that both thinkers held individuals' natural pride and ambition may elevate commercial honour from the pursuit of paltry distinctions into nobler *outwardly* selfless aristocratic forms. That is, commercial honour alone has the capacity to increase man's stature. In contrast to virtue, then, which demands self-renunciation, commercial honour carves the path of least resistance towards serving the common good because it is self-serving.[21]

Sharon Krause's classic commentary identifies in Montesquieu's work a more robust conception of honour, indispensable for guaranteeing freedom vis-à-vis the state in an increasingly egalitarian society.[22] The argument follows that although one's natural impulse for human recognition can attach itself to lower forms of ambition associated with mere survival, it can also attach itself to higher, more *human* ambitions associated with justice and morality.[23] The Viscount of Orte's example supports her claim. As we have seen,[24] the noble commander admired the Huguenots, who among them he found 'good citizens and brave soldiers',[25] and so he could not debase himself by committing such a vulgar act that would dishonour him on a visceral level. Orte's survival and personal wellbeing, which depended on obeying the will of the prince, mattered less to him since Charles IX demanded that he commit an act that did not correspond with his social standing. Krause explains that self-respect mattered more to Orte than mere survival. While he certainly acted in accordance with justice and morality, the argument follows that this did not make him a virtuous person in the classical sense, since his great act of defiance stemmed from self-love rather than altruism.[26]

Indeed, according to Montesquieu, it is the care for social standing that comes from a person's perception of value granted by the public that may support free, moderate government. He well understood the species of honour associated with wealth. And he equally considered the feudal honour associated with an unreflective love for one's higher social status in the political community. However, Montesquieu does not wholly reject the modes of honour associated with commerce and feudal aristocracy, which may explain why his interpreters often presume a theory of free, moderate government grounded in commercial or aristocratic self-interest alone, precluding the possibility of achieving honour that is neither wholly tied to commercial success nor to one's fixed position in society, but rather to one's *genuine* public spiritedness. As we shall presently see, Montesquieu held that the 'false' honours associated with wealth and fixed social standing may be harnessed to inspire a higher sense of honour accorded to those who enter the public sphere and demonstrate their genuine commitment to the public interest. That is, different modes of 'false honours' may be harnessed to enlarge the civic mind.

This meant that honour and virtue had to be moderated in political life because he observed that unchecked principled ambition yields an uncompromising commitment to the good that paradoxically leads to despotism. It is worth requoting a key passage from *The Spirit of the Laws*, which supports this counterintuitive facet of Montesquieu's moderation:

> I return to the beginning of my chapter. When in a century or a government one sees the various bodies of the state seek to increase their authority and to get certain advantages over each other, one would often be mistaken if their enterprises were considered a sure mark of their corruption. By a misfortune attached to the human condition, great men who are moderate are rare; and, as it is always easier to follow one's strength than to check it, perhaps, in the class of superior people, it is easier to find extremely virtuous people than extremely wise men.
>
> The soul takes such delight in dominating other souls; even those who love the good love themselves so much that no one is so unfortunate as to distrust his good intentions; and, in truth, our actions depend on so many things that it is a thousand times easier to do good than to do it well.[27]

Montesquieu seemingly shares Hobbes' anxieties concerning a politics based on classical notions of virtue. Indeed, although their bases differ, he avers the Hobbesian claim that we cannot turn the clock back to having a monolithic vision of the good as a foundation for political life. Hobbes suppresses the good in political life since it leads to divisiveness and war.[28] Similarly, Montesquieu realises that, even if one's vision of the good is legitimate, it becomes dangerous given the number of visions and political multiplicities that potentially exist in a pluralistic society. His distinction between the virtuous and the wise/prudent man, and his thoughts on why the latter is so rare, are especially apposite here. If one thinks one is serving the good, why would one want to exercise moderation? Given this dilemma, rather than suppress the good, as Hobbes prescribes in

Leviathan, Montesquieu's division of powers harnesses 'the superior's' principled ambition to serve the good, while suppressing the dangerous potentialities associated with this impulse. Montesquieu's division of powers aims to moderate, rather than eliminate, virtue, or any robust notions of the good in political life.

Aristocratic honour has the capacity to destroy the overall social fabric if left unchecked. If aristocratic honour animates legislators to be virtuous, it nonetheless has the capacity to become reckless, since, believing their virtue to be superior, it leads them to unproblematically dominate other wills. It becomes a mark of honour therefore, to increase one's strength as one glories in ennobling other souls. Therefore, principled ambition itself needs to be moderated. Here, Montesquieu echoes Machiavelli's observations concerning elites, and their propensity to oppress the people,[29] although they offer different solutions. Machiavelli held that a prince's success largely depends on his ability to fully suppress the elites, and to ally himself with the people, whereas Montesquieu held that elites still played an indispensable role in any form of free, moderate government. Correspondingly, he advances a robust conception of honour to anchor modern commercial society but regulates (moderates) it within a civic space, to constrain man's propensity to dominate.

Montesquieu's anxieties concerning the odious side of the aristocracy are prominent from the outset of *The Spirit of the Laws*. One recalls that in his tripartite distinction between republican, monarchical and despotic government,[30] he subdivides republican government into democracy, where 'the people as a body have sovereign power',[31] and aristocracy, where 'sovereign power is in the hands of a certain number of persons'.[32] Although Montesquieu is ambiguous over whether he favours the republican or monarchical form of government, it is most clear that aristocracy is the most problematic, since it has a greater likelihood of degenerating into a despotic regime than the other two constitutional forms. Although both republican forms require a renunciation of oneself, Montesquieu intimates his preference for the democratic model, stating that '[t]he more an aristocracy approaches democracy, the more perfect it will be'.[33] In the same chapter, he equally ranks monarchy above aristocracy, stating that honour, the monarchical regime's animating principle, sufficiently keeps the sovereign in check.[34] By contrast, no equivalent principle sufficiently checks the exorbitant power of a citizen who emerges among the nobility's ranks in an aristocracy.[35]

While Montesquieu is sceptical about the aristocratic republic being a viable political model for the modern age, aristocracy played a necessary intermediary role in modern political life. One recalls Montesquieu takes it for granted that in any society 'there are always some people who are distinguished by birth, wealth, or honours . . . [who] have no interest in defending [the common liberty]',[36] since their interest inevitably conflicts with that of the people. In the absence of a political body that represents elites' particular interests, they inevitably turn against the state.[37] It is why Montesquieu praises Solon and Tullius for permitting substantial class differentiation in republican Athens and Rome.[38]

Moderation could only be arrived at with the existence of adequate institutional buffers, as we observe in his account of moderate monarchy. On the one hand, the monarch, or executive, checks the nobility through its ability to suppress the institution if it oversteps its boundaries. On the other hand, the nobility checks the will of the monarch/executive. It is this agonistic, yet symbiotic, relationship between the two institutions that inform Montesquieu's famous aphorism: '*no monarch, no nobility; no nobility no monarch*'.[39] To summarise, Montesquieu embraces both commercial and aristocratic forms of honour, although commercial honour renders man too weak to *resist* despotism, and aristocratic honour, left unrestrained, leads to despotism. Next, we will see how Montesquieu balances aristocratic and commercial mores to establish a foundation of political morality and justice, commensurate with eighteenth-century exigencies.

In Book I of *The Spirit of the Laws*, Montesquieu states that human beings are naturally sociable and moral, and *feel* an attachment to the principles of justice. Montesquieu concomitantly identifies with the Molinist idea that accepts individuals' damned condition and therefore tolerates human vices.[40] Yet, interestingly for Montesquieu, *both* our higher and lower natures are potential sources of elevation. Montesquieu's distinction between man and beast in Book 1 of *The Spirit of the Laws* coheres with his broader distinction between higher and lower forms of honour that he details throughout the book. He writes: 'Be that as it may, [beasts] do not have a more intimate relation with god than the rest of the material world has, and feeling is useful to them only in their relation to one another, either with other particular beings, or with themselves' (emphasis added).[41] In contrast, a human being

> as a feeling creature . . . falls subject to a thousand passions. Such
> a being could at any moment forget his creator; God has called
> him back to him by the laws of religion. Such a being could at any

moment forget himself; philosophers have reminded him of himself by the laws of morality. Made for living in society, he could forget his fellows; legislators have returned him to his duties by political and civil laws.[42]

Indeed, individuals seek honours as means towards self-preservation, that is, self-interested honour. What makes them fully human, however, is their attachment to the principles of justice. It is the legislator's task 'to return him to his duties by political and civil laws'.

Montesquieu's avuncular note to his son provides clues to how legislators may enliven human beings' feeling of justice. Urging his son to pursue civic honours, Montesquieu explains that large societies contain a multiplicity of higher and lower honours. He writes: 'the political world is maintained by that restless inner desire possessed by everyone to leave the situation in which he is placed. It is in vain that an austere morality would efface the features that the greatest of all workmen has imprinted on our souls. It is up to morality, which would work on man's heart to regulate his sentiments, not to destroy them.'[43] Our desire for recognition is a component of the human totality that requires proper nourishment; it is a 'sentiment useful to society *when it is well directed*' (emphasis added).[44] Montesquieu further elaborates this idea in his comparative study of previous and contemporary regimes throughout *The Spirit of the Laws*, unearthing the political utility of various forms of commercial, feudal, martial and civic honours.

Montesquieu's definition of honour clarifies our understanding of how he directs the various honours inherent to large pluralistic nations. Honour is 'the prejudice of each person . . . it can inspire the finest actions; joined with the force of laws, it can lead to the goal of government as does virtue itself.'[45] 'Prejudice' connotes that honour cultures have their own rules, or logic of appropriateness, that correspond with the general spirit of a nation in a given moment. Our prejudices reflect the preconceived ideas of what others recognise as praiseworthy in our words, deeds and actions. The rules of honour relate to 'what is and not to what should be',[46] which explains why honour cultures manifest themselves distinctly between and within pluralistic nations. In honour-loving regimes, 'one judges men's actions here not as good but as fine, not as just but as great; not as reasonable but as extraordinary'.[47] Honour inspires good actions, in spite of human beings' impure motivations to be associated with a class that has risen above 'the sort of people who have been neglected through the ages'.[48] Moreover,

Montesquieu explains that in healthy, free and moderate regimes, human beings' desire for group identity outweighs their natural fear of death.[49] In well-ordered honour-loving societies which reward actions that are 'fine', 'great' or 'extraordinary', leading citizens are constitutionally incapable of following contemptible orders from superiors who ask them to commit injustices that debase their social standing. Accordingly, Montesquieu urges legislators to be mindful about maintaining the gravitas of their nations' honour-yielding public institutions.

An important characteristic of 'false honour', which interestingly mirrors Christian faith, is its capacity to simultaneously foster hier-archical reverence, *while* restraining the naturally despotic passions associated with princely authority. Readers discover that the passions which stem from an instinctual need for recognition provide more gravitas to a political order than those animated from belief in a higher existing power. Montesquieu observes that in moderate monarchies the structures of honour provide more reliable obstacles to the prince's otherwise boundless power. He writes: 'There is nothing in monarchy that laws, religion, and honor prescribe so much as obedience to the wills of the prince, but this honour dictates to us that the prince should never prescribe an action that dishonours [emphasis added] because it would make us incapable of serving him.'[50] It is one's sense of honour, rather than Christian charity, which better translates into magnanimous action. We have seen the Viscount of Orte's refusal to obey Charles IX's unchristian command to kill Huguenots.[51] And in 12.4, which discourages the inclusion of religious crimes in a nation's civil laws, Montesquieu provokes readers to ruminate over the merits of 'false honour' as a preferable human motivator over religiosity. He writes:

> The ill came from the idea that the divinity must be avenged. But one must make divinity honoured, and one must never avenge it. Indeed, if one were guided by the latter idea, where would punishments end? If men's laws are to avenge an infinite being, they will be ruled by his infinity and not by the weakness, ignorance, and caprice of human nature.
>
> An historian of Provence reports a fact that paints very clearly for us what this idea of avenging the divinity can produce in weak spirits. A Jew, accused of having blasphemed the Holy Virgin, was condemned to be flayed. Masked knights with knives in their hands mounted the scaffold and drove away the executioner in order to avenge the honour of the Holy Virgin themselves . . . I certainly do not want to anticipate the reader's reflections.[52]

Montesquieu lampoons the vigilante men for disgracing the nation's honour with their intolerance and 'pure morality'. Clearly, the honour-loving Orte better embodies the spirit of Christianity than Charles IX or the blasphemer's executioners, the latter of which acted in the name of Christianity! When juxtaposing the two anecdotes, we see how our love of honour, properly channelled, more reliably ennobles individuals than religion possibly can in the civic sense, if not also in the moral sense.

We saw in the previous chapter how Mandeville similarly opposed honour and religion to promote the former as a more reliable basis for moral and political action.[53] He traces the origins of contemporary points of honour to early medieval churchmen and leaders who appealed to their potentially dangerous subordinates' sense of pride in order to ensure their obedience and regulate their conduct.[54] Montesquieu rejected Mandeville's conspiracy theory by presenting modern honour as a source of restraint on both leaders and subordinates who cannot follow orders that violate a political community's shared principles of morality. Moreover, he rejects the Dutch philosopher's core premise, which presupposes that one's honour and shame necessarily derive from self-interest.[55] He suggests the possibility of more ennobled forms of honour in the modern commercial world. Individuals may aspire to serve in public office out of vanity and false pride, *but* the participatory aspect of civic life enlarges their sense of honour as it renders them genuinely other-regarding in their moral and political actions.

In Book 25, Montesquieu articulates a more nuanced understanding of human motivation, premised on the idea he introduces in Book 1, that human wills are divided. He writes:

> Men, rascals when taken one by one, are very honest as a whole; they love morality; and if I were not considering such a serious subject, I would say this is remarkably clear in the theatres; one is sure to please people by the feelings that morality professes, and one is sure to offend them by those that it disapproves.[56]

Indeed, individuals may enter public life wishing to be great, and to enforce their will upon others. However, once they enter the proverbial (political?) theatre, they develop a sense of responsibility towards one another. They long for personal recognition, but concomitantly realise their sense for the good when it is presented to them. This account shares an affinity with what Istvan Hont calls a

Grotian, Neo-Stoic outlook in seventeenth- and eighteenth-century political thought, which presupposes self-love and altruism with the caveat that 'every man was sooner sensible of the love he bears towards oneself than of that he bears towards others'.[57] Self-love is more immediate for Montesquieu, but when conditioned under proper institutional restraints it invigorates human beings' more sociable impulses. As such, Montesquieu's institutional restraints pacify honour to enable virtue in an eighteenth-century context.

Montesquieu's critique of religion throughout *The Spirit of the Laws* interestingly offers readers important insights concerning the place of honour in his political philosophy. Whereas Books 24 and 25 accommodate religion and emphasise its utility for encouraging civic restraint, Book 26 explains how the self-serving passions associated with 'false honour' more reliably aggrandise individuals' motivations than their religious impulses do. For instance, he juxtaposes Hinduism with Christianity to show that even the most devout religious adherents, who claim a hold on 'true honour', fall short of his standard for politics. With regards to Hinduism he writes:

> This honour is founded solely on religion; these distinctions . . . do not form civil distinctions [emphasis added]: there are Indians who would believe themselves dishonoured if they ate with their king . . . These sorts of distinctions are bound to a certain aversion for other men, an aversion quite different from the feelings that should arise from differences in rank and which among ourselves include love for one's inferiors. [emphasis added][58]

By contrast, '[t]he principles of Christianity, engraved in their hearts, would be infinitely stronger than the false honour of monarchies, the human virtues of republics, or that servile fear of despotic states.'[59] Montesquieu appears more congenial to Christianity since it at least encourages citizens to view each other as equally human in a moral sense. Yet, his tripartite regime distinction, which famously establishes the range of *possible* institutional configurations available to human beings, warns readers against constructing a system of government that presupposes angelic wills. As Montesquieu writes: '. . . however respectable may be the ideas which spring immediately from religion, they should not always serve as principles for civil laws, because civil laws have another principle, which is the general good of society.'[60] That is, virtue needs to be imperfectly felt to yield political goods.

Montesquieu held that 'false honour' may approximate genuine virtue even within a markedly modern commercial society, constituted of individuals primarily driven by self-interest. Individuals may enter public life with selfish intentions, but properly ordered societies do not legislate their motivations out of existence. Legislators must instead ground their politics on imperfect virtue. Citizens' desire to be remembered may be harnessed to produce a penchant for justice and the public good. In contemporary Europe, this means having to balance commercial and aristocratic mores. The next section examines Montesquieu's account of the Capetian monarch Saint Louis, who provides key signposts for approximating virtue in eighteenth-century France.

One recalls that in Book 28 of *The Spirit of the Laws*, Montesquieu praises Saint Louis for establishing a judicial system that eventually supplants the existing conflict resolution system in medieval France.[61] Prior to Saint Louis's reforms, men resolved their legal disputes through 'judicial combat', where they would challenge their accusers/witnesses to a duel if they felt falsely blamed for committing an injury. Saint Louis's set of reforms, known as the 'établissements', abolished this form of 'institutionalised honour', and introduced a wide range of judicial measures based on Roman right, derived from the Code of Justinian.[62] Among these measures, Saint Louis established a formal appeals process, which allowed one to declare false judgment without having to fight in a duel to defend one's honour.

Montesquieu emphasises that the Capetian monarch did not have the capability to introduce these measures throughout the entire French territories, since the local nobles had nearly complete sovereignty over their respective jurisdictions. However, once Saint Louis carved a more ennobled civic space in his own territory, other jurisdictions abandoned the vainglorious institution, in favour of his reforms. Montesquieu writes:

> He took away the worse by making the better felt. When one saw in his tribunals, and in those of the lords, a more natural, more reasonable way of proceeding, a way more in conformity with morality, religion, public tranquility, and the security of persons and goods, it was taken up and the other was abandoned.[63]

Saint Louis's genius is that he recognised human beings naturally pay fealty to a *noblesse* animated by a higher sense of honour; that is, by a commitment to morality, religion, public tranquillity and security. Again, once Saint Louis designed a civic space grounded in higher principles of justice, neighbouring fiefdoms abandoned the institution of judicial combat for his Roman-inspired reforms.

Saint Louis's example is germane to how Montesquieu reconciles commerce and virtue. Indeed, commercial self-interest and baser forms of honour govern most individuals in bourgeois society. Yet, the medieval reforms illustrate how the wider citizenry's natural reverence for those who defend their community's mores filters their own moral calculus in their day-to-day affairs. If political institutions are in place to harness an aristocratic ethos, citizens learn that lower forms of recognition pale compared to the higher long-lasting recognition associated with public service. These factors informed Montesquieu's view that commerce and virtue were indeed compatible, provided that a state's institutional arrangements preserved a civic space where higher forms of honour may flourish and receive due consideration. He divides the nobility and bourgeois society in a manner where both realms of human activity condition one another. This is why Montesquieu had a measured appreciation for France's system of venality. The feudal remnant institution allowed wealthy individuals in commercial society to purchase public offices at a sum established by the Crown. Such institutional arrangements may funnel a higher sense of honour to the wider citizenry, while pacifying the nobles' aristocratic impulses. Nobler and baser forms of honour may concomitantly inspire the public mind.

Montesquieu's scathing critique of France's monarchical system and its nobility in *Persian Letters* may leave one wondering whether he in fact preferred modern republican forms over hierarchical stratifications that the institution of venality perpetuated. For instance, in Letter 24, Rica writes to Ibben that, 'the king of France is the most powerful prince in Europe ... he has more riches ... because he extracts them from the vanity of his subjects ... He has been known undertake or sustain great wars having no funds other than honorary titles to sell.'[64] Here, Montesquieu alludes to how Louis XIV exploited early bourgeois aspirants who sought to purchase public offices handed out by the Crown, in order to exit the world of commerce and to achieve noble distinction in French society. Louis XIV used these revenues to fund his costly wars of imperial expansion, which would inevitably lead France towards despotism and decline domestically.

Although Montesquieu's anxieties concerning France's trajectory were explicit in his earlier works, it would be premature to conclude that he rejected France's constitutional model, whose grace he likened to the art of Raphael, in contrast to Michelangelo's prideful England.[65] Montesquieu held that multiple constitutional forms had the capacity to fuel despotism *or* promote free, moderate government. In spite of his earlier warnings that reflect his anxieties concerning Louis XIV's despotism, he later admires France's system of venality in *The Spirit of the laws*, since it '*encourages traders to put themselves in a position to attain* [nobility]' (emphasis added).[66] Venality disposes individuals away from the lower honours associated with paltry luxuries, and towards the greater honours associated with a fealty to the commonweal. Although public offices had to be limited, the hope of attaining these preferences and distinctions drove commercial growth and prosperity, in the process encouraging bourgeois citizens to modulate their behaviour according to the guiding principles of the institution they aspired to join. Montesquieu therefore supports a democratisation of aristocratic honour, in so far as achieving nobility has a merit-based foundation, being accessible to anyone who could afford the office, and, again, 'put themselves in a position to attain it'. Yet, he warns against excessively democratising aristocratic offices. As Louis XIV's reign in France and Spain's example demonstrate,[67] excess venality debases civic institutions and moreover reduces the number of available workers and labourers in commercial society, stifling economic growth and prosperity.

Montesquieu's own experience as an aristocrat serving in the Parlement de Bordeaux gave him an instructive vantage point for balancing traditional aristocratic mores and self-interested commerce.[68] For instance, the Parlement de Bordeaux's remonstrance of 1718, which protested against having bourgeois representation in the offices of the Hôpital St-André, is illustrative of the indispensable role of aristocrats in eighteenth-century commercial society. The Parlement feared the merchants' commercial interests would subvert the institution's ability to serve the public interest. Yet, it issued several subsequent declarations defending commercial self-interest, such as its remonstrance in 1725 regarding the establishment of the Compagnie des Indes.[69] Bourgeoisie merchants may pursue their interests while inadvertently contributing to the common good; although the *parlements* must regulate commercial activity when it threatens to undermine the common interest.

The *parlements*, mostly governed by members of France's *noblesse de robe*, had the technocratic, moral and cultural credibility to regulate mobile capital, as it demonstrated after the Regency reinstated its political powers in 1715. Its officers were the most educated among the different ranks of the nobility.[70] And although initially mocked for failing to grasp the intricacies of Law's System, their remonstrances proved to be prophetic once the system had collapsed and led to social disorder in Paris.[71] What is more, although an aristocratic sense of honour animated members of the *noblesse de robe*, there nevertheless remained a deep cultural link between them and the rest of commercial society. As Franklin Ford remarks, most magistrates were not distantly removed from the bourgeois class, and as a result, they retained similar manners of refinement, in contrast to the coarseness that animated members of France's other noble ranks.[72]

It would therefore be incorrect to conclude that Montesquieu envisioned a separate elite and a passive citizenry governed by a wholly different ethos. In a moderate government that leverages both baser and nobler forms of honour, the civic spirit animates all citizens, so long as the laws of the legislators nudge them towards their natural sense of duty to serve the public interest. Venality is indispensable because it produces widespread public spiritedness, offering all citizens in bourgeois society the possibility to escape the world of commerce – and, with that, the fleeting satisfaction associated with lower forms of honour – for a world of public duty, and an opportunity to achieve a deeper sense of human fulfilment.

In his discussion concerning political laws in republican democracies, Montesquieu writes: 'If a fixed body is established that is in itself the rule in mores, a senate to which age, virtue, gravity and service give entrance, the senators, who are seen by the people as simulacra of gods, will inspire feelings that will reach into all families.'[73] In eighteenth-century commercial France, the *noblesse de robe* performed a similar role to the ancient senators of Rome. For Montesquieu, the *parlements* were the depositories of laws and mores, and their honourable magistrates, whose political power was restored following the death of Louis XIV, were the simulacra that inspired feelings throughout the wider community. Moreover, the gravity of the community's mores, grounded in *shared* historical experience, makes the honours associated with serving the good less transient than commercial honours. This is why in *My Thoughts*, Montesquieu warns: 'Take away from a nation's general spirit the sentiments of honor, duty, love, and you do the same harm as when you take from a private individual all his principles.'[74] Following one's duties earns one deeper admiration, since it is self-actuating and immutable and corresponds with the community's shared principles of justice. People cannot help but honour it, and be drawn to it, precisely because it is more permanent and less dependent on luxury or social status.

Concluding Remarks

Montesquieu held that aristocratic honour was essential for embedding commerce within France's social and political structures. For this reason, he laments the decline of nobler forms of honour, and, with that, an overall sense of duty among citizens in eighteenth-century France. If honour is indeed the passion that animates monarchical government or modern commercial society, it cannot fully be underwritten by low forms of ambition and avarice. Rather, the community's political and moral anchors had to stem from a higher form of recognition disentangled from commercial self-interest. In the absence of higher forms of honour, nations inevitably lose their moral compass. And although commercial honour is indispensable for driving economic growth and prosperity, it alone is insufficient for achieving Montesquieu's political *summum bonum*: free, moderate government. Rather, it is non-commercial honour, which animates the civic spirit and ensures public order, tranquillity, and an overall respect for the laws. Moreover, if a nation's constitution ensures a civic space that enables the possibility of higher forms of recognition, it could circumscribe baser forms of honour. In sum, false honour can elevate itself into more noble forms if separate models of aristocratic honour inspire the public mind. Yet, if unrestrained, aristocratic honour has the capacity to become too moralistic and tyrannical as legislators would try to impose their own uncompromised notions of the good on the rest of society. Therefore, Montesquieu's ambitions for eighteenth-century France – while unlikely to measure up to the ancients in grandeur – are far greater for his own age than one would initially suppose.

Notes

1. Montesquieu, *Treatise on Duties*, in *Montesquieu: Discourses, Dissertations, and Dialogues on Politics, Science, and Religion* (Cambridge: Cambridge University Press, 2020), 127.
2. Montesquieu, *The Spirit of the Laws*, ed. and trans. Anne M. Cohler, Basia C. Miller and Harold S. Stone (Cambridge: Cambridge University Press, 1989), 4.5, 36.
3. Ibid., 35.
4. Ibid., 4.4, 35

5. Montesquieu, *My Thoughts*, ed. and trans. Henry C. Clark (Indianapolis: Liberty Fund, 2012), 93.

6. Cf. Chapter 3.

7. Robert Morrissey, *The Economy of Glory: From Ancien Regime France to the Fall of Napoleon*, trans. Teresa Lavender (Cambridge, MA: Oxford University Press, 2013), 80.

8. Cf. Robert Morrisey's discussion concerning Cicero's reception in eighteenth-century France. *The Economy of Glory*, 28–31.

9. Montesquieu, *Treatise on Duties*, 114.

10. Montesquieu, *Persian Letters*, trans. and ed. Stéphane Douard and Stuart Warner (South Bend: St. Augustine's Press, 2017), Letter 106, 173.

11. Montesquieu was not naive to Saint Louis's role in the French Crusades but recognises the Capetian monarch's importance for laying the foundations for free, moderate government in France. 'I never judge men by what they have or have not done as a result of the prejudices of their times. Most great men have been subject to them . . . Who are the fools who claim to be smarter than the great men who have been subject to them?' Montesquieu, *My Thoughts*, 227 [764].

12. Jean François de Saint-Lambert, 'Honneur', in *Encyclopédie, ou dictionnaire raisonné des sciences, des arts et des métiers, etc.*, eds. Denis Diderot and Jean le Rond d'Alembert, ed. Robert Morrissey and Glenn Roe (Chicago: University of Chicago: ARTFL Encyclopédie Project [Spring 2021 Edition]), 8:288.

13. 'l'amour de l'ordre est dans tous les hommes' (English translation my own). Ibid., 8:288.

14. 'le courage d'être pauvre' (English translation my own). Ibid.

15. 'l'agréable est honoré plus que le beau, l'utile & l'honnête' (English translation my own). Ibid., 8:290.

16. 'ne regne pas dans les secondes & dernières classes que la véritable honneur dans la première' (English translation my own). Ibid.

17. Céline Spector, 'Honor, Interest, Virtue: The Affective Foundations of the Political in *The Spirit of the Laws*', in *Montesquieu and His Legacy*, ed. Rebecca E. Kingston (Albany: SUNY Press, 2009), 50.

18. Ibid., 55.

19. Céline Spector, *Montesquieu: pouvoirs, richesses et sociétés* (Paris: Presses universitaires de France, 2004), 15

20. Ibid., 81.

21. Ibid., 5.17, 67.

22. Sharon Krause, *Liberalism with Honor* (Cambridge, MA: Harvard University Press, 2002).

23. Ibid., 43.

24. Cf. Chapter 3, 97–8.

25. Montesquieu, *The Spirit of the Laws*, 4.2, 33.

26. Krause, *Liberalism with Honor*, 45.

27. Montesquieu, *The Spirit of the Laws*, 28.41, 595.
28. Thomas Hobbes, *Leviathan*, ed. C. B. Macpherson (London: Penguin Classics, 1985), 697.
29. Machiavelli, *The Prince*, ed. David Wootton (Indianapolis: Hackett Publishing), 32.
30. Montesquieu, *The Spirit of the Laws*, 2.1, 10.
31. Ibid.
32. Ibid., 2.3, 15.
33. Ibid., 2.4, 17.
34. Ibid., 16.
35. Ibid.
36. Ibid., 11.6, 160.
37. Ibid.
38. Cf. Chapter 1.
39. Montesquieu, *The Spirit of the Laws*, 2.4, 18.
40. Michael Mosher, 'Monarchy's Paradox: Honor in the Face of Sovereign Power', in *Montesquieu's Science of Politics*, ed. David Carrithers, Michael Mosher and Paul Rahe (Lanham: Rowman & Littlefield, 2001), 195.
41. Montesquieu, *The Spirit of the Laws*, 1.1, 5.
42. Ibid.
43. Montesquieu, *My Thoughts*, 2.
44. Ibid.
45. Montesquieu, *The Spirit of the Laws*, 3.6, 26.
46. Ibid., 4.2, 34n.
47. Ibid., 4.2, 32.
48. Ibid.
49. Ibid., 6.9, 82.
50. Ibid., 4.2, 33.
51. Ibid.
52. Ibid., 12.4, 190.
53. Bernard Mandeville, *An Enquiry into the Origin of Honour, and the Usefulness of Christianity* (London: Brotherton, 1732), 20.
54. Ibid., 93.
55. Ibid., 6.
56. Montesquieu, *The Spirit of the Laws*, 25.2, 481.
57. Istvan Hont, 'The Language of Sociability and Commerce: Samuel Pufendorf and the Theoretical Foundations of the Four-Stages Theory', in *The Languages of Political Theory in Early Modern Europe* (Cambridge: Cambridge University Press, 1987), 267.
58. Montesquieu, *The Spirit of the Laws*, 24.22., 475.
59. Ibid., 24.6, 464.
60. Ibid., 26.9, 502.
61. Cf. Chapter 5, 126.
62. Montesquieu, *The Spirit of the Laws*, 28.45, 601.

63. Ibid., 28.38, 591.
64. Montesquieu, *Persian Letters*, Letter 24, 39.
65. Montesquieu, *The Spirit of the Laws*, 19.27, 333.
66. Ibid., 20.22, 351.
67. Montesquieu, *My Thoughts*, 133.
68. Rebecca Kingston. 'L'intérêt et le bien public dans le discours de parlement de Bordeaux', *Le Temps de Montesquieu*, ed. Michel Porret and Catherine Volpilhac-Auger (Geneva: Droz, 1998), 197.
69. Ibid., 91.
70. Franklin L. Ford, *Robe and Sword: The Regrouping of the French Aristocracy after Louis XIV* (Cambridge, MA: Harvard University Press, 1962), 188.
71. Ibid., 99.
72. Ibid., 76.
73. Montesquieu, *The Spirit of the Laws*, 5.7, 49.
74. Montesquieu, *My Thoughts*, 269.

Chapter 7

A Liberal Art for the Commercial World: Adam Smith and Adam Ferguson

The great Montesquieu pointed out the road. He was the Lord Bacon in this branch of philosophy. Dr. Smith is the Newton.

John Millar[1]

When I recollect what the President Montesquieu has written, I am at a loss to tell, why I should treat of human affairs: But I too am instigated by my reflections, and my sentiments; and I may utter them more to the comprehension of ordinary capacities, because I am more on the level of ordinary men. If it be necessary to pave the way for what follows on the general history of nations, by giving some account of the heads under which various forms of government may be conveniently ranged, the reader should perhaps be referred to what has been already delivered on the subject by this profound politician and amiable moralist. In his writings will be found, not only the original of what I am now, for the sake of order, to copy from him, but likewise probably the source of many observations, which, in different places, I may, under the belief of invention, have repeated, without quoting their author.

Adam Ferguson, An Essay on the History of
Civil Society[2]

It is my opinion, likewise, that Carthage ought not to be destroyed.

Scipio Nasica, cited by Adam Smith, The Theory
of Moral Sentiments[3]

A number of canonical figures who deeply admired Montesquieu were equally committed to protecting the integrity of the public sphere from commerce. Jean-Jacques Rousseau, Benjamin Franklin, John Adams, Alexis de Tocqueville and, more recently, Hannah

Arendt each revised Montesquieu's theory of free, moderate government to make political honours available to a broader citizenry.[4] However, they disagreed over the degree to which the commercial and political worlds needed to be kept separate. One will find a divergence on this question in the political thought of Adam Ferguson and Adam Smith who were considered heirs to Montesquieu in their immediate contexts. Both Scottish philosophers embraced modern commerce as the organising principle of eighteenth-century Europe. However, like Montesquieu, they were not unconcerned with the civic challenges posed by the new commercial order. In considering how Ferguson and Smith approximate political virtue in their respective works, this chapter delineates how each thinker appropriated Montesquieu's moderation to a more egalitarian, burgeoning commercial world of mass production and capital accumulation – one marked by the new civic challenges that advanced commercial specialisation introduced to European nations.

In *The Lost History of Liberalism*, Helena Rosenblatt traces how the term 'liberal' evolved between the Roman period and the twentieth century.[5] Rosenblatt associates the term with the language of virtue rather than the language of rights, in so far as 'being liberal' meant reining in the self-interested passions, 'showing devotion to the common good, and respecting the importance of mutual connectedness'.[6] This chapter will illuminate how Montesquieu and his Scottish counterparts aimed to preserve a classical spirit of 'liberalism'.

In Hume, we saw how commercial activity itself could be harnessed to moderate the passions and foster a sense of regard for others in civil society. And in examining the nature of honour and its function throughout Montesquieu's political writings, the previous chapters unearthed an analytically distinct idea of free, moderate government which rejects the premise that modern commerce alone may sufficiently generate a society's moral anchors. Adam Smith and Adam Ferguson shared Montesquieu's concerns about the anti-'liberal' impulses modern commerce may foster in citizens. However, Smith echoes Hume, identifying in commercial culture itself the sources for 'liberal' moderation. By contrast, as Rosenblatt explains, Ferguson 'deplored the mercenary values that he felt were spreading. Selfishness was threatening the very bonds of society, turning Scotland into a "servile nation of helots".'[7] Ferguson sought to preserve 'that habit of the soul by which we consider ourselves as part of the beloved community ...'[8] Building off these observations, this chapter traces Smith's and Ferguson's intellectual debt to Montesquieu, examining how each thinker distinctly arrived at moderate visions of politics that elevate the 'liberal' citizen while preserving the material freedom of modern commerce.

The Noble Frenchman and the Honest Scotsman

Mirroring Montesquieu, Smith's system of politics approximates a *via media* between ancient Rome and Mandeville's beehive. In *The Theory of Moral Sentiments*, he writes:

> Among civilised nations, the virtues which are founded upon humanity are more cultivated than those which are founded upon self-denial and the command of the passions ... The hardiness demanded of savages diminishes their humanity; and, perhaps, the delicate sensibility required in civilised nations sometimes destroys the masculine firmness of the character.[9]

Commerce itself may generate the cultural supports necessary for preserving free, moderate government. However, in his *Lectures on Jurisprudence*, Smith expresses concerns over the pathologies inherent to the modern commercial order. In an age of commercial specialisation, 'the minds of men are contracted and rendered incapable of elevation. Education is despised, or at least neglected, and the heroic spirit is almost utterly extinguished. *To remedy these defects would be an object worthy of serious attention.*'[10] Such anxieties echo throughout his writings, to the point that recent scholars have convincingly identified in his diagnosis, shared affinities between him and Rousseau.[11] Smith, of course, did not share Rousseau's anti-commercial vision of politics, which romanticises the citizens of the Greek polis and republican Rome as avatars for an era of genuine virtue and political freedom.

It is not that commerce provides the only means for inculcating moral and political virtue, for Smith. Rather, it carves the path of least resistance. Commercial sociability feeds our natural impulse to 'sympathise' with one another, enlivening the softer virtues of humanity, benevolence, openness, prudence and punctuality. Smith's notion of 'sympathy' constitutes one of two hinge-points in his moral philosophy. He writes that 'nothing pleases us more than to observe in other men a fellow-feeling with all the emotions of our own breast'.[12] Sympathy did not exclusively mean pity for another person's sorrow.[13] It manifests itself when individuals relate to one another's good fortune as well. As we enter society, human imagination allows us to place ourselves in another's position and experience another's passions, although at a lesser degree. Yet, we intuitively understand the impracticality of achieving perfect emotional harmony with another person, and 'flatten . . . the sharpness of [the emotion's] natural tone'[14] to establish a 'connection' with our fellow human beings, which would otherwise be lost. Greater distance from one's kin demands a further flattening of one's tenor. It is this internal regulation, or self-command, which calibrates our behaviour to the general norms of propriety that we establish through our commercial interactions.

Yet, certain harmonies confer greater pleasures than others. For instance, individuals have a penchant for seeking a common feeling of benevolence, while avoiding feelings of resentment towards one another.[15] What is more, sympathy may corrupt our moral behaviour. He writes: 'This disposition to admire, and almost to worship, the rich and the powerful, and to despise, or at least, to neglect, persons of poor and mean condition, though necessary both to establish and to maintain the distinction of ranks and the order of society, is, at the same time, the great and most universal cause of the corruption of our moral sentiments.'[16] Echoing Montesquieu's Troglodyte king in the unpublished sequel to his mythical allegory, Smith warns his readers that mass commercial society tends to revere wealth at the expense of virtue.

The remedy lies in the other hinge-point of Smith's moral philosophy: the 'impartial spectator', or the demigod within that regulates one's moral behaviour.[17] The impartial spectator serves as a governing mechanism for the establishment of moral intuition. It is a source of accountability that modulates our interactions with one another. One constantly gauges oneself from the perspective of the imaginary spectator, whose own sense of propriety builds on the norms and values established in society. The impartial spectator's moral possibilities are even greater than the standards of propriety rooted in our impulse to sympathise. Our most noble actions are derived from a type of self-regard, enjoying a degree of independence from the prevailing *doxa* of the community. We may praise, 'admire . . . worship, the rich and powerful . . . ' but the demigod within prefers a reputation that is praiseworthy. If properly nourished, the demigod within encourages great deeds, exercises sound moral and political judgement, and counterbalances 'the great and most universal cause of the corruption of our moral sentiments'.[18] From Smith's argument it follows that the impartial spectator's nourishment depends on conditions of well-ordered commerce. That is, legislators must preserve their nations' natural orders of rank, to enable the softer commercial virtues of honesty, prudence, moderation and punctuality. Recognising their currency for achieving upward mobility, citizens cultivate these virtues through habituation that is made possible by their day-to-day commercial interactions. Laws, therefore, must legislate against the formation of corporate monopolies and debasing modes of financial speculation, which, as we have seen, undermine the virtues of a well-functioning meritocratic society.[19] Without such protections, commerce becomes unethical, but still respected by the mere fact that it makes people rich.

Montesquieu did not share Smith's optimism that commerce itself may sufficiently produce modern nations' moral anchors. Commerce may atrophy the nobler impulses that motivate great deeds. In response to contemporary Europe's civic challenges, Book 4 of *The Spirit of the Laws* articulates a theory of political education that emphasises a culture of emulation. In well-ordered republics citizens emulate the passions of their elders, whereas in well-ordered monarchies 'the principal education is not in the public institutions where children are instructed; in a way, education begins when one enters the world.'[20] Here, individuals learn their nation's rules of politeness and honour through the example of the *honnête homme*, whose idealised version Montesquieu situates in the non-commercial *noblesse de robe*. Motivated by his self-respecting sense of honour, the *honnête homme* inspires fine, great and extraordinary actions, and possesses 'all the qualities and all the virtues required in this government'.[21]

Smith had little sympathy for this line of reasoning. Europe's aristocratic remnants threatened the modern order. Titled, hereditary classes impeded commercial and political progress and diminished the civic personality. The titled nobility has no place in Smith's progressive arc of modern liberty. They did not make efficient use of the vast property they owned,[22] and inculcated a spirit of dependence among the people.[23] Under such stultifying feudal arrangements 'it is impossible that they can be so well carried on by slaves and freemen, because they have no motive to labour but the threat of punishment and can never invent any machine for facilitating their business'.[24]

Echoing Hume, Smith traces the origins of modern liberty to the expansion of commerce, and the concomitant decline of the nobility,[25] thanks to Henry VII's reforms, which wrested property away from titled landholders, permitting commoners to become independent property-holders. Titled landholders incrementally negotiated away their burdensome property, and with that, their political power to pursue the baubles and trinkets yielded by commerce.[26] In turn, the political power of individual property owners increased in proportion to the redistribution of property. Smith writes: 'the Commons were now become very considerable, as they represented the whole body of the people; and as they knew the king could not want, they never granted him anything without in some degree infringing his privileges.'[27] They had a greater incentive to work the land. Their industry, innovation and labour conferred greater material wealth, further increasing their leverage against the Crown.

Indeed, Smith shared Montesquieu's view, that one's love of grandeur may be harnessed to inspire great deeds, but he argues that it is the commercial mores, rather than the aristocratic mores, which more reliably excite human beings' civic impulses. For Montesquieu, the spirit of commercial traffic and self-interest enervates human beings' social affections, whereas Smith held that a commercially dynamic society enlivens the public spirit. Indeed, titled aristocrats may have a genuine sense of *noblesse oblige*; however, they lack the wherewithal and technocratic competence to serve the public interest. Their '[s]uccess and preferment depend, not upon the esteem of intelligent and well-informed equals, but upon the fanciful and foolish favour of ignorant, presumptuous, and proud superiors; flattery and falsehood too often prevail over merit and abilities. In such societies, the abilities to please are more regarded than the abilities to serve.'[28] Commerce more reliably animates citizens. In the following passage, Smith explains how it is one's impulse for commercial improvement which incites public mindedness.

> Nothing tends so much to promote public spirit as the study of politics, – of the several systems of civil government, their advantages and disadvantages, – of the constitution of our own country, its situation, and interest with regard to foreign nations, its commerce, its defence, the disadvantages it labours under, the dangers to which it may be exposed, how to remove the one, and how to guard against the other.[29]

However, Smith shared Montesquieu's concern that principled ambition may become tyrannical, if left unrestrained. Yet, for

Smith, commerce itself contained the resources for taming one's civic impulses. A properly nourished impartial spectator tempers the spirited citizen's potentially destructive impulse for utility and constant improvement. Constantly attuned to society's customs, mores and prejudices, the demigod within compels the spirited citizen to accommodate his rational designs to the culture of the population.[30] Moreover, Smith warned that titled aristocrats fuelled a cultural pathology where 'the external graces, the frivolous accomplishments . . . are more commonly admired than the solid and masculine virtues of a warrior, a statesman, a philosopher, or a legislator'.[31] Indeed, commercial luxury expanded the branches of commerce. Baubles and trinkets, and the comforts of life, motivate industry and labour. '[I]t is well that nature imposes upon us in this manner. It is this deception which rouses and keeps in continual motion the industry of mankind.'[32] It is precisely why hereditary nobles of any rank – who never had to cultivate the commercial virtues to enjoy their social distinctions – debase commercial nations' political education. The virtues that originally endowed their families with titles fleeted away over generations. Subsequently, the aristocrat 'shudders with horror at the thought of any situation which demands the continual and long exertion of patience, industry, fortitude, and application of thought'.[33] What is more, the institution exacerbates economic inequalities, further poisoning the civic culture. As Smith writes, 'Many a poor man places his glory in being thought rich, without considering that the duties (if one may call such follies by so very venerable a name) which that reputation imposes upon him, must soon reduce him to beggary[.]' Pursuing his distinctions without learning the virtues requisite for achieving upward mobility, the poor man will become 'still more unlike that of those whom he admires and imitates, than it had been originally.[34]

Smith favoured the gentry because they were the most independent class of individuals, and therefore 'were least subject to the wretched *spirit of monopoly*' (emphasis added)[35] that one finds in merchants and manufacturers, and the *spirit of dependence* one finds in labourers. The gentry had a communicative spirit which yielded an overall generosity to their fellow citizens, and in constantly trying to improve their station in life, developed resilience and firmness of character, less common in modern commercial society. What is more, their commercial habits and spirited impulse for social and political progress are combined with a technocratic

competence required for properly administering the state apparatus. It is why

> [i]n all governments accordingly, even in monarchies, the highest
> offices are generally possessed, and the whole detail of the admin-
> istration conducted, by men who were educated in the middle
> and inferior ranks of life, who have been carried forward by their
> own industry and abilities, though loaded with the jealousy, and
> opposed by the resentment, of all those who were born their supe-
> riors, and to whom the great, after having regarded them, first with
> contempt and afterwards envy, are at last contented to truckle with
> the same abject meanness with which they desire that the rest of
> mankind should behave themselves.[36]

Smith held that the degree of admiration these paragons of commercial virtue would enjoy depended on their education. A more
broadly educated populace is a better judge of character and
authenticity. Otherwise stated, nobility in action and valour
depended on the people. Under such propitious circumstances,
they praise elites for their nurtured and enlightened demigod
within, instead of demagogues whose wealth, glamour and show-
manship perniciously generate currency in a culture of commercial
specialisation. In *The Wealth of Nations*, he writes: 'In free countries, where the safety of government depends very much upon the
favourable judgment which the people may form of its conduct,
it must surely be of the highest importance that they should not
be disposed to judge rashly or capriciously concerning it.'[37] Here,
Smith observed that, although specialised labour improved commerce, it also produced a parochial mindset among citizens. Specialisation diminishes the impartial spectator within, who, as we
have seen, naturally reveres honourable and praiseworthy behaviour. As a result, the labourer

> naturally loses, therefore, the habit of such exertion, and generally
> becomes as stupid and ignorant as it is possible for a human crea-
> ture to become. The torpor of his mind renders him, not only inca-
> pable of relishing or bearing a part in rational conversation, but
> of conceiving any *generous, noble, or tender sentiment*, and con-
> sequently of forming any just judgment concerning many even of
> the ordinary duties of private life . . . His dexterity at his own par-
> ticular trade seems, in this manner, to be acquired at the expense of
> his intellectual, social, and martial virtues. But in every improved
> and civilised society this is the state into which the labouring poor,

that is, the great body of the people, must necessarily fall, unless government takes some pains to prevent it.[38]

Specialised labour diminishes the civic and intellectual mind. It is why Smith held it necessary to provide working-class labourers with a baseline level of education. Literacy would allow the labouring poor to read newspapers and develop a more enlightened understanding of political issues, thus arming themselves against demagoguery that preys on the ignorant.

Smith moreover promoted religious belief as a source for counteracting the spiritless nature of specialised labour. He favoured a marketplace of religions from which individuals could freely choose, but only if in combination with their literacy, since their education would immunise them against superstition and enthusiasm. Their literacy would give 'them the benefit of religion, which is a great advantage, not only considered in a pious sense, but as it affords them subject for thought and speculation'.[39] It is irrelevant whether the faith people choose to follow is true or not. Belief in a higher power itself nudges citizens to think beyond their parochial interests, which counteracts the degenerative and dastardly effects of specialisation. In sum, literacy forges a greater degree of civic respect between the majority working class and their lawful superiors. Their education makes them more vigilant citizens, capable of detecting factionalism and sedition.[40] Moreover, Smith took it for granted that society's elites received a more holistic education, and had confidence that with a broadly educated populace, commercial society would permit a sense of honour and praiseworthiness to flourish among citizens. Leisure affords elites the freedom to contemplate a 'variety of objects', and, 'being attached to no particular occupation themselves, [are able] to examine the occupations of other people'.[41] It is why Smith was more concerned with the majority poorer classes. He warns that 'unless those few, however, happen to be placed in some very particular situations, their great abilities, though honourable to themselves, may contribute very little to the good government or happiness of society'.[42]

In spite of their fundamental differences, there exists a symmetry between Montesquieu and Smith's visions of politics, both of which extoll their respective nations' elites, who rein in the naturally despotic tendency of principled ambition at the top, while constituting a critically important source of their respective nations' political education. For Smith, it is Britain's gentry class, and for Montesquieu it is France's *noblesse de robe* who preserve the social

fabric. Nonetheless, Montesquieu and Smith each offer a historically grounded vision of politics that necessarily emphasises the
centrality of honour. As Smith writes:

> The different situations of different ages and countries are apt, in
> the same manner, to give different characters to the generality of
> those who live in them, and their sentiments concerning the par-
> ticular degree of each quality that is either blameable or praise-
> worthy, vary according to that degree which is usual in their own
> country and in their own times.[43]

Politics cannot be grounded in purely rational grounds, nor can it
be made manifest without paying homage to a particular nation's
historical configurations. Therefore, one cannot arrive at a viable
vision of politics ex-nihilo through abstract principles.

Montesquieu had greater reservations than Smith about the degree
to which the commercial virtues may temper one's behaviour in public life. He clearly differentiates the two spheres of human activity,
which in his estimation contain separate logics of appropriateness.
One recalls in Book 5 of *The Spirit of the Laws* that in democracies
'the spirit of commerce brings with it the spirit of frugality, economy,
moderation, wisdom, tranquility, order, and rule'.[44] However, the
tension between the following passages raises questions concerning
the extent to which commercial moderation could funnel into the
public sphere. In Book 21, Montesquieu famously writes:

> One has begun to be cured of Machiavellianism, and one will con-
> tinue to be cured of it. There must be moderation in councils. What
> were formerly called coups d'état would at present, apart from
> their horror, be only imprudences ... And, happily, men are in a
> situation that, though their passions inspire in them the thought of
> being wicked, they nevertheless have an interest in not being so.[45]

However, recall 28.41 where Montesquieu states: 'By a misfortune
attached to the human condition, great men who are moderate
are rare; and, as it is always easier to follow one's strength than
to check it, perhaps, in the class of superior people, it is easier to
find extremely virtuous people than extremely wise men.'[46] When
pressed against one another, these passages reveal the limits of commercial moderation in public life. Indeed, commerce cured the ills
of Machiavellianism, but it was in the interests of the prince vis-
à-vis other princes to moderate his passions, and citizens benefitted
from the windfall gains of liberty that resulted therefrom. However,

the difficulty of finding 'extremely wise men' in positions of power implies that people do not naturally reconcile themselves to compromise in the political world as they do in the commercial world. Merchants develop honesty and moderation as practical means for staying ahead, so long as an equal administration of justice prevents 'market failures' from occurring. In the commercial realm, moderation, honesty, tranquillity and wisdom are virtues that accommodate self-interest, in Montesquieu's estimation. However, commercial moderation has its limits in a realm that conditions people to think and act along Manichean lines. The civic sphere is a realm of common ground, which requires alternative sources of virtue. Political moderation depends on the sociable, other-oriented passions which are distinct from the passions associated with commerce.

In 6.9, Montesquieu intimates a more robust conception of moderation than what he associates with the spirit of commerce. He writes: 'In moderate states, love of the homeland, shame, and fear of blame are motives that serve as restraints and so can check many crimes.'[47] One's life is animated by the principles of virtue and honour. Remove these principles, and human beings lose the vivacity requisite for maintaining free, moderate government. It is therefore not commercial self-interest but rather the social principles which tame the unruly passions in civic life. It is noteworthy that in the same chapter Montesquieu measures free, moderate government by the extent to which citizens '[fear] the loss of life more than [they] dread death as such'.[48] Moderation in a state is reflected in the courage of its citizens, who willingly risk their physical security to preserve the fully human aspects of their lives. Yet how does one foster courage in a markedly modern commercial environment that encourages a spirit of inwardness, caution and calculation? It is a question that Adam Ferguson takes up nearly a decade later in his *Reflections Previous to the Establishment of a Militia*, where, like Montesquieu, he differentiates between debased political regimes, characterised by mere life necessity and physical security as primary motivators, and freer regimes, whose spirited citizens are animated by the more sociable, fully human passions.[49]

Adam Ferguson: Public Vigour in an Age of Commercial Specialisation

Ferguson shared Montesquieu's anxieties over the dehumanising aspects of modern commerce, but he considered honour as a second-order problem resulting from the specialisation of civic duties and tasks. Moreover, Montesquieu exclusively concerned himself with the self-interested aspects of modern commercial activity itself, whereas Ferguson's concerns shifted by the time he wrote his *Essay on the History of Civil Society*. He feared that specialisation, one of the rewards of human virtue in the evolution of commerce, vitiated the active spirit that animates citizens to meaningfully pursue their private and public endeavours. More specifically, he feared that commercial specialisation permeated non-commercial spheres of human activity. It was the bureaucratisation of public offices that presented the greatest obstacle for overcoming the wealth and virtue problem. He shared Montesquieu's premise that the public sphere needed to be protected from commerce, doubting that commerce itself contained the institutional and cultural resources for exciting the public spirit. In a direct repudiation of David Hume and Adam Smith, Ferguson mockingly writes: 'The care of mere fortune is supposed to constitute wisdom; retirement from public affairs, and real indifference to mankind, receive the applauses of moderation, and of virtue.'[50] Next, I will examine Ferguson's *Essay*, to demonstrate how he adapts and modifies Montesquieu's political moderation as the object of his commercial concerns shifted towards the problem of specialisation.

In his classic commentary, Richard Sher situates Adam Ferguson within a Presbyterian faction of intellectuals later known as the Scottish Enlightenment's 'moderate literati'.[51] Its members were united in their overall enthusiasm for the gains of modern commerce, but also in their equal commitment to a mode of patriotism whose theoretical foundations originate in the civic humanist tradition.[52] Even though the descriptor 'moderate' pertains specifically to a Scottish group of churchmen, some features within their moral and ideological outlook mirror Montesquieu's moderation.[53]

Both Ferguson and Montesquieu doubted that a separation of powers and good civil laws were sufficient for maintaining liberty, or that commerce itself could enliven human beings' social affections, as Hume and Smith held.[54] Rather, the requirements for liberty and happiness corresponded with a broader range of factors, particular to a population's circumstances. Neither Ferguson nor Montesquieu commit to a preferred regime. Their respective political philosophies articulate a pluralism grounded in the idea that political configurations must reflect human beings' divided wills.[55] In his *Institutes of Moral Philosophy*, Ferguson writes: 'A people in whom the virtuous and vicious are mixed; who admit adventitious distinctions in different degrees, and form states of various extent.

This is not a mere supposition, it is realised, and the most general description of mankind.'[56] Here, Ferguson echoes Montesquieu's response to the wealth and virtue problem, in so far as he aims to prevent commercial culture from constituting the only barometer of value that inspires the civic mind.[57] However, whereas Montesquieu emphasises how non-military honour-yielding institutions may be channelled within a commercial culture, Ferguson points to the citizen militia as the only reliable institution that could foster courage and discipline, and a truer sense of honour that supersedes commercial distinction in the public mind.[58] At the core of Ferguson's political theory, one finds a fusion between the virtue characteristic of rude ages and modern self-interested commerce. Alternatively, we saw in the previous chapter that Montesquieu considered false honour as a more reliable means for enlivening human beings' social affections. He would have doubted the practicality of Ferguson's synthesis. Therefore, it is how Montesquieu and Ferguson sought to excite their respective populations' sociable spirit that differentiates them.

Ferguson cites the examples of ancient Greece and Rome to reject the view that luxury and wealth necessarily corrupt republics.[59] He held that, in the face of commercial progress, citizens' naturally sociable impulses checked their proclivities for material wealth and paltry distinctions. Yet, despite Ferguson's overall equanimous disposition towards commerce, the relative ease of contemporary European life – which he attributes to the efficient specialisation of social, economic and civic tasks – preoccupied him throughout his *Essay*.

Ferguson begins his *Essay* by subverting various foundations of politics premised on the distinction between human beings' natural and artificial state. He writes that an individual's 'emblem is a passing stream, not a stagnating pool. We may desire to direct his love of improvement to its proper object, we may wish for stability of conduct; but we mistake human nature, if we wish for a termination of labour, or a scene of repose.'[60] Artificers by nature, human beings restlessly seek to improve their overall condition, and commercial activity is the principal motor that directs this preoccupation. However, it is the overall happiness of the political community, observable in the 'gladness and pleasure [citizens experience] with the concourse of men',[61] that fuels political, social and technological progress. Our affections towards one another as diverse citizens of a shared political community inspire the courage necessary for achieving real improvement in our labour, arts and politics. By contrast, societies animated by fear exclusively pursue personal 'safety, shelter, food, and the other means of enjoyment or preservation'[62] at the expense of real human progress. Such foundations paralyse citizens when 'placed in the midst of difficulties, and obliged to employ the powers they possess'.[63] Indeed, one may want to live a bourgeois life of ease, but only because one's disposition to constantly improve makes one lose sight of the fact that the activity of art itself is the reward.

Ferguson identified two mutually reinforcing sources of corruption in eighteenth-century Europe, paradoxically traceable to human beings' capacity for discovering new ways of improving their material condition: commercial specialisation and territorial enlargement. He shared Montesquieu's concern that, although commerce fosters peaceful social bonds, it may potentially sever those same bonds and yield a culture where individuals 'consider kindness itself a task', and 'introduce the spirit of traffic into the commerce of affection'.[64] He moreover writes:

> It is in [the commercial state] indeed, if ever, that man is sometimes found a detached and a solitary being: he has found an object which sets him in competition with his fellow-creatures, and he deals with them as he does with his cattle and his soil, for the sake of the profits they bring. The mighty engine which we suppose to have formed society, only tends to set its members at variance, or to continue their intercourse after the bands of affection are broken.[65]

However, the basis for his concerns differed from Montesquieu's. Montesquieu emphasised how commercial activity itself generates a more inward-looking disposition among individuals. Ferguson was primarily concerned about the ethos of specialisation that he witnessed permeating European nations' civic institutions.

Interestingly, Ferguson considered specialisation a source of corruption for 'polished societies' of antiquity as well. Referring to the ancients, he writes:

> Under the distinction of callings, by which the members of polished society are separated from each other, every individual is supposed to possess his species of talent, or his peculiar skill, in which the others are confessedly ignorant; and society is made to consist of parts, of which none is animated with the spirit that ought to prevail . . .[66]

He cites Pericles, who was concerned that Athenians increasingly viewed themselves as a society of craftsmen rather than citizens of a republic. As Ferguson explains, the 'Funeral Oration' exhorts Athenians to provide equal attention to affairs of state to avoid becoming victims of their own virtue. Pericles realised that advanced societies risk losing their vigour. As tasks increasingly become professionalised, citizens' more sociable faculties atrophy. Subsequently, they lose sight of the wider purpose underlying their vocations. Such conditions yield an overall spirit of malaise throughout the population:

> In their approach to this condition, and in the absence of every manly occupation, they feel a dissatisfaction and languor which they cannot explain: They pine in the midst of apparent enjoyments; or, but variety and caprice of their different pursuits and amusements, exhibit a state of agitation, which, like the disquiet of sickness, is not a proof of enjoyment or pleasure, but of suffering and pain . . . care of his buildings . . . literary amusement . . . sports . . . gaming . . . are employed to fill up the blank of a listless and unprofitable life. They speak of human pursuits, as if the whole difficulty were to find something to do: They fix on some frivolous occupation, as if there was nothing that deserved to be done . . .[67]

Our pursuits may have an equal baseness or nobility to them. One may find as much meaning and purpose in frivolous gaming as one finds baseness and meaninglessness in civil offices or speculative arts. In a public-minded society, a citizen discovers transcendent meaning in his/her activities and develops a sense of common humanity in his/her active pursuits. Here, one's axiology of value cascades out of one's vocation. By contrast, under conditions of unchecked specialisation, private individuals may pursue their callings, but they lose sense of the common place they occupy with their fellow citizens. Subsequently, their atomisation vis-à-vis the state vitiates the ardour and courage necessary for purposefully serving public offices, producing useful goods, or crafting meaningful poetry. A mechanised society untethers the natural association between one's activities and the commonweal. As a result, the only meaning one associates with one's vocation derives from material comfort.

Moreover, with the fragmentation of the public sphere, bureaucratic officeholders and professional soldiers simply become cogs of the state's machinery. Alienated from their service, public servants increasingly view their offices as mere instruments for preserving their own personal ends and lose the courage to risk their mere life necessities in the face of injustice. Commercial specialisation put European nations at risk of losing 'the objects that excite the spirit'.[68] Shorn of an active, sociable spirit, real prog-ress comes to a halt and despotism constantly looms as citizens become increasingly pusillanimous in the face of private and pub-lic adversity.

Despite his concerns, Ferguson had a measured but positive out-look regarding the merits of modern commerce.[69] The following passage helps readers work through this ambiguity in Ferguson's political outlook. He writes:

> The subdivision of arts and professions, in certain examples, tends to improve the practice of them, and to promote their ends. By having separated the arts of the clothier and the tanner, we are the better supplied with shoes and with cloth. But to separate the arts which form the citizen and the statesman, the arts of policy and war, is an attempt to dismember the human character, and to destroy those very arts we mean to improve.[70]

Emerging mills that produce better and cheaper clothing and more formidable ships for battle and trade were good for human devel-opment; however, commercial progress has reached a point of diminishing returns. The structures in place that helped ameliorate industry, military capacity and quotidian governance concomi-tantly diminished the vitality necessary for achieving real progress in the future. Ferguson's inclusion of antiquity's great republics among the world's most polished, pluralistic nations should give his interpreters pause. It suggests that contemporary European nations may follow their republican forerunners and continue to enjoy the fruits of commercial specialisation without 'dismember[ing] the human character'. As such, the examples of ancient Athens, Rome and even Sparta continue to provide important lessons for modern commercial society.

Ferguson's Affinity for Sparta

Ferguson's fascination with the classical republics of antiquity may prima facie suggest greater nostalgia for their heroism than one finds in the works of Montesquieu and his other Scottish counterparts. However, upon closer examination of his *Essay*, one discovers that Rome and Sparta did not rely on superhuman heroism for their flourishing, nor did Lycurgus and Romulus themselves make these societies great. Rather, their spirited citizens obviated the need for larger-than-life heroes.[71] When citizens perceive themselves as active players and spectators in a shared political theatre, their sociable impulses incite them to courageously pursue their modest ends. As Ferguson writes:

> The sovereign may dazzle with his heroic qualities; he may pro-tect his subjects in the enjoyment of every animal advantage or pleasure . . . but the benefits arising from liberty . . . are not the fruits of a virtue, and of a goodness, which operate in the breast of one man, but the communication of virtue itself to many; and such a distribution of functions in civil society, as gives to num-bers the exercises and occupations which pertain to their nature.[72]

Interestingly, for a thinker who admires the Spartan model, Ferguson adumbrates a more moderate conception of courage that rejects the superhuman glories one typically associates with Lace-daemonian honour, and which is grounded in the 'communication of virtue' among the populace. Here, he emphasises three aspects of ancient Sparta that continue to provide important lessons for modern civilised monarchies.

First, he explains that external rivals such as Athens were indispensable for maintaining the Spartan regime. The perceived threat Athens posed to Spartan citizens' shared liberty reminded them of 'the common ties of society'.[73] It ignited the social affec-tions, inspiring citizens to courageously defend their freedom and improve their condition. Here, Sparta had an edge over Rome. Rome's eventual domination of Carthage led to its decline. In their victory, they removed the principal catalyst of their progress. Subsequent territorial enlargement left Rome no choice but to fragment its public institutions to efficiently administer the grow-ing empire.

Second, given that modern commerce attenuates rivalries between European nations, Sparta's internal arrangements arguably provide more transposable lessons for eighteenth-century Europe than its insular geopolitical situation might suggest. The *Essay* echoes Mon-tesquieu's idea of constitutional liberty, although it invokes a differ-ent model in Sparta. Citing Plutarch, Ferguson writes:

> The Spartan legislator . . . appears to have sown the seeds of vari-ance and dissention among his countrymen: he meant that good citizens should be led to dispute. He considered emulation as the brand by which their virtues were kindled; and seemed to appre-hend, that a complaisance, by which men submit their opinions without examination, is a principal source of corruption.[74]

This passage explains the genius of Sparta's constitution, and its germaneness for maintaining public vigour in an age of commercial specialisation. Ferguson explains that to maintain the overall civic health of the state, public institutions must foster ongoing, irreconcilable tensions between the various social orders which naturally arise within a society. Under conditions of plurality, where power checks power, politics enlarges citizens. Citizens may enter civic life to defend the interests of their class, but, having a 'share in adjusting or preserving the political form of the state',[75] they develop a shared sense of the commonweal that conditions their overall outlook. By contrast, specialised civil offices may translate into efficient bureaucracies, but they concomitantly remove the sparks that stimulate affection beyond the immediate tribe.

Finally, Sparta's institutions foster a spirit of emulation that remains instructive for contemporary Europe. Ferguson disagreed with Adam Smith who thought formal education and literacy inoculate citizens against the more dehumanising outcomes of specialisation. Here, Ferguson's Machiavellian penchant for the citizen-soldier ideal[76] only partially explains how he hopes to counteract the pernicious effects of specialisation in commerce and manufacturing. Following Montesquieu, his theory carves out a civic space, which generates fealty and respect for, and provides direction to, the nobler individual pursuits. He writes:

> On the eve of such a revolution in manners, the higher ranks, in every mixed or monarchical government, have need to take care of themselves. Men of business, and of industry, in the inferior stations of life, retain their occupations, and are secured by a kind of necessity, in the possession of those habits on which they rely for their quiet, and for the moderate enjoyments of life. But the higher orders of men, if they relinquish to the state, if they cease to possess that courage and elevation of mind, and to exercise those talents which are employed in its defence and in its government, are, in reality, by the seeming advantages of their station, become the refuse of that society of which they once were the ornament; and from being the most respectable, and the most happy, of its members, are become the most wretched and corrupt.[77]

Ferguson and Montesquieu both perceived a reciprocal relationship between commercial and political institutions, and they sought to harness it in a way that safeguards against excessive commercial thinking in affairs of state, while directing citizens' public vigour. The maxim *corruptio optimi pessima* informs their respective visions of politics. Both held that the overall health of our public institutions reflects the quality of people who occupy the higher offices. As Ferguson writes:

> if those orders of men whose valour is required by the public, cease to be brave; if the members of society in general have not those personal qualities which are required to fill the stations of equality, or of honour, to which they are invited by the forms of the state; they must sink to a depth from which their imbecility, even more than their depraved inclinations, may prevent their rise.[78]

Otherwise stated, corruption occurs when elite impropriety debases the public sphere. The wider citizenry becomes corrupt as it no longer has a public touchstone to direct its nobler faculties. Here, Ferguson shared Montesquieu's concern about needing to protect elites from the pernicious effects of modern commerce. However, he doubted that Montesquieu's solution, which forbids elites from engaging in commerce, would be sufficient for preserving the dignity of the public sphere. Even in the absence of commercial ambition, bureaucratised public institutions operate like commercial enterprises, and, as such, engender among elites an atomistic understanding of the whole, leaving them unable to enlarge their virtue. They develop an impoverished understanding of their civic identities, unproblematically instrumentalising politics for personal ends. In this context, participants are unable to associate their particularity with the greater whole, having lost sight of their shared common space. Moreover, Ferguson did not share Montesquieu's view that false honour alone was a sufficient motivator to excite the public spirit. He writes, 'emulation may be directed to useful actions, and have effects serviceable to mankind; but is itself an unhappy disposition, a source of envy, and malice'.[79] He does not differentiate the commercial and non-commercial civil honours as Montesquieu does when he details his mixed monarchical regime in Parts II and III of *The Spirit of the Laws*, emphasising the greater 'happiness' in monarchies such as France vis-à-vis de facto 'republics' such as England.[80] In contradistinction to Montesquieu who sought to accommodate virtue in a world of 'smaller souls', Ferguson thought Britain had a greater capacity for genuine virtue,[81] which enabled him to draw greater lessons from antiquity's classic republics.

Indeed, Ferguson held that maintaining internal and external rivalry and strife was indispensable for liberty, but one cannot ignore the aristocratic dimension to his republican framework.

He underscores the critical importance of citizen militias for infusing a public spirit across the wider citizenry but accentuates the equal importance of preserving a dignified civic sphere that permits first citizens to harmonise their particularity with the public good. When the public sphere is diminished, even the 'noblest' pursuits become debased. Under such conditions, external rivals and internal despotic figures incite fear rather than courage among citizens. That is, shorn of a visible common space to stir the public imagination, citizens adhere to more diminished forms of freedom, satisfied by immediate personal safety that despots or external rivals may provide in return for their domination. In sum, the political theatre needs to maintain its gravitas to condition more ennobling forms of freedom.

Concluding Remarks

To recap, Montesquieu's examination of Europe's civilised monarchies in *The Spirit of the Laws* reveals how the structures of honour, properly harnessed, may nudge citizens towards having greater esteem for virtue and self-sacrifice than for material wealth and paltry distinctions. Smith believes this can be overcome through a baseline level of education under conditions of well-ordered commerce. Ferguson shares Montesquieu's penchant for aristocratic structures, but he considers honour as a second-order concern. As he writes:

> The same integrity, and vigorous spirit, which, in democratical states, renders him tenacious of his equality, may, under aristocracy or monarchy, lead him to maintain the subordinations established . . . he may . . . follow a principle of justice, and of honour, which the considerations of safety, preferment or profit, cannot efface.[82]

Modern commercial nations need ongoing rivalry and strife to properly order citizens' divided wills. Under these conditions, 'the individual will make a right choice of his conduct; [it] will lead him to lose in society the sense of personal interest; and, in the consideration of what is due to the whole, to stifle those anxieties that relate to himself as a part.'[83] For Ferguson, *formal* honours and distinctions alone are finite; they may resolve the problem of the divided will at the patrician level, but in an advanced age of commercial specialisation ongoing conflict and rivalry produce a more democratically apportioned volume of honour, where a greater number of citizens feel directly involved in a common project, regardless of their station in life.

Montesquieu and Ferguson established a *via media* in their respective works, which preserves the gains of modern commerce while emphasising the importance of certain pre-modern institutions for permitting individuals to live happy, fully human lives. It is what distinguishes them from David Hume and Adam Smith, who shared both Montesquieu's and Ferguson's commercial concerns, but identified European nations' moral bearings within commercial society itself. By contrast, Ferguson evokes the institutionalised rivalry and dissension that he draws from Rome's and Sparta's constitutions, whereas Montesquieu draws lessons from France's feudal constituents of honour on how to maintain a sociable spirit among citizens living in eighteenth-century commercial society. Here, Montesquieu and Ferguson's commonalities eclipse their differences. Both their theoretical constructs ensure the propriety of the public sphere, which they deemed paramount for avoiding a politics animated by the personal vainglory of elites and crass materialism of the wider population. On a more primordial level, Smith's, Montesquieu's and Ferguson's institutional prescriptions aim to enliven human beings' social affections, to moderate the self-interested passions that would otherwise nudge societies towards either less-than- or extra-human political configurations.

Notes

1. Cited in James Moore, 'Montesquieu and the Scottish Enlightenment', in *Montesquieu and His Legacy*, ed. Rebecca E. Kingston (Albany: SUNY Press, 2009), 191.
2. Adam Ferguson, *An Essay on the History of Civil Society*, 5th edn (London: T. Cadell, 1782), 108, http://oll.libertyfund.org/titles/1428.
3. Adam Smith, *The Theory of Moral Sentiments* (London: Henry G. Bohn, 1853), VI.II.II, 336, https://oll.libertyfund.org/titles/2620
4. Andrew Sabl, 'Commentary on "Montesquieu's Moderation"', *University of Toronto*, 30 Nov. 2018.
5. Helena Rosenblatt, *The Lost History of Liberalism: From Ancient Rome to the Twenty-first Century* (Princeton: Princeton University Press, 2018), 8.
6. Ibid., 8.
7. Ibid., 32.
8. Ibid., 33.
9. Smith, *The Theory of Moral Sentiments*, V.I.II, 297 and 304.

10. Adam Smith, *Lectures on Justice, Police, Revenue and Arms, Delivered in the University of Glasgow, by Adam Smith. Reported by a Student in 1763 and edited with an Introduction and notes, by Edwin Cannan* (Oxford: Clarendon Press, 1869), 259, http://oll.libertyfund.org/titles/2621

11. Istvan Hont's and Dennis Rasmussen's recent commentaries challenge conventional accounts that position Rousseau and Smith at opposite ends of the eighteenth-century commerce and virtue debates. Whereas Hont teases out Rousseau and Smith's 'epicurean' affinities, Rasmussen emphasises the 'stoic' foundations to their respective philosophies. Mark Hulliung's recent work depicts Rousseau as a thinker entrenched in Enlightenment ideals, but nonetheless rejects Hont's and Rasmussen's historiographies. Hulliung contends that 'underlying the questionable view that Rousseau was responding to commercial society was ahistorical thinking'. However, in his attempt to debunk links of continuity that Hont, Rasmussen and others have recently drawn between the Genevan and Adam Smith in particular, Hulliung himself inches toward ahistoricism. In his view, whereas Smith was engaged in debates concerning mercantilism, free trade and the merits of physiocracy, and considered the role of 'markets, banks, interest rates, prices, wages, rents, manufactures, wholesale and retail trades, imports and exports' (p. 11), Rousseau ignored these issues. However, such comparisons presume a disciplinary division between politics and economics that had not yet taken place during Rousseau's time. The fact that Rousseau was not an economist does not mean that some of his core concerns were not primarily economic. To further support his claim, Hulliung states that Rousseau was 'not so much [concerned with] commercial society as modernity in general, its possibilities and dilemmas' (p. 11). I am sceptical whether these two categories can be separated when engaging with Rousseau, since he was critical of modernity precisely because he believed it to be overly commercial. Response to Hulliung originally published in, Constantine Vassiliou, Review of Mark Hulliung's 'Enlightenment in Scotland and France: Studies in Political Thought', *Eighteenth-Century Scotland*, No. 33, Spring 2019: 30–1. Istvan Hont, *Politics in Commercial Society*, ed. Béla Kapossy and Michael Sonenscher (Cambridge, MA: Harvard University Press, 2015); Dennis C. Rasmussen, *The Promise and Limits of Commercial Society: Adam Smith's Response to Rousseau* (University Park: Pennsylvania State University Press, 2008); Hulliung, *Enlightenment in Scotland and France: Studies in Political Thought* (London and New York: Routledge, 2019).

12. Smith, *The Theory of Moral Sentiments*, I.I.II, 10.

13. Ibid., I.I.I, 5.

14. Ibid., I.I.IV, 23.

15. Ibid., I.II.IV, 52.

16. Ibid., I.III.III, 84.
17. Ibid., III.I.VI, 247.
18. Ibid., I.III.III, 84.
19. Cf. Chapter 2, 59–65.
20. Montesquieu, *The Spirit of the Laws*, ed. and trans. Anne M. Cohler, Basia C. Miller and Harold S. Stone. Cambridge: Cambridge University Press, 1989), 4.2, 31.
21. Ibid., 33.
22. Adam Smith, *The Wealth of Nations Vol 1*, ed. Edwin Cannan (London: Methuen, 1904), 363. http://oll.libertyfund.org/titles/237
23. Smith, *Lectures on Justice, Police, Revenue and Arms . . .*, 156.
24. Ibid., 231.
25. Smith, *Lectures on Justice, Police, Revenue and Arms . . .*, 47.
26. Smith, *The Wealth of Nations*, I.III.IV, 387.
27. Smith, *Lectures on Justice, Police, Revenue and Arms . . .*, 44.
28. Smith, *The Theory of Moral Sentiments*, I.III.III, 87.
29. Ibid., IV.I.I, 267.
30. Ibid., V.I.I, 289.
31. Ibid., I.III.III, 87.
32. Ibid., IV.I.I, 263.
33. Ibid., I.III.II, 78.
34. Ibid., I.III.III, 88.
35. Smith, *The Wealth of Nations*, I.IV.II, 426.
36. Smith, *The Theory of Moral Sentiments*, I.III.II, 78.
37. Smith, *The Wealth of Nations*, II.V.I, 273.
38. Ibid., 268.
39. Adam Smith, *Lectures on Justice, Police, Revenue, and Arms, Part II*, 256.
40. Ibid.
41. Smith, *The Wealth of Nations*, II.V.I, 268.
42. Ibid.
43. Smith, *The Theory of Moral Sentiments*, V.II, 296.
44. Montesquieu, *The Spirit of the Laws*, 5.6, 48.
45. Ibid., 21.21, 389–90.
46. Ibid., 28.41, 595.
47. Ibid., 6.9, 82.
48. Ibid.
49. 'Every Instance of Shame or Degradation seen in the View of a Punishment, awakens the Care of our own Honour and Reputation. Instances of Imprisment, corporal Punishment, or pecuniary Fines, tend to excite our Fears, and beget an Attention to sordid Considerations. If the Cry of Shame from a dishonoured Nation cannot break the Heart of an Offender; nor the Applause which tends an honourable Action fire and stimulate the Mind, we have Reason to be solicitous for the Fate of our Country.' Adam Ferguson, *Reflec-*

tions Previous to the Establishment of a Militia (London: Printed for R. and J. Dodsley in *Pall-mall*, 1756), 43.

50. Ferguson, *An Essay on the History of Civil Society*, 429.
51. It is a term Sher himself borrows, to also include Hugh Blair, Alexander Carlyle, John Home, William Robertson within this moderate group of thinkers. Richard Sher, *Church and University in the Scottish Enlightenment: The Moderate Literati of Edinburgh* (Princeton: Princeton University Press, 1985), 8.
52. Ibid., 324–6.
53. Namely, in Montesquieu's distinction between moderate regimes, which are *animated* by the sociable principles of virtue and honour, and despotic regimes, which are animated by individual fear alone.
54. Cf. Alexander Broadie, *Agreeable Connexions: Scottish Enlightenment Links with France* (Edinburgh: West Newington House, 2012), 190.
55. Cf. Lisa Hill, *The Passionate Society: The Social, Political and Moral Thought of Adam Ferguson* (Dordrecht: Springer, 2006), 90.
56. Adam Ferguson, *Institutes of Moral Philosophy (1769)* (Eighteenth-Century Collections Online, Gale, University of Toronto Libraries), 222.
57. Ferguson, *Reflections Previous to the Establishment of a Militia*, 10.
58. Ibid., 16.
59. Ferguson, *An Essay on the History of Civil Society*, 414.
60. Ibid., 11.
61. Ibid., 27.
62. Ibid., 74.
63. Ibid.
64. Ibid., 147.
65. Ibid., 31.
66. Ibid., 364.
67. Ibid., 434.
68. Ibid., 352.
69. Cf. Marco Geuna, who correctly discerns that despite the Highlander's sometimes harsh criticism of contemporary conditions, he shares Hume's and Smith's embrace of commerce, as evidenced by his involvement in various social circles that encouraged progress in the arts and sciences. Marco Geuna, 'Republicanism and Commercial Society in the Scottish Enlightenment: The Case of Adam Ferguson', in *Republicanism: A Shared European Heritage*, vol. II, ed. Quentin Skinner and Martin Van Gelderen (Cambridge: Cambridge University Press, 2002), 183. I disagree with Geuna's conclusion that Ferguson's republican framework precludes anachronistic concepts such as alienation. Although Ferguson indeed accepted the 'social division of labour as a characteristic trait of modern commercial societies' (ibid., 183), he was nonetheless attuned to its inherent pathologies, as a number of selected passages in this chapter illustrate.

70. Ferguson, *An Essay on the History of Civil Society*, 384.
71. Ibid., 98 and 157.
72. Ibid., 456.
73. Ibid., 367.
74. Ibid., 102.
75. Ibid., 213.
76. Ibid., 452.
77. Ibid., 434.
78. Ibid., 407.
79. Ferguson, *Institutes of Moral Philosophy*, 72.
80. Montesquieu, *The Spirit of the Laws*, 19.
81. Ferguson, *Institutes of Moral Philosophy*, 73.
82. Ferguson, *An Essay on the History of Civil Society*, 398.
83. Ibid., 398.

Conclusion: Moderate Liberalism for a Commercial World in Transition

This book has emphasised the critical importance of honour in foundational liberal thought, explaining how a feudal propensity for social distinctions can preserve civic virtue within an emerging inward-looking liberal order. Chapters 1 and 2 examined the institutional and intellectual context of early eighteenth-century public and private finance in France to help illuminate the entry point to this important facet of Montesquieu's theory of moderation. His response to John Law's economic system in particular reveals a preoccupation with questions concerning the relationship between commerce and liberty, and the role of the nobility in market society (Chapter 1). In examining these themes, Montesquieu observed certain trends in eighteenth-century political economy which threatened to turn commerce into a handmaid of despotism: *despite it being a source of political moderation, commerce itself needed to be moderated.*

While Montesquieu appreciated the existing nobility's public-minded mores, he equally valued the increasing quality of life delivered by modern commerce. It is in this context that he revises James Harrington's republican project (Chapter 3). In a post–Financial Revolution climate, Harrington's republican vision was too utopian in its failure to recognise tangible commercial threats to political freedom. Eighteenth-century financial innovation may have helped stimulate commerce and reduce the public debt. However, it opened new avenues leading to political despotism, unidentifiable through a mid-seventeenth century lens. More specifically, the 'monied interest' threatened to supplant the principal source of France's political education, namely, the *noblesse de robe*, whose intermediary check on the sovereign was indispensable for France's liberty. John Law's System undermined France's intermediary bodies, threatening to eliminate the nobility's economic lifeline. Having considered these material circumstances, Montesquieu's theory of moderation proposes a modified republican vision suited to a modern commercial context.

To approximate republican virtue, a nation's institutions, manners and mores needed to correspond with the new commercial reality. Even though Montesquieu described both republics and monarchies as models of free, moderate government, in the face of financial innovation, he deemed the honour-loving archetype more viable for France and most of its continental European neighbours. In light of this realisation, his works are preoccupied with how legislators could harness existing monarchical institutions in a manner that allows a sense of personal honour to translate into genuine virtuous behaviour.

It is commonly understood that the principal aim of Montesquieu's constitutional prescriptions is to cool human beings' more despotic passions. However, readers often miss that they equally aim to enliven human beings' other-regarding passions, which he deemed requisite for preserving liberty. Any account of Montesquieu's moderation must therefore consider the principal passions that underlie his political philosophy. Chapters 4–7 examined underexplored affinities between Montesquieu and key figures of the Scottish Enlightenment to gain deeper insights into this underappreciated perspective in foundational liberal thought. Here we learned that, in opposition to Hume and Smith's shared view, Montesquieu held that honour and virtue – the two foundational principles that sustain free, moderate government – cannot be borne by commercial society alone. He rather emphasises the critical role pre-commercial institutions and manners play for counteracting the more despotic passions in human beings. Yet, those sources themselves needed to be moderated – an aspect of Montesquieu's constitutionalism often overlooked by his readers. This realisation informed Montesquieu's pluralistic conception of honour, which necessarily includes 'lower' and 'higher' forms of distinction for staving off contemporary manifestations of despotism.

Montesquieu is well known as a theorist of constitutional balance that especially loomed large in the United States' founding, often cited for his influence on both the Federalists and the anti-Federalists. However, his impact on John Adams – who adapts Montesquieu's theory of honour to an American context – merits further scholarly attention. As Mayville writes: 'Similar to Montesquieu's description of monarchies as channeling the desire for prominence by the use of titles and preferments, Adams insisted that republics needed titles to govern the passion for distinction.'[1] Adams witnessed the emergence of a new commercial elite in America that led him to moderate earlier republican sensibilities that he shared with his fellow founders.[2] Echoing Montesquieu's concerns about England and France, Adams feared that a new aristocracy, distinguished by its wealth and success in entrepreneurship, threatened the long-term prospects of the American republic. This new class 'not only exert[s] all [its] own subtlety, industry, and courage, but [it] employ[s] the commonalty to knock to pieces every plan and model that the most honest architects in legislation can invent to keep them within bounds.'[3] To counterbalance this tendency in political life, and to preserve virtue in the American republic, Adams follows Montesquieu in attempting to reimport some of Europe's monarchical structures and customs into the American republican vision. He tolerates hierarchical stratifications to check oligarchic honour. Indeed, ambition needed to counteract ambition, as 'Publius' famously held, but this was insufficient for preventing the republic from degenerating into an oligarchy. *Distinction needed to counteract distinction.*[4] The wisdom of Montesquieu and John Adams on this question is more germane than ever if one considers the extent to which an oligarchic ethos has infused itself in America's political culture today.

Benjamin Franklin embodied this important facet of Montesquieu's thought at the Federal Convention of 1787. This may seem counterintuitive given that he urged his fellow delegates to institute a unicameral legislature, betraying the criteria for constitutional liberty that Montesquieu formally details in 11.6 of *The Spirit of the Laws*. Instead, Franklin draws attention to monarchical France's principal institution of liberty and honour, namely, the *parlements*. He states:

> I do not however mean to recommend this as an eligible mode for our Judiciary department. I only bring the instance to shew that the pleasure of doing good & serving their Country and the respect such conduct entitles them to, *are sufficient motives with some minds* to give up a great portion of their time to the public, without the mean inducement of pecuniary satisfaction. [emphasis added][5]

To be sure, Franklin did not share John Adams's propensity for titled distinctions. But, in his view, the ancien régime demonstrated the possibility (granted, for only two more years!) of keeping political and commercial honours separate in the modern world; of carving a civic space within the commercial world that generates fealty and respect for the nobler pursuits. As Franklin states: 'we shall never be without a sufficient number of wise and good men to undertake and execute well and faithfully the office in question.'[6] One may assess the overall health of our public institutions by examining the quality of characters who fill their highest offices. Conversely, the wider citizenry will become corrupt and inward-looking without a non-commercial, public touchstone in place to enliven their social affections. As such, Franklin advises his fellow delegates to avoid building institutions 'where a post of honor is at the same time a place of profit'.[7]

Despite Montesquieu's egalitarian sensibilities,[8] he could not conceive of another means for protecting the gains of modern commerce in his own time, without tolerating some hierarchical stratifications and hereditary titles. Honour is not honour when it loses its exclusivity. It is why Montesquieu bemoaned Louis XIV's exploitation of France's venal institutions to fund his territorial ambitions.

We have also seen that, even though Hume and Smith categorically rejected the idea of maintaining a titled nobility, their response to the financial bubbles of 1720 reveal a sensitivity towards disruptions to their nation's delicate distinction of ranks. They each presumed a meritocratic order of rank was necessary to inspire the commercial virtues that supported free, moderate government. What differentiates Hume and Smith from Montesquieu is a shared belief that well-ordered commerce itself may foster a sense of social responsibility among Britain's commercial elites. In opposition to David Hume and Adam Smith, who consistently held that commercial distinctions were categorically superior to non-commercial distinctions, Montesquieu sought to preserve a non-commercial civic space that inspires nobler pursuits without stifling the 'lower' distinctions that drive commercial activity. Adam Ferguson shared Montesquieu's view, that European nations cannot survive without a non-commercial aristocratic ethos that inspires the public mind. Yet, Ferguson would have been opposed to French venality. It professionalised virtue, appealing to the baser human faculties, and generated a spirit of passive indifference among citizens. In his Machiavellian penchant for social strife, institutional rivalry and citizen militias, Ferguson democratically apportions honour without fully accepting modern commerce as the central organising principle of European society as his Scottish counterparts had.

The idea of honour guiding human behaviour continues to inform political life today as a series of financial crises have led some theorists to raise questions concerning the impropriety of elite behaviour. In *Why Liberalism Has Failed*, Patrick Deneen writes: 'At its inception, liberalism promised to displace an old aristocracy in the name of liberty; yet, as it eliminates every vestige of an old order, the heirs of their hopeful anti-aristocratic forebears regard its replacement as a new, perhaps even more pernicious, kind of aristocracy.'[9] In *Why Honor Matters*, Tamler Sommers suggests that 'illiberal' honour cultures may paradoxically aid in maintaining justice within a liberal order.[10] Contemporary Western legal frameworks do not address this emotional component of the human totality. Sommers observes that by marginalising honour, Western political cultures fail to produce the interpersonal magnanimity requisite for inspiring great deeds from citizens.[11]

Indeed, in his later writings Montesquieu is congenial towards Christianity as a source of civic restraint, and his theory of honour underpins both republican *and* monarchical legal systems – his two archetypal forms of moderate government. Such observations may lead interpreters to situate him within a broader tradition in the history of ideas, which embraces *illiberal* institutions and manners as necessary props for sustaining the practices of liberalism. For instance, Christopher Brooke provocatively writes that, for Montesquieu, '[b]ehaving like arseholes in public, and being known to behave like arseholes in public, is a key ingredient in sustaining that esprit de corps'.[12] Montesquieu defends aristocratic privilege by granting nobles a degree of immunity against public criticism and tolerating their hereditary titles. In Brooke's reading of Montesquieu, such concessions are a small price to pay in a climate of intractable socioeconomic inequality.[13] He nonetheless acknowledges the normative value of Montesquieu's defence of aristocratic privilege, in so far as it provides a framework for moderating the excesses of a class that unapologetically seeks to protect its own interests at the expense of the commonweal. Even though Brooke seemingly comes to terms with Montesquieu's 'elitism', his normative concerns should give readers pause. Considering the tribal nature of current-day political life, where market forces rather than public-mindedness drive elite activity, why should readers turn to a thinker whose theory reinforces the inequalities elites themselves perpetuate? While Montesquieu harnessed existing institutions to channel elite ambition towards public ends, these institutions had a deeper function than to appease elites' parochial interests. Montesquieu integrates elites within the body politic to unearth a genuine sense of social responsibility in them that would redound upon the broader population.

Montesquieu's theory of honour in fact promotes emergent proto-liberal practices. For instance, one recalls that he tolerates France's venal institutions because they foster a hierarchy of value in the public psyche that favours civic honours over paltry distinctions, without discouraging commercial activity. He appreciates the 'egalitarianism' of the institution, in so far as material wealth, not bloodlines, determined who held venal offices. The institution elevated the *noblesse de robe* whose members' education in law and the commercial arts made them most equipped for both managing increasingly complex affairs of state and reining in the excesses of modern commerce. Their bourgeois lineage carried with it a modern, proto-liberal ethos, which harmonised well with eighteenth-century norms.

Obviously, monarchical structures and customs cannot provide the antidote to America's oligarchical tendencies. As such, one may question the normative value of Montesquieu's idea of honour. However, Montesquieu wrote in a dialectical manner, which exhorts contemporary and future readers to reflect on how existing institutions may be harnessed to produce an *esprit de corps* in their nations. This historical grounding of his political thought reflects his pluralism. The constituents of liberty vary from nation to nation. In his own time, the *noblesse de robe* and France's venal system were constitutive of its liberty. Such institutions were not ends in themselves but instruments for producing public spiritedness in Bourbon France.

More broadly, Montesquieu and his Scottish counterparts provoke readers to reflect on how the material changes delivered by the unrelenting pace of commercial progress are transforming our societal relations and affecting our liberty more generally. Their theories offer readers lenses for recognising the market forces shaping inequalities that are not as recognisable in commercial society: What new orders of 'elites' are we yielding? How are their commercial activities fuelling the dysfunctional features of liberal modernity? What new privileges and responsibilities do current-day commercial circumstances impose on already existing elites? How do we channel elites' demands for 'preferences and distinctions' to accommodate the commonweal? These questions are invariably topical today,[14] as varied forms of populism continue to question the liberal state's ability to balance the pursuit of wealth and public welfare. We have seen throughout this book that the conceptual language available to respond to these abiding civic challenges in the history of political economy could be traced to the early modern period.

Prima facie, Montesquieu's moderate vision may seem somewhat quixotic, as we could think of many examples of businesspeople whose elevated positions of social responsibility did not translate into their civic aggrandisement. This reality reflects both the strength and weakness of his theory. The introductory chapter described Montesquieu's vision of free, moderate government as a 'modest' *summum bonum*. He took it for granted that each typology of free, moderate government contained the seeds of corruption. The most we could hope for from our vestigial sources of liberty is to increase the longevity of our existing liberal democratic institutions.

To recap, Montesquieu shared his Scottish contemporaries' embrace of modern commerce, professing that contemporary regimes needed to reflect this more humane reality. Yet, he often qualified his praise with a tone of lament. One recalls his often-cited passage in 3.3 that '[the political men] of today speak to us only of manufacturing, commerce, finance, wealth, and even luxury.' Then, in 3.5 he writes, 'The state continues to exist independently of love of the homeland, desire for true glory, sacrifice of one's dearest interests, and all those heroic virtues we find in the ancients and know only by hearsay.' To be sure, such passages affirm the Bordeaux aristocrat's preference for the modern world over the ancient world. He doubts the practicality of establishing government on ancient principles. His lament is an exhortation to future legislators, urging them to be more modest in their political ambitions.

Montesquieu and Ferguson agreed with Hume and Smith's shared premise: fortunately, modern conditions do not effectively spawn, nor require, heroic figures. However, the vitiating effects of commerce on the more sociable human faculties deeply troubled them. Both bemoaned the 'feeling of exact justice'[15] that animated modern commercial citizens. They observed that the inward-looking behaviour of contemporary English and Dutch citizens especially atrophied their deeper human faculties. As Montesquieu writes, there one finds 'traffic in all human activities and moral virtues; the smallest things, those required by humanity, are done or given for money.'[16] A spirit of contractual reasoning and bargaining conditions social interactions and runs the risk of permeating all spheres of activity, crowding out deeper *human* feelings of empathy and the desire to please.

In *Dangerous Minds*, Ronald Beiner alarms readers about a renewed affinity in the West for the superhuman heroism that later thinkers such as Friedrich Nietzsche nostalgically revived in their political writings.[17] Beiner seeks to understand Nietzsche's seductiveness fully to combat the more unsavoury aspects of his project and legacy. In doing so, he urges us to attune ourselves to how dangerous movements on the political Far Right are fuelled by a sense of malaise and anomie, for which Nietzsche's writings provide a cure.[18] Yet, he warns that cutting out the Nietzschean roots which underlie current-day fascistic branches is insufficient when the seed has already spread. In a clarion call to readers, Beiner states: 'We must read the great anti-liberal theorists . . . *not* in order to appropriate them for liberal or leftist intellectual projects, but in order to come to a deeper understanding of precisely why they turn their backs on bourgeois liberalism and hence why many of our fellow citizens are readily tempted to do the same.'[19] As such, I would argue that our own theories of liberalism must plant more attractive gardens.

Montesquieu and his Scottish counterparts offer us valuable conceptual resources for restoring our liberal foundations on more fertile grounds. They presumed that the fellow feeling and empathy we experience in our face-to-face interactions themselves provide the foundations for free, moderate government. To be sure, they did not provide a fully articulated ontology of morality. Yet morality is not wholly arbitrary in their respective theories of politics either. It is rather the impulse of sociability made manifest. Hume and Smith embraced commercial self-interest as the primary mover, believing that existing exchange relations alone nourished human beings' sociable impulses. Nearly a century later, Alexis de Tocqueville accepted their premise and channelled 'commercial sociability' through egalitarian institutions of civic learning such as town halls and churches, which he understood as microcosms of the nation. Considering how the unrelenting pace of technology steadily fosters interference within even our most primordial social bonds, it is doubtful such intermediary bodies – or their modern-day equivalents – on their own can help enlarge the civic mind, as Tocqueville had once envisioned. In its aim to encompass the upside of commercial dynamism while preserving the primacy of the commonweal, Montesquieu's moderate liberalism offers an alternative basis for feeding our sense of interpersonal magnanimity and maintaining the integrity of our public institutions.

Notes

1. Luke Mayville, *John Adams and the Fear of American Oligarchy* (Princeton: Princeton University Press, 2016), 136–7.
2. Ibid., 7.
3. John Adams in ibid., 8.
4. 'Are riches . . . to be the only distinction? Is there any distinction more degrading than riches?' John Adams in ibid., 144.
5. Benjamin Franklin, 'Remarks at the Federal Convention', *Madison's Notes at on the Debates at the Federal Convention* (New Haven: The Avalon Project, 2008), 2 June 1787.
6. Ibid.
7. Ibid.
8. As evidenced in his sanguinity about Europe entering an age of Saturn where 'there was neither master nor slave', with everyone viewing each other as equals in a moral sense. Montesquieu, *The Spirit of the Laws* , ed. and trans. Anne M. Cohler, Basia C. Miller and Harold S. Stone (Cambridge: Cambridge University Press, 1989), 15.7, 252.
9. Patrick Deneen, *Why Liberalism Failed* (New Haven: Yale University Press, 2018), 33.
10. Tamler Sommers, *Why Honor Matters* (New York: Basic Books, 2018), 14.
11. Ibid., 74.
12. Christopher Brooke, 'Arsehole Aristocracy (or: Montesquieu on Honour, Revisited)', *European Journal of Political Theory* 17.4 (2018), 400.
13. Ibid., 399.
14. Recently, many have drawn from a causal thread in Peter Turchin's famous analysis of social instability, to explain the United States' polarisation, claiming that the United States is suffering from an overproduction of elites, who have vastly more communicative power than our Enlightenment forefathers would have ever imagined. Cf. Graeme Wood, 'The Next Decade Could be Even Worse', *The Atlantic*, Dec. 2020; Michael Lind, *The New Class War: Saving Democracy from the Managerial Elite* (New York: Penguin Random House, 2020); Amy Chua, 'Tribal World: Group Identity is All', *Foreign Affairs*, July/ August 2018, https://www.foreignaffairs.com/articles/world/2018-06-14/tribal-world; Steven W. Webster and Alan I. Abramowitz, 'The Ideological Foundations of Affective Polarization in the U.S. Electorate', *American Politics Research* 45.4 (2017): 621–47.
15. Ibid., 21.11, 376.
16. Ibid., 20.2, 339.
17. Ronald Beiner, *Dangerous Minds: Nietzsche, Heidegger, and the Return of the Far Right* (Philadelphia: University of Pennsylvania Press, 2018).
18. Ibid., 27.
19. Ibid., 93.

Bibliography

Andrew, Edward. 2015. 'Locke on Consent, Taxation, and Representation', *Theoria* 62.2 (2015): 15–32.

Arendt, Hannah. 'What is Freedom?' *Between Past and Future: Six Exercises in Political Thought*. New York: The Viking Press, 1961.

Aristotle. 'The Politics', in *A New Aristotle Reader*, ed. J. L. Ackrill, trans. J. L. Ackrill. Princeton University Press, 1988.

Aristotle. *The Politics*, ed. Carnes Lord, trans. Carnes Lord. Chicago: The University of Chicago Press, 2013.

Baker, Geoff. 'Man fears 2nd attempt on life after pipe bomb failed', *The Gazette* [Montreal], 16 Apr. 1994. https://advance-lexis-com. ezproxy.lib.uh.edu/api/document?collection=news&id=urn:contentIt em:3SR8-X150-002G-H3W9-00000-00&context=1516831.

Bandoch, Joshua. 'Montesquieu's Selective Religious Intolerance in *Of the Spirit of the Laws*', *Political Studies* 64.2 (2016): 351–67.

Beiner, Ronald. *Civil Religion: A Dialogue in the History of Political Philosophy*. New York: Cambridge University Press, 2011.

Beiner, Ronald. 'Civil Religion and Anti-Clericalism in James Harrington', *European Journal of Political Theory* 13.4 (2017): 388–407.

Beiner, Ronald. *Dangerous Minds: Nietzsche, Heidegger, and the Return of the Far Right*. Philadelphia: University of Pennsylvania Press, 2018.

Beiner, Ronald. *Political Philosophy: What It is and Why It Matters*. Cambridge: Cambridge University Press, 2014.

Benrekassa, Georges. 'Moderation', in *A Montesquieu Dictionary*, ed. Catherine Volpilhac-Auger. Lyon: ENS Lyon, September 2013.

Bibby, Andrew S. *Montesquieu's Political Economy*. New York: Palgrave MacMillan, 2016.

Boesche, Roger. 'Fearing Monarchs and Merchants: Montesquieu's Two Theories of Despotism', *The Western Political Quarterly* 43.4 (1990): 741–61.

Braun, Theodore. 'La chaîne secrète: A Decade of Interpretations', French Studies 42 (1988): 278–91.

Brewer, John. The Sinews of Power: War, Money and the English State, 1688–1783. New York: Routledge, 1989.

Broadie, Alexander. Agreeable Connexions: Scottish Enlightenment Links with France. Edinburgh: John Donald, 2012.

Brooke, Christopher. 'Arsehole Aristocracy (or: Montesquieu on honour, revisited)', European Journal of Political Theory 17.4 (2018): 391–410.

Callanan, Keegen, 'Une infinité de biens: Montesquieu on Religion and Free Government', History of Political Thought 35.4 (2014): 739–67.

Carrese, Paul O. Democracy in Moderation: Montesquieu, Tocquevill, and Sustainable Liberalism. Cambridge: Cambridge University Press, 2016.

Carrithers, David. 'Montesquieu and the Spirit of French Finance: An Analysis of His Mémoire sur les dettes de l'état (1715)', in Montesquieu and the Spirit of Modernity, ed. David W. Carrithers and Patrick Coleman, 15–32. Oxford: Voltaire Foundation, 2002.

Chamley, Peter. 'The Conflict between Montesquieu and Hume: A Study of the Origins of Adam Smith's Universalism', in Essays on Adam Smith, ed. Andrew S. Skinner and Thomas Wilson, 274–305. Oxford: Clarendon Press, 1975.

Cheney, Paul. 'Montesquieu and the Scottish Enlightenment', in A Montesquieu Dictionary, ed. Catherine Volpilhac-Auger. Lyon: ENS Lyon, September 2013.

Cheney, Paul. Revolutionary Commerce: Globalization and the French Monarchy. Cambridge, MA: Harvard University Press, 2010.

Chernow, Ron. Alexander Hamilton. New York: The Penguin Press, 2004.

Chua, Amy. 'Tribal World: Group Identity is All', Foreign Affairs, July/August 2018.

Cléro, Jean-Pierre. 'HUME ET MONTESQUIEU: sur deux chapitres de "L'Esprit des lois" traduits en anglais', Revue française d'histoire des idées politiques 35 (2012): 73–91.

Condorelli, Stefano. 'The 1720 Bubble: A European Perspective', ISECS Conference, Rotterdam, 27 July 2015.

Craiutu, Aurelian. A Virtue for Courageous Minds: Moderation in French Political Thought. Princeton: Princeton University Press, 2012.

de Dijn, Annelien. 'On Political Liberty: Montesquieu's Missing Manuscript', in Political Theory 39.2 (2011): 181–204.

Defoe, Daniel. The Chimera: or, the French way of paying national debts, laid open: Being an impartial account of the proceedings in France, for raising a paper credit, and settling the Mississippi stock. London: Printed for T. Warner, 1720.

Deneen, Patrick. 'The Ignoble Lie: How the New Aristocracy Masks its Privilege', *First Things* (2018), https://www.firstthings.com/article/2018/04/the-ignoble-lieDeneen, Patrick. *Why Liberalism Failed*. New Haven: Yale University Press, 2018.

Derfel, Aaron, Ann Carroll and Eddie Collister. 'Police disarm car bomb that caused traffic chaos', *The Gazette* [Montreal], 12 Nov. 1993. https://advance-lexis-com.ezproxy.lib.uh.edu/api/document?collection=news&id=urn:contentItem:3SR8-XFB0-002G-H2JG-00000-00&context=1516831

Desserud, Donald. 'Commerce and Political Participation in Montesquieu's Letter to Domville', *History of European Ideas* 25 (1991): 135–51.

Desserud, Donald. 'Virtue, Commerce and Moderation in "The Tale of the Troglodytes": Montesquieu's Persian Letters', *History of Political Thought* 4.12 (1991): 605–26.

Dutot, Nicolas. *Réflexions politiques sur les finances, et le commerce*, vol. 2. The Hague: Les Frères V. et N. Prévost , 1754.

Ferguson, Adam. *An Essay on the History of Civil Society*, 5th edition. London: T. Cadell, 1767. http://oll.libertyfund.org/titles/1428.

Ferguson, Adam. *Reflections Previous to the Establishment of a Militia*. London: Printed for R. and J. Dodsley in *Pall-mall*, 1756.

Ferguson, Adam. *Institutes of Moral Philosophy*. Eighteenth-Century Collections Online, 1769.

Fetters, Ashley 'The Five Years That Changed Dating', *The Atlantic*, 21 Dec. 2018.

Forbonnais, François Veron de [n.d.]. 'Commerce', in *Encyclopèdie, ou dictionnaire raisonne des sciences, des arts et des métiers, etc.*, ed. Denis Diderot and Jean le Rond d'Alembert. Chicago: University of Chicago: ARTFL Encyclopédie Project.

Ford, Franklin L. *Robe and Sword: The Regrouping of the French Aristocracy after Louis XIV*. Cambridge, MA: Harvard University Press, 1962.

Fukuyama, Francis. *The End of History and the Last Man*. New York: Free Press, 1992.

Geuna, Marco. 'Republicanism and Commercial Society in the Scottish Enlightenment: The Case of Adam Ferguson', in *Republicanism: A Shared European Heritage*, vol. II, ed. Quentin Skinner and Martin Van Gelderen, 177–96. Cambridge: Cambridge University Press 2002.

Gonthier, Ursula Haskins. *Montesquieu and England: Enlightened Exchanges, 1689–1755*. London and New York: Routledge, 2016.

Haakonssen, Knud. 'Introduction', in David Hume, *Political Essays*, ed. Knud Haakonssen, xi–xxx. Cambridge: Cambridge University Press, 1994.

Haakonssen, Knud. 'The Structure of Hume's Political Theory', in *The Cambridge Companion to David Hume*, ed. David Fate Norton and

Jacqueline Taylor, 341–80. Cambridge: Cambridge University Press, 2008.

Hammersley, Rachel. *The English Republican Tradition and Eighteenth Century France*. New York: Manchester University Press, 2010.

Hanvelt, Marc, 'Politeness, a Plurality of Interests and the Public Realm: Hume on the Liberty of the Press', *History of Political Thought* 33.4 (2012): 627–46.

Harari, Yuval Noah. *21 Lessons for the 21st Century*. New York: Penguin Random House, 2018.

Harrington, James. *The Commonwealth of Oceana*, vol. 1, in *The Political Works of James Harrington*, ed. J. G. A. Pocock, 155–359. Cambridge: Cambridge University Press, 1977.

Harrington, James. *A Discourse upon this Saying*, vol. 2, in *The Political Works of James Harrington*, ed. J. G. A. Pocock, 735–46. Cambridge: Cambridge University Press, 1977.

Harrington, James. *The Political Works of James Harrington*, 2 vols, Cambridge: Cambridge University Press, 1977.

Harrington, James. *Pour Enclouer le Canon*, vol. 2, in *The Political Works of James Harrington*, ed. J. G. A. Pocock, 727–34. Cambridge: Cambridge University Press, 1977.

Harrington, James. *The Prerogative of Popular Government*, vol. 1, in *The Political Works of James Harrington*, ed. J. G. A. Pocock, 389–566. Cambridge: Cambridge University Press, 1977.Harrington, James. *A System of Politics*, vol. 2, in *The Political Works of James Harrington*, ed. J. G. A. Pocock, 833–54. Cambridge: Cambridge University Press, 1977.

Harris, James A. *Hume: An Intellectual Biography*. Cambridge: Cambridge University Press, 2015.

Hill, Lisa. *The Passionate Society: The Social, Political and Moral Thought of Adam Ferguson*. Dordrecht: Springer, 2006.

Hirschman, Albert O. *The Passions and the Interests: Political Arguments for Capitalism before its Triumph*, Twentieth Anniversary Edition. Princeton: Princeton University Press, 1997.

Hobbes, Thomas. *Leviathan*, ed. C. B. Macpherson. London: Penguin Classics, 1985.

Hobbes, Thomas. *Leviathan in The English Works of Thomas Hobbes of Malmesbury; Now First Collected and Ed. Sir William Molesworth, Bart*, vol. 3. London: Bohn, 1839–45. http://oll.libertyfund.org/titles/

Hoffman, Philip T. 'Early Modern France, 1450–1700', in *Fiscal Crises, Liberty, and Representative Government*, 226–52. Stanford: Stanford University Press, 1994.

Hont, Istvan. *Jealousies of Trade*. Cambridge: Harvard University Press, 2005.

Hont, Istvan. 'The Language of Sociability and Commerce: Samuel Pufendorf and the Theoretical Foundations of the Four-Stages Theory', in

The Languages of Political Theory in Early Modern Europe, 253–76. Cambridge: Cambridge University Press, 1987.

Hont, Istvan. *Politics in Commercial Society*, ed. Béla Kapossy and Michael Sonenscher. Cambridge, MA: Harvard University Press, 2015.

Hoppit, Julian. 'The Myths of the South Sea Bubble', *Transactions of the Royal Historical Society*, 6th series, vol. 12 (2012), 141–65.

Hulliung, Mark. *Enlightenment in Scotland and France: Studies in Political Thought*. London and New York: Routledge, 2019.

Hulliung, Mark. *Montesquieu and the Old Regime*. Los Angeles: University of California Press, 1976.

Hume, David. *History of England from the Invasion of Julius Caesar to the Revolution in 1688*. Indianapolis: Liberty Fund, 1983.

Hume, David. *Essays Moral, Political, Literary*, ed. Eugene F. Miller. Indianapolis: Liberty Fund, 1987.

Hume, David. *To President de Montesquieu: Londres, 10 avril 1749*, vol. 1 in *The Letters of David Hume, 1727–1765*. Oxford: Oxford University Press, 1932.

Hume, David. *A true account of the behaviour and conduct of Archibald Stewart, Esq: late Lord Provost of Edinburgh. In a letter to a friend*. London: Eighteenth Century Collections Online, 1748.

Israel, Jonathan. *A Revolution of the Mind: Radical Enlightenment and the Intellectual Origins of Modern Democracy*. Princeton: Princeton University Press, 2009.

Kaiser, Thomas E. 'Money, Despotism, and Public Opinion in Early Eighteenth-century France: John Law and the Debate on Royal Credit', *The Journal of Modern History* 63.1 (1991): 1–28.

Kelley, Duncan. *The Propriety of Liberty: Persons, Passions and Judgment in Modern Political Thought*. Princeton: Princeton University Press, 2011.

King Jr., Martin Luther. 'Letter from a Birmingham Jail', African Studies Center–University of Pennsylvania, 16 Apr. 1963. www.africa.upenn.edu/Articles_Gen/Letter_Birmingham.html

Kingston, Rebecca. 'L'intérêt et le bien public dans le discours de parlement de Bordeaux', *Le Temps de Montesquieu*, ed. Michel Porret and Catherine Volpilhac-Auger, 187–204. Geneva: Droz, 1998.

Kingston, Rebecca. 'Montesquieu on Religion and on the Question of Toleration', in *Montesquieu's Science of Politics*, ed. David W. Carrithers, Michael A. Mosher and Paul A Rahe, 375–408. New York: Rowman & Littlefield, 2001.

Kingston, Rebecca. 'Religion', in *A Montesquieu Dictionary*, ed. Catherine Volpilhac-Auger. Lyon: ENS Lyon, September 2013.

Krause, Sharon. *Liberalism with Honor*. Cambridge, MA: Harvard University Press, 2002.

Krause, Sharon. 'Two Concepts of Liberty in Montesquieu', *Perspectives on Political Science* 34.2 (Spring 2005), 88–96.

Lane, Melissa. *Eco-Republic: What the Ancients can Teach us about Ethics, Virtue, and Sustainable Living.* Princeton: Princeton University Press, 2011.

Larrère, Catherine. 'Montesquieu économiste? Une lecture paradoxale', in *Montesquieu en 2005*, ed. Catherine Volpilhac-Auger, 243–66. Oxford: Studies on Voltaire and the Eighteenth Century, 2005.

Larrère, Catherine. 'Montesquieu on Economics and Commerce', in *Montesquieu's Science of Poltiics: Essays on The Spirit of the Laws,* 335–74. Lanham: Rowman & Littlefield, 2001.

Larrère, Catherine. 'Montesquieu: tolérance et liberté religieuse', *Montesquieu, l'état et la religion*, 153–71. Sofia: Éditions Iztok-Zapad, 2007.

Law, John. *Idée générale du nouveau Système des finances*, vol. 2, in *Œuvres complètes*, ed. Paul Harsin. Paris: Sirev, 1934.

Law, John. 'Réponse de Law aux objections présentées à sa proposition [19 octobre 1715]', in *Œuvres complètes*, ed. Paul Harsin. Paris: Sirev 1934.

Law, John. 'Réponse de Law aux plaintes du Parlement-April 27, 1720', in *Œuvres complètes*, ed. Paul Harsin. Paris: Sirev, 1934.

Lettres patentes du Roy. 'Portant privilege en faveur du Sr. Law & sa compagnie, d'éstablir une banque generale', in *Actes royaux 1716 Avril–Juillet*, 2 et 20 May 1716. Paris: de L'Imprimerie Royale. 3. [Article 1]. 1716.

Lewis, Michael. *Moneyball: The Art of Winning an Unfair Game.* New York: W. W. Norton & Co., 2004.

Lind, Michael. *The New Class War: Saving Democracy from the Managerial Elite.* New York. Penguin Random House, 2020.

Locke, John. *A Letter Concerning Toleration and other Writings*, ed. Mark Goldie. Indianapolis: Liberty Fund, 2010.

Machiavelli, Niccolo. The Prince *and Selections from* The Discourses, trans. and ed. David Wooton. Indianapolis: Hackett Publishing Company, Inc., 1994.

McDaniel, Iain. *Adam Ferguson in the Scottish Enlightenment.* Cambridge: Harvard University Press, 2013.

McGee, Patrick. 'Car emissions scandal: loopholes in the lab tests', *Financial Times*, 5 Aug. 2018.

MacPherson, C. B. *The Political Theory of Possessive Individualism.* Oxford: Oxford University Press, 1962.

Mandeville, Bernard. *An Enquiry into the Origin of Honour, and the Usefulness of Christianity.* London: Brotherton, 1732.

Mandeville, Bernard. *The Fable of the Bees or Private Vices, Publick Benefits, 2 volumes*, ed. F. B. Kaye. Indianapolis: Liberty Fund, 1988.

Mandeville, Bernard. 'The Grumbling Hive: or, Knaves turn'd Honest', in *The Fable of the Bees: or Private Vices, Publick Benefits, Vol 1*. Indianapolis: Liberty Fund, 1988.

Mayville, Luke. *John Adams and the Fear of American Oligarchy.* Princeton: Princeton University Press, 2016.

Melon, Jean-François. *Essai politique sur le commerce*, ed. Francine Markovits. Caen: Presses universitaires de Caen, 2014.

Montesquieu. *Considerations on the Causes of the Greatness of the Romans and Their Decline*, trans. David Lowenthal. Indianapolis: Hackett Publishing Company Inc., 1999.

Montesquieu. *Considerations on the Grandeur and Declension of the Roman Empire*. Vol. 3 Evans, in *The Complete Works of M. de Montesquieu*, 1721. Online Liberty Fund.

Montesquieu. 'Considérations sur les richesses de l'Espagne', in *Œuvres complètes*. Gallimard, 1951.

Montesquieu. *Letter from Montesquieu to David Hume: A Bordeaux, 19 may, 1749*, vol. 1 in *Life and Correspondence of David Hume*, ed. John Hill Burton. Edinburgh: William Tate, n.d.

Montesquieu. 'Letter to Domville', in *My Thoughts*, trans. and ed. Henry C. Clark, 595. Indianapolis: Liberty Fund, 2012.

Montesquieu. 'Lettre sur les dettes de l'État', in *Œuvres complètes*. Paris: Gallimard, 1949.

Montesquieu. *My Thoughts*, trans. and ed. Henry C. Clark. Indianapolis: Liberty Fund, 2012.

Montesquieu. *Notes on England*, trans. Iain Steward. Oxford University Comparative Law Forum 6, 2002. https://ouclf.law.ox.ac.uk/.

Montesquieu. *The Persian Letters*, vol. 3 in *The Complete Works of M. de Montesquieu*. London: T. Evans, 1777.

Montesquieu. *The Persian Letters*, trans. Margaret Mauldon. Oxford: Oxford University Press, 2008.

Montesquieu. *Persian Letters*, trans. and ed. Stéphane Douard and Stuart Warner (South Bend: St. Augustine's Press, 2017).

Montesquieu. *Réflexions sur la monarchie universelle*, vol. 2 in *Œuvres complètes*. Paris: Gallimard, 1951.

Montesquieu. *The Spirit of the Laws*, ed. and trans. Anne M. Cohler, Basia C. Miller and Harold S. Stone. Cambridge: Cambridge University Press, 1989.

Montesquieu, *Treatise on Duties*, in *Montesquieu: Discourses, Dissertations, and Dialogues on Politics, Science, and Religion* (Cambridge: Cambridge University Press, 2020).

Moore, James. 'Hume's Political Science and the Classical Republican Tradition', *Canadian Journal of Political Science* 10.4 (1977): 809–39.

Moore, James. 'Montesquieu and the Scottish Enlightenment', in *Montesquieu and His Legacy*, ed. Rebecca E. Kingston, 179–95. Albany: SUNY Press, 2009.

Morrissey, Robert. *The Economy of Glory: From Ancien Regime France to the Fall of Napoleon*, trans. Teresa Lavender. Cambridge: Oxford Press, 2013.

Mosher, Michael. '"Empires of Imagination": Montesquieu, the Financial Crisis of 1720 and the Future of Inequality', paper presented at the

14th Congress of the International Society for Eighteenth-Century Studies, Rotterdam, The Netherlands, 28 July 2015.

Mosher, Michael. 'Monarchy's Paradox: Honor in the Face of Sovereign Power', in *Montesquieu's Science of Politics*, ed. David Carrithers, Michael Mosher and Paul Rahe, 198–229. Lanham: Rowman & Littlefield, 2001.

Murphy, Antoin E. 'Introduction', in *Histoire du systême de John Law*, ed. Nicolas Du Tot. Paris: L'Institut national d'études démographiques, 2000.

Murphy, Antoin E. 'John Law and the Scottish Enlightenment', in *A History of Scottish Economic Thought*, ed. Alexander Dow and Sheila Dow, 9–26. London: Routledge Taylor and Francis Group, 2006.

Murphy, Antoin E. *John Law: Economic Theorist and Policy-Maker*. Oxford: Clarendon Press, 1997.

Nacol, Emily. *An Age of Risk: Politics and Economy in Early Modern Britain*. Princeton: Princeton University Press, 2016.

Nacol, Emily, and Constantine Christos Vassiliou. 'The Plague of High Finance in Montesquieu's *Persian Letters*', in *The Spirit of Montesquieu's Persian Letters*, ed. Constantine Christos Vassiliou, Alin Fumurescu and Jeffrey Church (Lanham: Lexington Books, 2023 [forthcoming]).

Nelson, Eric. *The Greek Tradition in Republican Thought*. Cambridge: Cambridge University Press, 2004.

O'Brien, Patrick. 'The Political Economy of British Taxation', *Economic History Review* 41.1 (1988): 1–32.

Orain, Arnaud. *La Politique de merveilleux: une autre histoire du Système de Law (1695–1795)*. Paris: Fayard, 2018.

Orwin, Clifford, Michelle Clarke, Harvey Mansfield and Erica Benner, interview by Paul Kennedy. 'Machiavelli: The Prince of Paradox', *CBC Ideas*, 6 November 2013.

Paganelli, Pia. 'Vanity and the Daedalian Wings of Paper Money in Adam Smith', *New Voices of Adam Smith*, ed. L. Montes and E. Schliesser. London: Routledge, 2006.

Pangle, Thomas. *The Theological Basis of Liberal Modernity in Montesquieu's Spirit of the Laws*. Chicago: Chicago University Press, 2010.

Pernoud, Régine. *Histoire de la bourgeoisie en France: les temps modernes*. Paris: Éditions du Seuil, 1962.

Plutarch. 'The Life of Lycurgus', in *The Parallel Lives*, trans. Bernadotte Perrin. Cambridge, MA: Loeb Classical Library, 1914.

Pocock, J. G. A. *Historical Introduction*, vol. 1, in *The Political Works of James Harrington*, ed. J. G. A. Pocock, 1–160. Cambridge: Cambridge University Press, 1977.

Pocock, J. G. A. *The Machiavellian Moment: Florentine Political Thought and the Atlantic Republican Tradition*. Princeton: Princeton University Press, 2003.

Pocock, J. G. A. *Political Thought and History: Essays on Theory and Method*. Cambridge: Cambridge University Press, 2009.

Pocock, J. G. A. *Virtue, Commerce, and History*. Cambridge: Cambridge University Press, 1985.

Rahe, Paul. *Montesquieu and the Logic of Liberty: War, Religion, Commerce, Climate, Terrain, Technology, Uneasiness of Mind, the Spirit of Political Vigilance, and the Foundations of the Modern Republic*. New Haven: Yale University Press, 2009.

Rasmussen, Dennis C. *The Pragmatic Enlightenment: Recovering the Liberalism of Hume, Smith, Montesquieu, and Voltaire*. Cambridge: Cambridge University Press, 2014.

Rasmussen, Dennis C. *The Promise and Limits of Commercial Society*: *Adam Smith's Response to Rousseau*. University Park: Pennsylvania State University Press, 2008.

Rosenblatt, Helena. *The Lost History of Liberalism: From Ancient Rome to the Twenty-first Century*. Princeton: Princeton University Press, 2018.

Rousseau, Jean-Jacques. 'A Discourse on the Moral Effects of the Arts and Sciences', in *The Social Contract and Discourses by Jean-Jacques Rousseau*, trans. G. D. H. Cole. Toronto and London: J. M. Dent and Sons, 1923.

Rowlands, Guy. 2013. *The Financial Decline of a Great Power: War, Influence, and Money in Louis XIV's France*. Oxford: Oxford University Press.

Sabl, Andrew. 'Commentary on "Montesquieu's Moderation"', *University of Toronto*, 30 Nov. 2018.

Sabl, Andrew. *Hume's Politics: Coordination and Crisis in the History of England*. Princeton: Princeton University Press, 2015.

Sandel, Michael. *The Tyranny of Merit: What's Become of the Common Good*. New York: Farrar, Straus and Giroux, 2020.

Seitter, Walter. 'Montesquieu, Pléthon. Politique et religion dans l'Empire byzantine et dans un projet de réforme tardo-byzantin', *Montesquieu, l'état et la religion*. Sofia: Éditions Iztok-Zapad, 2007.

Shackleton, Robert. *Montesquieu: A Critical Biography*. Oxford : Oxford University Press, 1961.

Shklar, Judith. *Montesquieu*. Oxford: Oxford University Press, 1987.

Sher, Richard. *Church and University in the Scottish Enlightenment: The Moderate Literati of Edinburgh*. Princeton: Princeton University Press, 1985.

Sher, Richard. 'From Troglodytes to Americans: Montesquieu and the Scottish Enlightenment on Liberty, Virtue, and Commerce', in *Republicanism, Liberty, and Commercial Society, 1649–1776*, ed. David Wootton, 368–402. Stanford: Stanford University Press, 1994.

Skinner, Quentin. *Visions of Politics: Regarding Method*, vol. 1. Cambridge: Cambridge University Press, 2002.

Smith, Adam. *Lectures on Justice, Police, Revenue and Arms, Delivered in the University of Glasgow, by Adam Smith. Reported by a Student in 1763 and edited with an Introduction and notes, by Edwin Cannan.* Oxford: Clarendon Press, 1869.

Smith, Adam. *Theory of Moral Sentiments.* London: Henry G. Bohn, 1853. https://oll.libertyfund.org/titles/2620

Smith, Adam. *The Wealth of Nations,* ed. Edwin Cannan. London: Methuen, 1904. http://oll.libertyfund.org/titles/237

Sommers, Tamler. *Why Honor Matters.* New York: Basic Books, 2018.

Sonenscher, Michael. *Before the Deluge: Public Debt, Inequality, and the Intellectual Origins of the French Revolution.* Princeton: Princeton University Press, 2007.

The South Sea Bubble, and the Numerous Fraudulent Projects to which it gave rise in 1720, Historically Detailed as a Beacon to the Unwary against Modern Schemes. London: for Thomas Boys, Ludgate Hill, 1825.

Spector, Céline. 'Honor, Interest, Virtue: The Affective Foundations of the Political in *The Spirit of the Laws*', in *Montesquieu and His Legacy,* ed. Rebecca E. Kingston, 49–80. Albany: SUNY Press, 2009.

Spector, Céline. *Montesquieu: pouvoirs, richesses et sociétés.* Paris: Presses universitaires de France, 2004.

Strauss, Leo. 'Persecution and the Art of Writing', *Social Research* 8.1 (1941): 488–504.

Sullivan, Vickie B. *Montesquieu and the Despotic Ideas of Europe: An Interpretation of 'The Spirit of the Laws'.* Chicago: University of Chicago Press, 2017.

Terjanian, Anoush Fraser. *Commerce and Its Discontents in Eighteenth-century Political Thought.* Cambridge: Cambridge University Press, 2013.

Thomas George, 'Liberal Education and American Democracy', *The American Interest,* 24 August 2015. https://www.the-american-interest.com/2015/08/24/liberal-education-and-american-democracy/

Tocqueville, Alexander de. *The Old Regime and the Revolution,* trans. and ed. John Bonner. New York: Harper & Brothers, 1856.

Tolonen, Mikko. 'The Gothic Origin of Modern Civility: Mandeville and the Scots on Courage', *Journal of Scottish Philosophy* 12.1 (2014): 51–69.

Trenchard, John. *An examination and an explanation of the South-Sea Company's scheme, for taking in publick debts.* London: Printed, and sold by J. Roberts.

Trenchard, John. *Some Considerations Upon the STATE of our Publick Debts in General, and Of the Civil List in Particular.* London: Printed, and sold by J. Roberts, 1720.

Vassiliou, Constantine. '*Le système de John Law* and the Spectre of Modern Despotism in the Political Thought of Montesquieu', *Lumen* 38 (2019): 161–78.

Walsh, Jonathan. 'A Cultural Numismatics: The "Chain" of Economics in Montesquieu's *Lettres persanes*', *Australian Journal of French Studies* 46 (2009): 139–54.

Ward, Lee. 'Female Modesty and Commerce *in Persian Letters*', in *The Spirit of Montesquieu's* Persian Letters, ed. Jeffrey Church, Alin Fumurescu and Constantine Vassiliou (Lanham: Lexington Books, 2023 [forthcoming]).

Webster, Steven W. and Abramowitz, Alan I. 'The Ideological Foundations of Affective Polarization in the U.S. Electorate', *American Politics Research* 45.4 (2017): 621–47.

Wood, Graeme. 'The Next Decade Could be Even Worse', *The Atlantic*, 20 Dec. 2020.

'The world has become obsessed with elites', *The Economist*, 17 Dec. 2016.

Wright, J. P. 'Hume on the Origin of "Modern Honour"', in *Philosophy and Religion in Enlightenment Britain: New Case Studies*. Oxford: Oxford Scholarship Online, 2012.

Index

Adams, John, 153, 179–80
Arendt, Hannah, 96–7, 98, 153–4
aristocratic government, 5, 9;
　　see also nobility; parlements
Aristotle, 58, 79, 80
Athens, 13, 37, 72, 78, 79, 81,
　　107, 134–5, 140, 168, 169

Bank of England, 27, 29, 72
Banque générale, 30, 35
Banque royale, 31
Bayle, Pierre, 85
Beiner, Ronald, 185
Bibby, Andrew, 2, 33, 38
Boulainvilliers, Count of, 125
Brooke, Christopher, 182

'Cato', 17, 61–2, 64
Cato's Letters, 60, 61–2
Cheney, Paul, 5, 66
China, 95–6, 100, 117
Cicero, 135
citizens
　civic virtue, 4–5, 9, 13, 73, 74
　religion and civil liberties, 85
civic virtue, 4–5, 9, 13, 73, 74
climate, 37, 38, 50, 57, 58–9,
　　116–18, 117, 123–4

commerce
　commerce and virtue debates, ix,
　　2–3, 11–16, 51, 146, 162–3
　commercial honour, ix, 6–7, 120,
　　124–5, 128, 129, 136–7, 140
　commercial revolution, 58–9
　commercial sociability, 93, 108,
　　123, 155–6
　as communication, 3–4
　and despotism, 11–12
　and moderation, 8, 162
　'Tale of the Troglodytes', 11–16,
　　156
Conseil de Finance, 29
cosmopolitanism, 4, 92, 110, 117
Craiutu, Aurelian, 8

Deneen, Patrick, xi, 182
despotism
　and extreme liberty, 97
　and Law's System, 5–6, 33, 34,
　　36–7, 39, 40–1, 57, 59, 60
　and modern commerce, 5–6,
　　9–10, 11–12, 84
　and religion, 83–5
Domville, William, 124
Dubos, Abbé Jean-Baptiste, 125
Dutot, Nicholas, 31–2, 43

economics
  France's monetary and fiscal
    challenges, 54–5
  paper money, 27, 28–9, 31–2,
    34, 36, 50–1, 56, 57, 59
  state debt, 54
empires of commerce, 50, 51–3,
  52–3, 61, 61–2, 83
empires of conquest, 50, 51–3, 52,
  59, 61, 83
England
  taxation in, 27–8, 56
  factionalism, 128–9
  gentry, x, 51, 77, 91–2, 159–60,
    161–2
  legislature, 94
  liberty, 95, 96–7, 99–100
  in Montesquieu's thought, 2,
    3, 59–60, 92, 93–4, 94, 100,
    100–2, 118, 127, 128–9
  nobility in, 42–3
  paper-based economy, 27, 29
  public credit, 26, 27, 29, 55–6
  South Sea Bubble, 59–60

Ferguson, Adam
  on commercial specialisation,
    163–4, 166–8
  on corruption, 165–6
  on honour, 172–3, 181
  political moderation, 164–5,
    170–2
  on Sparta, 168–70
feudalism
  feudal honour, 118–19, 121–2,
    123, 137–8, 173, 179
  in France, 34, 42
  France's system of venality, 55,
    126–7, 146–7, 148, 181, 183
  Henry VII's land reforms, 72,
    116, 122–3, 124
  tax farming, 27–8, 60
  see also nobility
Ford, Franklin, 148

France
  French commerce, 93, 108, 123
  in Hume's thought, 92–3, 106–10
  moderate government, 92
  in Montesquieu's thought, 100–2
  political economy, 25, 28–9,
    31–2, 54–5, 59
  see also commerce of luxury;
    Law's System ('Le système');
    parlements
Franklin, Benjamin, 153, 180–1
Fukuyama, Francis, xi, 20

gentry
  in Harrington's thought, 77
  in Hume's thought, 51, 91–2
  in Smith's thought, x, 51,
    159–60, 161–2
Gordon, Thomas, 60, 61

Harrington, James
  ancient prudence and commerce,
    72, 78–9, 82, 106–7
  on the Dutch republic, 77–9
  Montesquieu's response to,
    71–6, 79, 85–6, 97, 99, 135,
    178
  on religion, 74–5, 76, 82
  republicanism, 71–2, 76–82, 178
Henry VII, 72, 116, 122–3, 124,
  157
Hirschman, Albert, 4
Hobbes, Thomas, 12, 14, 97–9,
  138–9
Holland, 26, 29, 57, 72, 77–9, 105
honour
  aristocratic honour, ix, xi,
    139–40, 147–9
  commercial honour, ix, 6–7, 120,
    124–5, 128, 129, 136–7, 140
  in Ferguson's thought, 172–3,
    181
  feudal honour, 118–19, 121–2,
    123, 137–8, 173, 179

and market society, 74–5, 76,
82–4, 86, 108–9
Smith on religion, 161
republican government
classical republican government,
37, 71, 135, 140
in Harrington's thought, 71–2, 97
and high finance, 61–2, 64–5, 66
Hume on English
republicanism, 102–3, 104,
105, 107, 109, 128
and moderate government, 9,
10–11, 139
republican virtue, 3, 10–11, 73,
74
republicanism and modern
commerce, 76–82
Rosenblatt, Helena, 154
Rousseau, Jean-Jacques, 153, 155

Saint-Lambert, Jean François de,
136
slavery, 57–8
Smith, Adam
on commercial sociability, 155–6
on education, 160–1
on the gentry, 51, 159–60, 161–2
the impartial spectator, 156–8
on Law's System, 63
moderate government, 155
on the nobility, 157–9, 181
on religion, 161
on the South Sea Bubble, 51, 62,
63–6, 181

social distinctions, 27–8, 50–1,
55, 56–7, 60; see also gentry;
nobility
Sommers, Tamler, 182
South Sea Bubble
Montesquieu's response to, 51,
59–61, 64–6
Smith's response to, 51, 62,
63–6, 181
Spain, 52–3, 59, 61, 100
Spector, Céline, 33, 136
Sullivan, Vickie, 79–80

'Tale of the Troglodytes', 11–16,
156
Tocqueville, Alexis de, 42–3, 153,
185
Trenchard, John, 60, 61, 63

virtue
civic virtue, 9, 13, 73, 74
commerce and virtue debates,
2–3, 11–16, 51, 146, 162–3
and moderate government,
9–10, 91, 93, 96–9, 179,
181
and modern honour, 91, 93,
96–9, 116, 124, 136, 136–91
in Montesquieu's thought, 91,
93, 96–9, 116, 124, 136
'Tale of the Troglodytes', 11–16

War of the Spanish Succession, 4,
5, 26, 29, 54, 63, 93

EU representative:
Easy Access System Europe
Mustamäe tee 50, 10621 Tallinn, Estonia
Gpsr.requests@easproject.com

www.ingramcontent.com/pod-product-compliance
Lightning Source LLC
Chambersburg PA
CBHW070844300326
41935CB00039B/1441